Parts of an Andrology

PARTS OF AN ANDROLOGY

On Representations of Men's Bodies

LAWRENCE R. SCHEHR

Stanford University Press
Stanford, California 1997

Stanford University Press
Stanford, California

© 1997 by the Board of Trustees of the
Leland Stanford Junior University

Printed in the United States of America

CIP data are at the end of the book

Original printing 1997
Last figure below indicates year of this printing:
06 05 04 03 02 01 00 99 98 97

*For Jean-François Fourny and Caryl Lloyd,
in deepest friendship*

Acknowledgments

Many people have had the courage to read this material, make comments, keep me to the straight and narrow, and generally ask all the right questions. Again, in no order but alphabetical, let me thank them here: Martine Antle, the late George Bauer, David Bell, Frédéric Canovas, Mary Donaldson-Evans, Dominique Fisher, Jean-François Fourny, Calvin Jones, Kevin Kopelson, Caryl Lloyd, Neill Matheson, Charles Porter, Pierre Saint-Amand, Ralph Sarkonak, and Charles Stivale. Margaret Waller and Stephen Whitworth were especially generous with their time in reading earlier versions of this manuscript. And I should like to thank Daniele Davini for introducing me to Moravia's novel *Io e lui*.

Institutional support came from Bernard J. Quinn, chair of the Department of Foreign Languages at the University of South Alabama, the College of Arts and Sciences and its dean, Larry Allen, and Vice-President John Morrow of the University's Academic Affairs Office. Through their efforts I was able to use the University's Faculty and Service Development Award to best advantage. Without their help and support, I would not have had the time to finish this book.

I have continued to benefit from the professional support and dedication of Helen Tartar and Peter Kahn of Stanford University

Press. Let them be thanked again, along with Ann Klefstad, who did such a splendid job with copyediting. Some of this material has appeared in earlier forms. The pages on Bonnetain and Roth appeared in "Fragments of a Poetics: Bonnetain and Roth," in *Solitary Pleasures*, eds. Paula Bennett and Vernon Rosario (New York: Routledge, 1995). Some of the material on Hocquenghem appeared in "Defense and Illustration of Gay Liberation," *Yale French Studies* 90 (1995–96); the pages on Foucault appeared in an earlier form in "Foucault's Body," *Bulletin de la Société Américaine de Philosophie de Langue Française* 6.1–2 (1994): 59–75. The material on the AIDS-infected body appeared in *Studies in Twentieth-Century Literature* 20.2 (1996): 405–30; and several pages on Guibert appeared as part of an article in French in *Le Corps textuel*, edited by Ralph Sarkonak (Paris: Lettres Modernes, 1997). I would like to thank all of the above for permission to reuse this material.

L.R.S.

Contents

Parts of an Andrology

Introduction: On Plemystography

Men's bodies are detachable. . . . A man and his body
are soon parted.

—Margaret Atwood

Seeing, now, that there were no curtains to the window, and that the street being very narrow, the house
opposite commanded a plain view into the room, and
observing more and more the indecorous figure that
Queequeg made, staving about with little else but his
hat and boots on; I begged him as well as I could, to
accelerate his toilet somewhat, and particularly to get
into his pantaloons as soon as possible.

—Herman Melville

The novel is set in Rome, a modern Rome, recovered from the repression of Fascism, the strife of the war years, and the bleakness of
the fifties. It is a city of reasonable prosperity, of middle-class values,
and of middlebrow tastes; indeed, it is a consumer society that is very
much a part of modern, late capitalist Europe. It is a city where sexual liberation has occurred, where the traditional moralizing role of
the Catholic church is ignored by the characters in the book, who
prefer to follow their own moral consciences and to make their own
choices. It is a modern world in which sex is not a hidden topic,
where sexual matters are freely discussed, and where the ideological
myths of virginity and fidelity have been forgotten. Sex and sexuality
are no longer in the closet, no longer whispered about behind closed
doors, but are the frequent subject of conversations: marriages, affairs, seductions, paternity, relationships, the contents and the structures of the sexual revolution.

The two protagonists, or characters, or figures—I am not yet sure
what to call them, for reasons that will soon become clear—are engaged in one of their many conversations. The tone varies from ban-
tering to serious, from pleading to conspiratorial, but the subject is

always sex. In an early conversation, one of the protagonists is egging the other on, by trying to get him to look at a *Playboy*-like magazine on sale at a newsstand. The other balks, finding this behavior inappropriate for a 35-year-old man, especially at eight in the morning. Finally he acquiesces, and starts to look at the magazine. This does not occur without a bit of embarrassment, for the man running the newsstand "rudely and ironically" asks him if he is going to buy what he is looking at. Caught red-handed, he is ashamed, buys the magazine, and gets in the car. But this is not the end, for the conversation continues with the other protagonist, who has not yet tired of prodding the first to action. The interlocutor continues his acts of cajoling, his taunting, his challenges: "Later, at home, when you've finished working, we'll look at it closely, page by page" (12–13).

Such conversations occur throughout the book, with one of the protagonists trying to get the other to engage in sex. And never mind the homoerotic overtones that seem to surge out of the suggestion that they look at the magazine together, for the two protagonists are not two individuals out for fun. They are a man and his penis. And it is the penis that makes these suggestions throughout, a penis that proves to be a master at casuistry and an expert at convincing, conniving, and cajoling, as well as being a superb individual in his, or its, own right. The book is Alberto Moravia's one-joke novel, *Io e lui*, and the latter title character is the penis of the former title character.

Are there one or two characters? It seems a simple question, a necessary question, an obvious question. Prey to his own Bahktinian polyphony, Federico, the "io" of the title, insists that he is, or more correctly, that they are and are not one. Responding to the voice of his other, to his master's voice, Federico says, "First of all, enough with this plural. We are not 'we'; we are 'I' and 'you.' And then, you know, it is better for you not to talk to me. I hate you" (13). Separate yet joined, they are, for him, certainly not a dynamic duo, a pair, bosom buddies, a "we" of complicity. They are separate: two individuals, two voices, and yet they are joined at the hip, so to speak. For "lui," however, it is an endless game involving a "we" of connivance and conspiracy, Siamese twins who must act in concert. The reader is faced with a dilemma: are they / is Federico one or two? Depending on the point of view of the protagonist, depending on the point of view with which the reader is sympathetic, a different answer will arise. The resolution of the two viewpoints is possible, however. If it is not a question of one soul in two bodies, the "we" of friendship as Cicero or Montaigne might have it, it is a question of two souls, or better yet, two voices in one body. Not two individuals, not a duo, but somewhere in between.

Before we go any further, before I bring my reader, whoever he or she may be, any further along this primrose path of seemingly phallocentric dalliance, I ask for a bit of indulgence on two counts. If the reader will bear with me for a little while, I do promise to explain the mysterious title of the chapter, though not quite yet. And I assure you that this book is not about penises. The book deals with representations of the human male body, the body of a man, of men, in various narrative frameworks from the mid-nineteenth century, a moment that concretizes our conception of the male subject in narrative, to the end of the twentieth century, a point at which many of the assumptions made about that subjectivity have come under challenge. Specifically, I have engaged the figure of the white male subject, the subject on whom Western universals have long been predicated, a subject whose mastery and exemplarity have often been brought into question in the last twenty-five years.

Discussions of the body have become an important topic in current critical writing. Recent books on the interrelations of the body and poiesis include a collection of excerpts from philosophical treatises on the representation of the body, edited by Bruno Huisman and François Ribes; Anne Deneys-Tunney's study of the representation of the body, and most often the female body, in seventeenth- and eighteenth-century French writing; a collection of essays on the body, or fragments of a historiography of the body, edited by Jean-Christophe Goddard and Monique Labrune; Veronica Kelly's and Dorothea E. Von Mücke's collection on the interrelationship between body and textuality in the eighteenth century; and Juliet Flower MacCannell's and Laura Zakarin's excellent anthology on the representation of the body in philosophy. Collections and overviews of the philosophical topos of the body have come out in France as the subject has taken on an allure; these include a study of the depiction of the body in Plato, Descartes, Nietzsche, and Merleau-Ponty, by Serge Le Diraison and Eric Zernik; a study on the philosophical representation of the body in mainline philosophy, by Jean-François

Schaal, and an anthology of excerpts assembled by Odile Quéran and Denis Trarieux. By and large, these French collections and studies tend not to distinguish the specificity of the male body as a distinct object and talk about "le corps de l'homme" when they mean the human body. The subject I have elected to explore is both different from and more specific than the philosophical topos of the human body in general: it is the figure of the vulnerable white male body. In other words, I am seeking to provide a counterpoint in gender studies to readings of the representation of the female body. To look at the construction of this figure, I have chosen to examine a varied group of works that are discontinuous among themselves, but that are also representative of the discontinuity in their intermittent representations of the male body. Especially in nineteenth-century narrative, from which I am taking Edgar Allan Poe and Guy de Maupassant as authors who wrote particularly astutely on the subject, there is never a continuity of representation of the male body. The writings I have chosen by Poe and Maupassant are flickering, episodic investigations into that for which classicism has no language: a male body as subject, as sentient feeling, as the subject of torture or of aesthetic adulation. It is not until the twentieth century that one gets the possibility of continuous representation of this male subject. Though often at center stage in works where it is treated as a metonymy of its own phallic and phallocentric power, the male body has not nearly as often been seen relative to pleasure and pain, to aesthetics, to human vulnerability. Few works put the body on stage without first automatically imbuing it with the capacity for power.

Moravia's game is not at all far-fetched, for it asks us to think about the penis in particular, and the body of the male in general. Is the penis something hidden, something shameful, something different? Is it part of the man? Does it have its own mind, the lusting figure of a literate id in this case? Or does Moravia's "lui" offer a discourse that desublimates the male body itself? For what defines the male body, at least phenomenologically, is the presence of the penis, visible yet hidden, seemingly the last taboo (though Guy Hocquenghem will posit a more radical unclothing of the male body), yet the sine qua non of the male body itself. I would like to think that my book is about that body, though I know it is about the penis as well, about its *escamotage*, its camouflage, its parade as phallus, as phallic symbol—not at all the same thing—about its appearance, guilty or innocent, one organ among others, or singular organ, standing there, erect like a monument. It is for that reason that I have started with a reference to Moravia, who violates one of the last taboos of nonpornographic Western writing by treating the penis not as some mighty phallic sword—although many amusing remarks are made about it in a deconstruction of that fiction—but as a member of the vulnerable male body.[1]

So my book is about that, to be sure; it is about an account of that body, a count of that body, a measuring of that body. Counting the presence of the penis, measuring the penis, not about the myth or nonmyth of the enormous size of the African member, for example, when compared to that of the white male, but about having the penis stand up and be counted. How can we count it, if the major ideological role of the penis is to hide behind a phallic veil, when what you see is always more than what you get? As Naomi Schor says, "To subject the penis to representation is to strip the phallus of its empowering veil, for . . . while the phallus can be said to draw its symbolic power from the *visibility of the penis*, phallic power derives precisely from *the phallus's inaccessibility to representation*" (*Bad Objects* 112).

As we have already seen in the brief excerpt from *Io e lui*, this counting is nearly impossible. How can we count the body or make an account of the body, if we do not even know if it is a question of two or one, not the sublime argument of the dualism of body and soul, but the earthbound, physical, even banal counting of bodies, numbering them as individuals, marking them off, defining territoriality? For we are, as the reader will no doubt suspect, prey to concepts of number and space, descriptions of counts and accounts that are implicitly or explicitly predicated on a kind of numbering system of discrete integers that we have always taken for granted.

Integers are axiomatic to counting, and we have not often paused to think just what we predicate on that numbering system when we count, be it in literature or philosophy, according to such a system. Body after body and page after page. The numbering system of discrete integers, if itself not inherently phallocentric, lends itself to support a model of territoriality, of phallic power, of definitions of self that depend on a discrete division between self and other. Indeed, the system of integral numbers as the equivalent for phallic exchange is the basic element of the entire ideological system and economic system of the West. Modern western men, the quintessential accountants of culture and history, number heads, territory, space. They divide the world into what is theirs and what is tributary to them, such as "their wives" and "their children," both fitting into the realm of the proper, and some territories of the other, uncounted, unmanned until such an other becomes an object to be acquired. These children of the famous "mommy-daddy-me" scenario, written of so brilliantly by Gilles Deleuze and Félix Guattari in their epoch-making book *L'Anti-Oedipe* (60–162), provide us with the notion of the integral subject exercising "his" liberty, and "her" liberty only derivatively, in an integral fashion. The Oedipal subject is a whole integer, a unique, singular free being. That this image of the Oedipal subject comes about most clearly in the nineteenth century, during an era in which the constraints on the subject are put into question and the integral nature of his subjectivity begins to be challenged, is an irony of an ideological system that sees the liberty of the subject as a sign of his (and, only derivatively, her) free will and the construction of a system as a reflection of some collective sum of the free wills of its integral parts.

Writing of the coupling of this Oedipal individual, otherwise known as *Homo oeconomicus* in a reproductive economy, Alphonso Lingis says: "Each enters the contract with an eye to his or her own interest; he offers his penis as a check drawn on a phallic mortgage and demands an absolute of gratification; she sees in his penis the means to acquire the unconditional love of an infant" (127). So we might say that there is in fact a flickering moment in this history, a moment at which integrality is assured by the sacrifice of a body part to the whole. A man is whole if he has hidden his penis behind the mask of phallic power, which is the guarantee, in the traditional capitalist social structure, that the individual reflects the ideology of the whole and that the family unit is the integral reflection of the economic system. For Michael Kimmel, writing "Consuming Manhood" (Goldstein 12–41), in order for a man in nineteenth-century puritanical America to become a real man, a "Marketplace Man," it would be necessary to control the flows of desire and of fluids filling his body. Liquids, the ex-carnation of the feminine, weaken the system, destroy solids and integral counting, and make the world a more difficult place for a man to become a man. This is, to be sure, a male model, a phallic model, and a numbering system devised by men for men. To stand up and be counted as a productive member of society, a man was supposed to put his penis in a trust fund, because it was the physical sign of a disruptive voice; it was the incarnation of flows of desire; it upset the body count.

Alberto Moravia's Federico wonders, insists, divides the unit of the individual, the composite into a separate "you" and "I," while he attempts to maintain the integral nature of the body, a maintenance of obvious necessity to him as an individual. He is not a "we"; he is not some rhizomatic process of intersubjectivity of the self, of the individual, but a distinction, clearly marked. Yet this is a duplicitous, doubling distinction: he names his other self with the same name and calls it "Federicus Rex" (84). Same and other. And I would venture to say that the system that defines the other as other, at least in the realm of literature, is the one we all know and think of as the phallocentric hierarchy, the system of measurement and norm, the system of integers and their parts. Moravia gives us what we have been expecting, the phallic description, the measure of the man: "Twenty-five centimeters long, eighteen centimeters in circumference, and weighing two and one half kilograms" (84). The system we expect is the system that is in place, the order of the body that uses the phallus as a norm, as a standard, a model and modeling tool for textuality. It is a clear division between self and other, a marking of territory, a measuring-out of space.

But what if it were not Federico who were right, but Federicus Rex? That is, what if men were not really Oedipal, economic subjects except at the cost of a member, that particular member? If the voice given the penis in this novel has any validity as a subject, or even as a fleeting, partial subject, as a voicing of desire and its flows, it is because it can bring out the hidden elements that are suppressed when men start to count. More generally, though, the voice of that desublimated penis underscores two different, though not unrelated, consequences. The first is that the penis is ultimately metonymic of the male body itself, which has been sacrificed in its individuality in order to belong to the system. To be *Homo oeconomicus*, to be a good

Oedipal subject, to be a corporate man, or to be incorporated into the ideological structure as a man—this is at the expense of the individual body as a zone in which there are flows of desire that are not always neatly categorized or channeled. At the same time, Moravia's work points out that the individual is somehow always tied to others, to other flows of desire; the unitary, singular, integral numbering of men is a specious concept that is useful only to the accountants of the world.

The title I have given this chapter will now become clearer, for it comes from the description of a process of determining the exact nature of sexual perversions, as if they could be categorized by numbers. Writing of sexual offenders taken to the Pinel Institute near Montreal, Jacqueline Remy notes:

> They are taken to a laboratory to undergo a "plemystography," an examination that allows for the identification of the exact object of their fantasies. In full view, they are asked to masturbate while listening to porn scenarios of all sorts—sadistic, non-sadistic, hetero, homo, with children of all ages—and their erections are measured by means of a mercury ring link to a sophisticated machine. As for those trying to fool themselves, the technician answers: "And your penis lies?" (30)

Now there is clearly a philosophical imperative here, but it is not my intent to focus on the philosophical or scientific bases on which this system of plemystography is founded, nor even to speculate on how such biopolitical measurement will help the judiciary system or penological reform deal with "sexual offenders." For me the system is predicated both on the essentialization of a fantasm (or an induced fantasm or simulacrum) to the exclusion of metonymic tripping or metaphoric/fetishistic displacement, and on the necessarily measurable nature of the reaction, which returns me to the argument about counting and the integral nature of the individual. And on a purely experimental note, one would have serious questions about the use of sound instead of visual imagery to test the waters, as if the fantasm (or perversion) were always necessarily linguistically codified. The deperversion of the narrator and protagonist in Stanley Kubrick's film *A Clockwork Orange*, based on the novel by Anthony Burgess, is at least a more advanced version of this plemystography, as it creates aversion through a general association of stimuli, both coenaesthetically and synaesthetically: the deperversion is accomplished through a screening of visual fantasms, an audio of the protagonist's favorite composer, Beethoven, and a nausea-producing drug. There is a Kafkaesque machine that categorizes and counts our perversions—and I would assume that in such a phallocentric universe every exhibition of sexuality, even the norm itself, is by definition a perversion—by measuring the hard-ons of sexual offenders. Obviously, in such a system, all men are guilty of some sexual perversion, or would be deemed so. And the system works—that is, one gets a detailed plemystographic answer—because it is only the "guilty" who are monitored. The system of testing and naming does not inscribe, but it pre-inscribes, it pre-scribes sexual behavior. It is the ultimate tool in the game of phallocentric ideology, the final figure of that power system, for it is a cogent means of denying the validity of ecstasy under which representation is engulfed. Plemystography says that we must never allow the ecstasy of the body to subsume representation, for representation must remain as the telltale sign of the inscription of power on the body. Flows of desire are viewed as morally repugnant, because they insist on being flows, because they are economically counterproductive; they must therefore be measured and categorized, banned or channeled, marked or eliminated by a digital system that transforms the visual into the metric. Again, this concept of a machine reinforcing the unity of the subject is at the heart of my study and in the next chapter, we will see to what extent this kind of machine is undercut by a different concept of the machine, and even a different concept of pain itself. But is it not true that, in a general sense, the machine is always there, ready to measure the guilty with its monitors?

The phallic model presupposes the possibility for power, measurable and demonstrable, but it is always a power that operates on the other. It is power that is visited outside the subject. In the works I am examining here, parts of a somewhat occluded history of the male body, representation is of the subject within himself, in his subjectivity, in his submission to, or escape from, a law outside him that defines the possibilities of pleasure, pain, *jouissance*. Even in the tale by Poe, "The Pit and the Pendulum," where there is no real question of sexuality or erotics, the force of the law is the same: it is for that reason that I am looking at the male body in pain and the male body in pleasure as being phases of the same phenomenon. And Poe's genius, here as elsewhere, is to help his reader visualize the apparatus that makes the subject a subject. Yet that is not the only possible ramification of the model of pleasure and pain to which I am subscribing. Moravia's more modern Federicus Rex is neither fully other nor fully different from the possessor of the body to whom, or to which, he, or it, is attached. Self and other are not that distinct; the division between them is one of parceling and false divisions. If the description in numbers defines space, the description in language describes pleasure: "Yes, there is no doubt, I am well-supplied, superlatively endowed, nature was generous with me. With no false modesty I can brag of having an absolutely exceptional sex organ, for its proportions, sensitivity, promptness, power, resistance" (63). To describe his penis in language, the narrator must maintain it as his, part of him, attached to him. Though he resorts to what we would consider a traditional vocabulary of power, even of phallic power, the ways of literature interfere with a complete internalization of that model: "Robust and massive like an oak tree, with all the veins standing out" (64). This was the same language used to introduce "lui" in the first pages of the book: "Enormous, rigid, congested, like a tree that rises alone and gigantic from the middle of a plain, beneath a low, suffocating sky, 'lui' stands up from my stomach almost vertically, showily raising the bed sheet" (7). The majesty of this organ of pleasure is not resolvable into some dimensional engineering problem; there is a comparison, a literary device, that joins two different bodies. Pleasure itself is not integral, but a gasp of literary desire: "'lui' explodes between my fingers like a bottle of champagne that has just been uncorked" (67).

The construction of the phallocentric system of power and order that is at the heart of our modernity affects the order of desire as well. It forces desire to relate to a hysterocentric order of values, but that hysterocentrism is tributary to the phallic order itself. In other words, the woman and her incarnation of desire are seen as products or constructions of a phallocentric system that invests her with desire as the representation of men's desire for women, the collective becoming momentarily incarnate by one of its members. In this phallocentric order of power, man's desire is for a woman, for the possession, in its fullest economic sense, of her body, counted as a conquest, as chattel, as possession. Her body is present but it is always marked by the signs of the male investment in it, the codes of the male possession of it. Forbidden is her desire, not as one of Eve's daughters, but as one of Lilith's; the only desire she is allowed is one deemed complementary to, or reflective of, what a man wishes. Equally forbidden is the male body, sign of its own vulnerability, of its own noncodifiable desires, of its own nonphallic nature. There is a whole history of desire, of male desire, that does not appear as such in the official annals of encoding, and even more, as we shall see below, in the postmodern deconstructions of the phallocentric model, especially as it is figured in gender studies. A simple model for the depiction of desire I am proposing is the following: male desire leans—in the sense of Freudian *Anlehnung*—on the phallocentric model of power just as the various drives discussed by Laplanche lean on the parts of the female body. All fealty to psychoanalytic models aside, male pleasure leans on the construction of male power. As René Girard pointed out thirty years ago, though to quite different ends, in his ground-breaking study *Mensonge romantique et vérité romanesque*, literature sometimes tells the truth where science and ideology cover it up. In this case, I would say that nineteenth-century science and biopolitics—to use Michel Foucault's term—consigned much of male desire and the male body as well to the realm of the pathological. In literature, at least, models of male desire and models of the male body exist that are ambiguous, nondisjunctive, and non-integral. And even if they are, at least initially, propped upon the phallocentric model that we have all accepted as the model to be critiqued and deconstructed, it is neither sufficient nor appropriate to sweep away a model of desire with it. And a certain twentieth-century philosophical investigation of desire and its incorporation in the form of the body, including the work of Sartre, Merleau-Ponty, and Foucault among others, illuminates complementary aspects of the humanistic tradition.

Before continuing, I would just like to add a word or two about pronouns and their consequences. As much as many might not like it, this book is about pronouns referring to beings with penises and there are problems with attempting to make a wholly inclusive discourse that is not politically incorrect while reflecting the intellectual object of investigation. Consider Monique Wittig's *Les Guéril-lères*, whose poetics is in part lost in English translation because there is no equivalent in English for the French pronoun "elles." Here, then, I consider a writer like Guy Hocquenghem, whose support of women's issues is, I think, unchallengeable. Yet, though *solidaire* with lesbian concerns and with the women's liberation movement occurring in France in the late sixties and early seventies, when much of his own writing on gay liberation was published, Hocquenghem tends to restrict his arguments to male homosexual desire. At the same time, I do not believe that he is making an appeal to universalize his position. Rather, I think he is attempting through his polemics to have "homosexual desire" stand on its own two feet, so to speak, neither subject to a dominant heterosexual other nor to a reproductive model tacitly accepted as a universal. In short, whether thinking about Hocquenghem, or any one of a number of other writers I discuss in this book, I find myself agreeing wholeheartedly with Leo Bersani. Bersani asserts his disquiet in the face of a complaint by a lesbian colleague who complained that much of his talk marginalized women: "Since much of what I said had to do with gay men's sexuality and, more specifically, with gay men's love of the cock, her entirely accurate comment became entirely puzzling when voiced as a complaint" (8). His cogent point in *Homos* is quite simply that "*any* perspective, direct or vicarious, would be to some extent exclusionary" (8). In other words, no pronoun is truly universal; no position can include all possible perspectives. And therefore all pronouns and all positions exclude something or someone; as I have discussed above, the position of the universal, liberal, modern subject depends on the exclusion of flows of desire, of whatever is deemed pathological within the dominant ideology.

Now the two systems of phallic power and of secret desire do coexist; there is no purity, even within what one might call a literary work of pleasure. The link between the two systems is too long historically, too tight ideologically. Indeed one might well argue, as Michel Foucault does in the first volume of his *Histoire de la sexualité*, that the model of pleasure is allotted its marginalized space within the confines of a larger general system of phallic power. It is a space in which phallocentric economic power says that it has no interest; it is a space in which there would be no return on investment.

Flow is allowed to occur as long as it does not damage the floodgates protecting the citadels of power. Some literature too confirms this as it examines pathological cases that flow negatively, as is the case of Herman Melville's "Bartleby the Scrivener," or unproductively, as is the case of Charles Dickens's Uriah Heep in *David Copperfield*. Only when these unproductive flows interfere with the functioning of the dominant apparatus are they stanched. But literature also offers, as early as the nineteenth century, a literary work of pleasure and pain, a text of a singularity in which the phallic system, even in its own endless redundancy and inanity, no matter how dominant it is, cannot explain what is at work in the writing. It would seem foolish to try to explain away Poe's "The Pit and the Pendulum" simply by references to a power structure. More recently, the system of pleasure has begun to come into its own. As Leo Bersani says:

> If it is time to sing the praise of the penis once again, it is not only because a fundamental reason for a gay man's willingness to identify his desires as homosexual is love of the cock (an acknowledgment profoundly incorrect and especially unpopular with many of our feminist allies), but also because it was perhaps in early play with that much-shamed organ that we learned about the *rhythms* of power, and we were or should have been initiated into the biological connection between male sexuality and surrender or passivity—a connection that men have been remarkably successful in persuading women to consider nonexistent. (*Homos*, 103)

So in Moravia's novel, along with a discourse of positive desire interwoven with the strands of self-aware literary endeavor, one finds the simplest, even the most simplistic, version of a phallocentric ideology, a territory marked, a pissing contest, a game of king of the hill, a banal version of phallic power:

> While I am urinating, I hold "him" up with my palm, testicles and all; with my hand, I figure out and estimate his weight, I measure his volume with my eyes. Yes, whoever can make genitals of this mass dance in his hand, he could not be an average man, a man of little, a man like the others. Nor could he be a failure, a wishy-washy moral and intellectual impotent. (62–63)

Within Moravia's own enterprise, the phallocentric ideology that defines stereotypical male subjectivity, given here as a sarcastic reflection, finds its equivalent in his novel *The Conformist*. This work concerns a "little" man, a latent homosexual, who joins up with the Fascists to feed his own need for power, to compensate for his inadequacies, to be no longer a little man. It is the quintessence of an ideology, a game of make-believe, a myth of mass male hysteria. Elsewhere, the lassitude of his book *La Noia* will find its way, in a complete reversal of value, into the celebratory passages of *Io e lui*, which make unbridled pleasure a good thing. Even within Moravia's writing, we have two versions of what it is to be a man. In one, that of *La Noia* in the negative and that of *Io e lui* in the affirmative, the subject is one of sentient feeling, of flowing desire, be it of disgruntled lassitude or of unbridled, desublimated libido. In the other, the simultaneous elision of singularity and the construction of the subject is accomplished through an appeal to the phallocentric system of power and ideology. For many critics there is no choice, for, as I have already noted, it may be that the system of pleasure is always found to depend on a phallocentric system of power. As Kaja Silverman notes, "'exemplary' male subjectivity cannot be thought apart from ideology, not only because ideology holds out the mirror within which that subjectivity is constructed, but because the latter depends on a kind of collective make-believe in the commensurability of penis and Phallus" (15). Yet, as much as that ideology is difficult to extirpate, a writer such as Moravia shows us a system of desire that transcends this Lacanian mirror tendered by ideology, a Lacanianism, by the way, that Judith Butler categorizes as a kind of "slave morality" (*Gender* 57). In the main, Moravia constructs *Io e lui* to provide a space for a "desublimated" game of pleasure—the word is Moravia's own and provides the title of the first chapter of the novel—a space in which the pleasure of the penis far outweighs, immeasurably outstrips, the power of the phallus.

My book takes Moravia's chapter title about the "desublimated" penis as a serious clue. This book is a series of essays exploring literary and philosophical works to see the traces of this body of pleasure and pain, this body of which the penis as desublimated and described by Moravia is simply the most visible figure. I am hypothesizing that numerous works, well within the traditional canon of Western literature, can be read as figures of that other model, a nonphallocentric model, as signs of a zone of pleasure or pain, of bodily immanence, and even, as will become clear in the last chapter, of a game of power and pleasure that is predicated not on a phallocentric model but on what we might term a deconstruction of that model. There are multiple ways of approaching this body of pleasure and pain, as the variety of readings that follow clearly show.

Some critics are currently proposing models for reading and understanding that are not necessarily predicated on that phallocentric model. Susan Bordo, for example, posits a descriptive mode that, while including the penis as penis, distances the images of phallic swordsmanship: "Let's not look to the figure of the 'soft' penis. This would seem the most obvious route to re-visioning masculinity; but we're trying to refuse 'hard/soft' now. So, let's rather allow the imagination to play with the figure of the *aroused* penis—aroused (as in a state of *feeling*), rather than 'erect' (as in a state of accomplishment and readiness to perform)" (in Goldstein, 296). Just as radically, like a number of other critics, Gayatri Spivak calls for a reading of the queer body as a *mise-en-question* of phallocentric models, and specifically, "to undo our banishment of Eros from the ethical field" (in MacCannell and Zakarin, 51). Again, while the language is different, the strategy suggested by Bordo and Spivak is the same: dislodging an entrenched phallocentric order without falling into the traps of a simple opposition, for the oppositional space, like that of pleasure within the phallic model, is always already circumscribed by the dominant model.

Some may find these utopian positions. Let us consider, for a moment, the specter of the "queer body" in Spivak's quote. Notions of homo- and heterosexuality are intimately bound up with one another. Would the queer body somehow exist out there separate and apart from those notions? The queer body and the queer look or gaze might be a means of effecting, as Spivak suggests, a critique of the phallocentric model, even if it is derivative therefrom. So the queer body, itself a critique of the division between homo- and heterosexuality, stands as a criticism of any model that defines identity along such a line of cleavage, as if the two situations did not depend on one another for their contours, as if the two were completely separated by the line of demarcation between them. In *Male Impersonators*, his excellent study of the representation of masculinity in several fields of popular culture, Mark Simpson shows to what extent a homoerotic component is necessary to the construction of masculinity in various fields, including the obvious like bodybuilding and the construction of Tom Cruise as a superstar, and the less obvious like advertising and rock music. Can we be so sure that we are actually looking at the "straight" body or the "queer" body untainted or unmarked by its other? Similarly, as intriguing as the idea of the "aroused" penis may be, we can never be sure that it, always ready to be played with by the imagination, is not just a displacement of a phallocentric model of a perpetual motion machine, the production of outcome without an expense of spirit. More cogently, I am not sure how we can at this point abstract a figure on a large-scale theoretical level that will not be tied to the ideological system from which it comes. As Bersani shows, the straight system orients gay desires. But it also orients straight desires, desires for a postphallic world, and all other moves of a similarly idealistic bent. So the queer body may be just one more incarnation of a system of desire that allows, in its chronological development of an ever-changing array of consumer products, for the space in which a queer body and queer looks can exist.

Freedom from this system of ideological constraints comes not at a deep theoretical level from which some subsequent freedom can be deduced, but on a local level, repeatedly, as an act of remarking or rebellion. If this act occurs often enough—not as integers but as a sum—it will change the model. And this is not just within the contemporary context of current literary criticism or cultural studies, but with a retrospective glance at what has gone before. I am proposing therefore that a careful rereading of a number of works through a perspective that seems endlessly to "queer" the straight lines of canonic models may very well offer glimpses, at least, of a secret history of desire and of the body.

In the remainder of this introductory chapter, I should like to look at some recent contexts and examples of the desublimation of the penis. After that, I will generalize matters and propose considering a desublimation of the male body itself as a locus of desire. It is my contention that the penis has been the most hidden of male body parts because of the ideological as well as the psychoanalytical temptation to turn the penis into its evil twin brother, the phallus.[2] Over the last quarter century, that model has been consistently dismantled or deconstructed by writers, thinkers, and critics of all sorts, from Louis Althusser to Luce Irigaray, from Adrienne Rich to Jacques

Derrida, from Herbert Marcuse to Gilles Deleuze. That their readings are contemporary with—and among the sources of—a revision in understanding the literary and philosophical subject and a greater focus on political change, should come as no surprise to anyone, for the model critiqued is one that has served to repress women, gay men, and people of color, among others. What has not so often been noted, and what constitutes my point here, is that with the multiple, visible act of repression, the model simply does not allow for the expression of male desire—even or especially in its white heterosexual variety—in any form other than its "always-already" translated form of phallic power. Women are objects to be conquered and counted as are, in one way or another, all "others." Indeed, for Queequeg to be naked is no problem, even if his legs are "marked, as if a parcel of dark green frogs were running up the trunks of young palms" (816). Queequeg is brute force, the white man's other, physical power incarnate with no capacity to seize the phallocentric ideological structure for himself. The black man is the white man's victim, a naked figure who can, whether in Melville, René Crevel, or Robert Mapplethorpe, signify the white man's fears and fantasies, be paraded more safely unclad than clad. In *Mon corps et moi*, René Crevel puts a naked black man on stage who is wearing nothing more than a pair of white underpants that "stretches from thigh to thigh under the burden of African genitals" (64).

Thus, for me, there is an additional impetus in getting beyond the position that literary and philosophical endeavors are endlessly imprisoned within that model and that, consequently, captive to it, all these discourses can do is deconstruct it. Feminist critiques have shown that it is possible to posit a nonphallocentric universe, even if the origin of the critique comes from within the phallocentric model. It stands to reason that the last bastion of this phallocentric system needs also to be undercut through a deconstruction, so that there is a masculism or an andrology that goes beyond the phallocentric model as well. And again, I underline that such an andrology has been present in literature for well over a century at least and that this andrology will have two components. First is that the discrete model of counting and cataloguing the self and the other meets a challenge in a nonintegral mode of understanding. Second, the discourse of pleasure (or of pain), albeit propped on a phallocentric model, can take on a life of its own and leave that model behind because it is ultimately, through its *jouissance*, a deconstruction of the prop. Recent arguments about the status of the individual as a performer of his or her own selfhood seem to be the intertwining of both these strands. Consider the arguments advanced by Judith Butler in *Gender Trouble* concerning what she perceives as a discontinuity existing in the realm of sex, sexual practice, gender, object choice, and performance. For Butler, separating sex from gender, the latter becomes "the cultural meanings that the sexed body assumes" (6). Therefore there is no necessary continuity between man and masculine and the male (sexed body) or between woman and feminine and the female body. Indeed, the situation of the transgendered individual shows a radical split between the discursive structures of, for example, a woman, and the male body that woman inhabits. Moreover, this split does not necessarily reflect any sexual behavior: the same transgendered individual can be lesbian in his/her sexual behavior, for example. Again, however, this does not happen at the level of some Lacanian rule about lack; it happens in each individual instance.

The desublimation of the penis seems to have happened, at least in the consciousness of the public, with great éclat. And for that I should like to start in the pages of the *New York Times*. If something has made the *New York Times*, it is, as the saying goes, "fit to print." It is out of the underground, the purported closet, the depths of ignominy, the hidden world; it has surfaced, seen the light, come out into the clear black-and-white print of the daily or Sunday paper. Now it is perhaps only serendipitous that in the confessional culture of the present-day United States, in the performative culture that is, I would add, the same thing, penises appeared in profusion on the scene in what Camille Paglia calls in *Vamps and Tramps* "The Year of the Penis" (1). I am thinking of John Bobbitt, of course, and also Michael Jackson, whose penis was photographed for evidence in a legal case. Jackson's crotch-grabbing, like that of the Boston rapper Marky Mark, splayed in his Calvin Kleins for all to see on buses and billboards, whose display is eminently discussed by Mark Simpson (153–62), did all it could to outline in black and white what we had previously only assumed was there. And somewhat earlier, though basically in the same time period, could be found the discussions, on television, in the papers, and at every water cooler in the country, of the alleged comments by Clarence Thomas to Anita Hill on the size of his own penis and on that of the porn star Long Dong Silver. Yes, in fact, these boys had penises; well, Michael Jackson and Marky Mark did, even if John Bobbitt temporarily was relieved of his. The thing is that this appeared, not only as reported news stories in the New York *Times*, which, after all, one might have expected: stories of one superstar, one star *du jour*, a Senate hearing on a candidate for the Supreme Court of the United States, and a *fait divers* of an unusual nature followed by an equally hysterical trial. But it appeared at a meta-level, in discussions of the word "penis" itself, in discussions of the manifestations of such a word in this time and place, in everything short of a full-color picture. The nominally conservative columnist William Safire, in his guise as defender of the language every week in the *New York Times*, writes a whole column on the word "horny," and segues from the political comment that inspired his article, a statement on "Meet the Press," to a mention of the case of John and Lorena Bobbitt. Safire provides us with a statistic as he comments on yet another editorial: "The writer didn't need to use the word, but *penis* was used in the paper 12 times in the opening weeks of the year, compared with no uses in the same period last year." After providing the etymology of the word "penis," Safire goes on to note that "*Penis* surfaced two years ago in our living rooms in the Clarence Thomas hearings during Anita Hill's testimony, which also necessitated exhaustive etymological research into the slang synonym *dong* in this space." The word "penis" resurfaced in Michael Jackson's videotaped statement defending himself from charges of child molestation, and became part of life's daily language in the avid coverage of Lorena Bobbitt's trial. Safire concludes on two notes. The first relates to the size of the penis, or at least to that of its signifier: "July 13, 1993, will be remembered as the day the word *penis* appear in 30-point type in the New York Times." And the final paragraph is "Standard English has no dirty words. The word *penis*—severed or reattached, flaccid or erect—is as innocent, and as usable in polite company, as the hornyhead chub."

Another week, the *Times* has an article on the value of the penis. Bruce Handy starts his article with the question "What *is* a penis worth?" He goes on to speculate on a "reliable theory of penis value" in which he examines the purported aphrodisiac powers of tiger penises, the cost of John Bobbitt's surgical reattachment, the price of constructing "a phallus" for transsexuals, the annual income of porn stars who can "complete two 'scenes' a day, three to five days a week." He concludes with speculation on the whereabouts of John Dillinger's penis and the somewhat sad fact that there are some things more valuable than a penis, including a Jeff Koons sculpture and "a really huge truffle." Now I would posit that this concentration on the penis, for all its humor that mitigates the shock value, is a reflection of the fact that our society, or at least middlebrow and middle-class society, have accepted not only the diminished value of phallocentric ideology but also a replacement of it: a philosophy of desire.

This means, on the one hand, that there is a renewed emphasis on the male body itself, not just as a locus of congealed ideological power, but also as a locus of desire. Holly Brubach notes the recent "outbreak of naked men on billboards, in magazines and on the sides of buses." Interestingly, the gaze of the other looking at those naked men is an ambiguous, shared one. It is the author's male lunch date who remarks "the pecs on that guy"; the guy in question is Marky Mark. Yet when the author fantasizes herself in a hotel room in Venice with the model from the ad for Zino, who is "wearing his muscles with nonchalance," the fantasy goes nowhere; she muses that "a woman's libido" may be "wired differently" from that of a man. Clearly a desire that is the fictional construct produced by the systems of a world hellbent on selling something, that desire at its origin is a creation of a system that gives the viewers simulacra to desire. The desire is socially constructed and socially engineered. But the desire, thus foisted on the public, takes on a life of its own, for the perspective on any such case is necessarily queer, involving some blending of once distinct positions. For the desire to succeed as a vehicle for an economy in which the viewer's desire is provoked to resemble some fictional creation, the desire must mime all positions, thereby denying the uniqueness and the difference of individual subjects. For me to buy underwear, I must look at Marky Mark more queerly than ever before.

Equally important is that, even at the level of a world of simulacra produced from within the superstructural vehicles of advertising, there has been a successful challenge to the categories of phallocentric division: self and other, of course, as we have seen in the Moravia novel, but also man/woman, heterosexual/homosexual, and the like. Moravia himself points this out, for the discourse of pleasure necessarily implies a break with the model at hand: "I knew he was voyeuristic [*guardone*], sadistic, masochistic, homosexual (sure, even that; I haven't spoken about it yet, but the time will come for me to do so), fetishistic . . . but not an exhibitionist" (149). Moravia allows not only what used to be unthinkable—the prospect of one's own "homosexuality"—but also permits that category to dissolve in its descriptive chain into all the others.

Consider the old game of comparing penises to see who has the biggest one. The simplest explanation would be to see the game as a game of phalluses: the biggest penis means the biggest phallus means being king, not queen, of the hill. So the game would be some reminder of a more animal-like state in which the most male gets the best chance to breed and reproduce. But there is a queerer view, for some could see in this adolescent game the insidious structuring of all heterosexual men as latent size queens. And certainly, such an explanation of compulsory or "impulsory" homoeroticism makes sense: guys *do* look at other guys and the only ones not permitted to do so, in the United States at least, would seem to be queer men in the military. Moravia explicitly marks the game as a sexual one between two men, therefore as homoerotic and homosexual, because in this world of penis and instrument of pleasure, the simplistic division of the world into hetero- and homosexual no longer holds water:

I tell Maurizio, or more accurately, "lui" speaks with my mouth: "I have no difficulty in showing that nature truly was very generous with me. But you must do the same."
    "And why is that?"
    "Because some things are done only in pairs." (171)

So the game of comparing penises, in a world of "you show me yours, I'll show you mine," becomes the equivalent of a sexual act between the two men: "some things are done only in pairs." Federico sees himself as liberated, even if it is through the desublimated voice of his other, "lui." But not all the characters have arrogated such freedom to themselves. This same Maurizio is still caught in the old system of sublimation, that is, of clear division into hetero- and homosexuality, while Federico and, *a fortiori*, Federicus Rex have moved beyond that into a state of desublimated, free-flowing desire. Imprisoned in this old-fashioned binarism, Maurizio asks Federico if he's not a bit of a fag [*frocio*]. As soon as Maurizio leaves, "lui" is in a state of erection (173). "Lui" knows no such categories. As many theorists including Deleuze, Guattari, and Hocquenghem have pointed out, desire is not always already channeled into those socially engineered categories that seek to name it. Desire is, and it flows. Even if Federico, at various times, becomes a backslider into the world of heterocentric, phallocentric ideology, "lui," the book's real militant, remains steadfast in a commitment to a freeing of desire from the shackles of an out-of-date ideology: "When will you understand, superficial, light man, that I am desire and that desire desires everything [*tutto*]" (229).

Peter Lehman's excellent study, *Running Scared*, is one of the first books to examine the representation of the male from a generalized position that is not a priori sexualized as hetero or homo (though the author's point of view generally seems to be heterosexual), but is gendered as male.[3] There are a few lapses into a heterocentric discourse, which seem more a lack of attention than a prejudice: he notes that Almodóvar and Fassbinder are "self-acknowledged gay filmmakers" (126); that he would not make a remark about someone being a "self-acknowledged straight filmmaker" is clear. Lehman generally maintains a viewpoint that is, as Michel de Certeau might put it, outside the realm of the written, and not in dialectical opposition or relation to the written. Lehman focuses on the representation of the male body in cinema, though his most interesting chapters, to me, are not primarily about the visible, but about the audible. These three chapters deal with that most taboo of subjects, penis size (105–68). Lehman's point throughout is that to show the penis means to demystify the phallus, to show that sometimes a penis, large or small, is only a penis and not the magical organ of power: "In a patriarchal culture, where the penis is hidden, it is centered. To show, write, or talk about the penis creates the potential to demystify it and thus decenter it" (28). Hence the taboo on the representation of male nudity that is largely (though, of course, not completely) the law of cinema. It is to Lehman's credit that he tackles the question of aberrant discourses, jokes, myths, and prejudices about the size of the penis, that most mystical of measurements, the one that seems, in the abstract, to be the index of phallic power. Also to his credit, he does not exclude pornographic imagery, as the representation of the penis is one of the mainstays of pornography. One might conclude that this pornographic reversal depends on an identification, and an assent by the viewer, that the penis in view is in fact the phallus, not only of power, but of pleasure. The male body then, body of pleasure and/or of pain, is itself desublimated, not only as far as it relates to a question of restricted sexuality, but even more important, to what would be definable as a generalized economy of sexuality. Even in the first sense, there is a change. Alice Jardine's oft-quoted remark bears repetition:

What else? Well, there's men's relationship *after feminism*, to death, scopophilia, fetishism (we've had a beginning today), the penis and balls, erection, ejaculation (not to mention the phallus), madness, paranoia, homosexuality, blood, tactile pleasure, pleasure in genera, *desire* (but, please, not with an anonymously universal capital D), voyeurism, etc. Now this *would* be talking to your body, not talking *about* it. (61)

In thinking about the desublimated body, the body of desire, one does well to consider Deleuze and Guattari's well-known concept of privatization of the body. In the *Anti-Oedipe*, Deleuze and Guattari underscore how our organs became privatized, and since, according to them, the anus was the first organ to undergo that transformation, the anal model was used for subsequent acts of privatization (167–68). They start with the anus because, for them, this organ captures and is captured by the ideology of normalization in which the penis is always already hidden. It is no wonder then that the deprivatization of the anus, with which I deal in detail in the pages on Guy Hocquenghem, has elicited so much commentary. Consider the famous case of Robert Mapplethorpe, who had the nerve not only to produce a series of nude photographs of black men whose large penises are quite apparent as well as the equally famous picture of a white man, entitled "Mr. 10½," but also, and more despicably according to censorious detractors, to show a picture of his own asshole. Meyer quite matter-of-factly (and rightly so) describes Robert Mapplethorpe's infamous self-portrait: "The 1978 *Self-Portrait* offers

Mapplethorpe, outfitted in a black leather vest, chaps and boots, penetrating his asshole with a bullwhip" (362). Meyer goes on to say that the bravado of the photograph derives largely from the spectacle of its anality and from the fact that the asshole on offer is the photographer's own. By offering, indeed flaunting, his anus to the camera while also self-penetrating it, Mapplethorpe presents his body as a sadomasochistic receptacle of both the bullwhip and the viewer's gaze. Within the history of art, one is hardpressed to recall another self-portrait, whether painterly or photographic, which depicts its artist as anally penetrated. (363)

The spectacle of the anus is itself the most naked of the figures of this story of the sublimation or desublimation of the male body; and for me Deleuze and Guattari seem, though without saying it, masculist in intent. One might consider that Deleuze and Guattari also choose that organ because it is shared, as are all other organs except for reproductive ones, by both sexes. But Deleuze and Guattari focus on the construction of the patriarchal economy, one that assigns women a position as chattel and as vehicles for reproduction, and not one that assigns them the possibility of privatizing their organs. Indeed, one could forcefully argue that one of the signs of the classical patriarchal economy was that women had no right to privatize their own organs, and that the changing economy of the nineteenth century that would lead to the modern era was actually the first time that women's private parts began to belong to them. I would add that Hocquenghem himself, in his reading of Deleuze and Guattari, points out the availability of the woman's anus, as opposed to that of the man. The asshole, so to speak, has nowhere to hide; it is either privatized or out there in the open. But the penis has the luxury of having an alter ego in the phallus. In fact, I would go so far as to say that it makes no sense to talk about the privatization of the penis when it has fully disappeared behind the phallus of power, dissolving into it, sheathed in an imaginary condom of tensile strength, erectile capacity, and infinite power.

The disappearance of the penis into the phallus is part and parcel of the construction of normalized male desire. In his chapter on "Male Sexualities," Arthur Brittan finds one of the cornerstones of masculinist ideology to be the idea that "A man is only a man in so far as he is capable of using his penis as an instrument of power" (47).

This move to power by the simple virtue of having a penis founds a whole ideology of dominance. Most importantly, for Brittan, male sexual narratives depend on the belief by men that their sexuality as it is projected and acted out is reality. There are thus sexual scripts, "the means whereby men learn to name their internal states, so that they come to believe that the name is identical with the internal state (desire)" (60). R. W. Connell agrees:

The body-as-used, the body I am, is a social body that has taken meanings rather than conferred them. My male body does not confer masculinity on me; it receives masculinity (or some fragment thereof) as its social dedication. Nor is my sexuality the eruption of the natural; it too is part of a social process. In the most extraordinary detail my body's responses reflect back, like the little mirrors on an Indian dress, a kaleidoscope of social meanings. (83)

At the same time, as I have stressed all along, there is a body of desire, of pleasure and/or of pain, that is simultaneous with, though not commensurate with the body of power. It is this body of power that eventually determines for us the system against which much of contemporary literary and cultural criticism has rebelled in critiques of masculinist ideology, phallocentric discourses, and antifeminist desire. One example would be the homosocial condition of which Eve Kosofsky Sedgwick writes and another would be the male-male friendship focused on by E. Anthony Rotundo in his work. In *American Manhood*, Rotundo (75ff) develops the idea of an intimate male-male friendship arising among middle-class youth in nineteenth-century America. This friendship could extend as far as affectionate physical gestures and even romantic bonds, but usually, or seemingly, stopped short of full physical satisfaction, even if there was the occasional kiss, or even the very literal act of "sleeping together" (84), which was, as Rotundo points out, an everyday occurrence, and of which Melville's Ishmael makes much in the beginning of *Moby-Dick*, when faced with the possibility of having to sleep with Queequeg:

No man prefers to sleep two in a bed. In fact, you would a good deal rather not sleep with your own brother. I don't know how it is, but people like to be private when they are sleeping. And when it comes to sleeping with an unknown stranger, in a strange inn, in a strange town, and that stranger a harpooneer, then your objections indefinitely multiply. (809–10)

Of course, having spent the night with "Queequeg's arm thrown over me in the most loving and affectionate manner. You had almost thought I had been his wife" (820), Ishmael changes his tune. In any case, what was common early to mid-century becomes suspect by the end of the century. Much later in his book, Rotundo (278) notes the disappearance of such romantic friendships toward the end of the century as the "homosexual," the stigmatized character of a classifying society, became more and more visible as a singular type. By implication, then, these romantic friendships, once deemed innocent, seemed to push the edges of what was acceptable heterosexual behavior, and the separation between homosexuals and heterosexuals became ever more distinct. So it is not that there is a direct repression of homosexuality as such. Even less is there the woefully misnamed phenomenon of "homophobia": such repression as there is is the result of the firm establishment of an ideological system that finds one dominant sexuality as its economic vehicle, a phallic male sexuality that, by its very nature, pushes away all other possibilities. That is to say, it is not only heterosexual women's sexuality that is distanced by a categorization of that sexuality as impossible—"normal women have no sexual desire"—or fantastic—"women are hysteric"—but also all other sexualities, including homosexual sexuality in both its male and female varieties. If certain of these sexualities become stigmatized, it is neither out of a direct fear—"homophobia"—nor out of a totalitarian act of repression, but because they are seen, indeed scapegoated ideologically, as containing values contrary to the ideology. Women's sexualities and homosexual male sexuality are a challenge to a socioeconomic construct that depends on phallic power, choice of reproductive and productive venues, and the integral division into self and other already mentioned. Just as women's sexualities and homosexualities are repressed or "repressed" by the dominant ideological structure that creates "man" in the Enlightenment and post-Enlightenment era, all nonphallic versions of male sexuality, be they heterosexual or homosexual, are distanced. The power of the phallic model means that any system of bodies of pleasure or pain, any system that involves the organ of pleasure, the game of jouissance, the bliss of the male body, as well as that of the female body for the female subject, as source or object of desire is eclipsed as well.

An excellent literary example is Alfred Jarry's 1902 novel *Le Sur-mâle*. It starts with the possibilities of a discourse of pleasure. The protagonist André Marcueil, who "had never seen his genitals" (39) is taken to a tailor, though he does not understand why twelve-year-old boys can no longer be clothed by a dressmaker. The tailor, how-ever, has a problem, because there is a problem in the fitting: "Something below the waist and very near the waist, was making a big disgraceful fold" (40). Trying to make allowances both right and left, the tailor does no better in fitting the suit, for "between *on the left* and *on the right*, there is another direction: *up*" (40). Organ of discomfort for the tailor and for André's mother, who figures out she has eight years "to correct his deformity" (40), André's special penis becomes the incarnation of the antisocial, the nonreproductive, and the seditious. Nothing can be done to cure his priapism, neither physical exercise, drugs, nor repeated sexual activity; not even "vices 'against nature'" (41). Since it appears that this condition has been inherited, there is nothing to be done except to become the phallus of force, the superman of the title, the master bicycler, racer, he-man for all time. At least in that way, the dangers of pleasure will finally have been subsumed in the biggest phallus in the world.

So as masculinity becomes defined in terms of a phallic model of power in which pleasure is always a translation of that power, the model of pleasure for the sake of pleasure, or pain, for that matter, as we shall see in "The Pit and the Pendulum," is eclipsed by the all-dominating model. That phallic masculinity is, for my money, a perversion of maleness, for several simple reasons. It dismisses a model of pleasure that does not find its anchor in a model of power; it artificially separates sexualities, grosso modo, homo- and hetero-, of the male variety, with no valid reason other than an ideological stricture. And it is so powerful a model, if not to say compelling, it forces our readings against it into aberrant categories. As Victor Seidler says: "what is significant is not the category of 'masculinity' *per se*, but rather the ways in which the category normalizes a distorted life experience, and creates a distance from men's capacity for a fuller experience" (8). So the model is so capacious as to make all other possibilities themselves seem to be aberrations. All escape from the model becomes a distortion, a perversion of desires, for the institutionalization of desire, the effect of the subject, is always subsumed under this phallic totalization. As Brittan notes, albeit a bit naively,

The fact that the penis is valorized in Western culture does not mean all men attach the same meaning to sexuality. The script is not omnipotent; men are not aroused in the same way, nor are they likely to perform in a uniform manner. . . . For example, a gay person cannot easily transcend the parameters of the dichotomous model of sexuality. In his relationship with other gay men, he may find that he has to take either an active or passive role. (61)

More seriously, the pervasiveness of the phallic model leads someone like Judith Butler to castrate her own work in hopes of coming up with a performative theory of sexuality. In a parenthetic remark, Butler notes: "I have consigned the penis, conventionally described as 'real anatomy' to the domain of the imaginary" (*Bodies* 61). She goes on to say that this consignment may be considered a "liberation." For whom? Certainly not for the poor Bobbitt-like man walking around without a penis for the sake of a liberating theory. Indeed, Butler is well aware that she is doing this, not out of some vengeance on the domination of the male member, but because of the pervasiveness of the phallic model that finds its unique, yet totalizing voice in the myth of the penis magically transformed into a phallus: "If the Phallus only signifies to the extent that it is *not* the penis, and the penis is qualified as that body part that it must *not be*, then the Phallus is fundamentally dependent upon the penis in order to symbolize at all. Indeed, the Phallus would be nothing without the penis" (*Bodies* 84). As Butler goes on to suggest, there is no necessary relationship between the penis and the phallus and in her informative writing on the lesbian phallus proposes other possibilities:

The question, of course, is why it is assumed that the Phallus requires that particular body part to symbolize, and why it could not operate through symbolizing other body parts. The viability of the lesbian Phallus depends on this displacement. . . . To suggest that the Phallus might symbolize body parts other than the penis is compatible with the Lacanian scheme. (*Bodies* 84)

Now this allusion to Lacanianism, which, I repeat, she has earlier characterized, in a Nietzschean fashion, as a slave morality, is certainly a valid possibility. It is a means of liberating her own writing from the game of the phallus, for it is a way of reminding us that phallus means lack: "Indeed, if men are said to 'have' the Phallus symbolically, their anatomy is also a site marked by having lost it; the anatomical part is never commensurable with the Phallus itself. In this sense, men might be understood to be both castrated (already) and driven by penis envy (more properly understood as Phallus envy)" (*Bodies* 85). Thus by placing the penis in the realm of the imaginary, she is taking a strategy that repeats the castration of one and all, men and women alike.

Removing the penis is an act of castration at worst, an act of mutilation at best. And even if it serves to liberate gender theory from the yoke of the phallus it recapitulates that act of imposition that is phallic theory. Moravia knows this, as "io" threatens "lui" that he will castrate himself, to be like Abelard and Origen, but ultimately, of course, so taken is he with the idea of pleasure, of eros, that he does not perform that act (174). Now I cannot with one sweeping gesture simply install a theory of nonphallic erotics in the place massively occupied by phallic power. Indeed, Peter Middleton, who provides a comprehensive discussion of "Theories of Modern Masculinities" (113–65) in his book *The Inward Gaze*, points to one of the pitfalls of a male-oriented gender studies: "The problem facing men when they try to reflect upon themselves, without self-deception, is that they use the same intellectual methods that once justified men's power. It is then especially hard to interrelate subjectivity and power without either exaggerating the ease with which men can change, or denying culpability" (7). Middleton goes on to suggest using the idea of the gaze: "Laura Mulvey's (1985) influential image of men's power as the male gaze offers one possible way of exploring the problem, because it triangulates vision, knowledge and power. The act of looking is overdetermined as an act of scopophilia, and as the establishment of the boundary between the subject and its other." Here I cannot follow him, for I suspect, quite frankly, that the gaze, the tool of scopophilia, precisely because it continues to insist on boundaries, is part of the phallic power game. And indeed, Judith Butler seems to me to support this same system in her discussion of the congealing of material into boundaries: "What I would propose in place of these conceptions of construction is a return to the notion of matter, not as site or surface, but as a process of materialization that stabilizes over time to produce the effect of boundary, fixity, and surface we call matter" (*Bodies* 9).

So I would say that we have not progressed very far, even if we have been able to substitute a kind of performative model for a phallocentric eternity, or a progressive model, with various sites for the phallus, including a lesbian phallus, for an "erected" construction. No, I would still suggest that such models are all too indebted to the phallic system. And that, at the same time, we need to disengage a system of erotics from a system of power. In his book on the adventure tale, Martin Green contrasts what he terms "potestas" with "eros." Like eros, "potestas describes a set of relationships, but the latter have to do with force not love, domination not desire" (5). And although, he adds, the fields are often linked, or even confused, as in the case of traditional male-female relationships that depend as much on potestas as on eros, or in the erotic figuring of the adventurer as an erotic icon, the fields for him remain by and large opposite. Green goes on to say that this confusion is not simply solipsistic; far from it. As Green writes:

In both cases [eros and potestas], moreover, when one person either desires or dominates another, a reciprocal action occurs whereby the second person either resists, or accepts the position of being desired or dominated, or, on the other hand, seeks the position of desiring or dominating a third. (As this phrasing suggests, the two systems go together often. One often both desires and dominates the same other.) (7)

The system of phallic power subsumes the erotic, or the system of desire, or the system of the sensate, in an overwhelming fashion. Try as we may to come up with a theory that is not phallocentric, we inevitably fall into the pit of phallocentrism and find ourselves looking down on the body to be executed in a tale by Poe or by Kafka, in a novel by Octave Mirbeau. Our look, our scopophilia itself repeats both the panoptical prison of reason looking in on madness, the healthy looking in on the sick in the ward, the sane looking at the ship of fools sailing off, the "free" looking in on the imprisoned. And yet there are parts, body parts, parts of the canon, parts of an other andrology. It is my contention that even if, by and large, the discourse of dominant phallocentrism is inevitable, there exist works that propose an other discourse, a discourse, shall we say, of the penis instead of the phallus. In loftier terms, the same possibility that allows someone like Jacques Derrida to perform an extensive deconstruction of phallocentrism from within its confines is the force that produces such literary and nonliterary works. Derrida's own biography, and I would add, his work on friendship, escape the phallic to be written in the realm that allows for a novel like Moravia's *Io e lui*. It should be no surprise that aside from the pun on the word "parts" in my title, there is a serious reason for it. I would venture that a complete andrology is impossible, because the very gesture of totalization, or its rhetorical equivalent of visualizing a "lack," is the supreme phallocentric gesture. And to try to create a full andrology would help me hurtle headlong into the abyss of phallocentric lack. So I have opted for a more modest path, by choosing a number of works, most of which are familiar to all educated readers, in which I can describe, albeit partially, an andrology. In the next chapter I look at Poe's story, "The Pit and the Pendulum." While Poe's story may not immediately imply to some a problematics of the male body, I am suggesting that in fact it is only about that, about the limits of that body, its edges, indeed its number. And in that chapter, I elaborate a theory of enumeration that is not dependent on the game of integers. In my study of Proust, in *The Shock of Men*, I suggested a suitable figure for exploring metaphorics is the image of the complex number figured on Argand planes. Here, without dealing with the realm of imaginary numbers, I reduce the question to the most well-known "irrational" number, π. But as the reader will see, that particular number, situated between the integers 3 and 4, is not at all an arbitrary or "irrational" choice. At the same time, I might suggest that our reading of Poe could be greatly illuminated by a requestioning of his textuality. How is it that the founder of the mystery story seems also to be the one whose system is based on an irrational number? One possible solution is that in the mystery story, there is a link between subject and other, say, victim and murderer, formed by clues, which cannot be resolved into a simple binary pair: the victim is linked to the murderer and vice versa. At the same time, the detective remarks those clues and thus traces a second irrational number on top of the first.

In the third chapter I treat a novel of pleasure, the wonderfully titled *Bel-Ami* by Guy de Maupassant, a work about a social climber in French society. I suggest that this novel, though in a rosy light when compared to Poe's black abyss, can also be read as a figure of pleasure. Indeed, the whole novel is about Georges's rise to power because he is an object of beauty and a figure of pleasure—not a walking phallus, but an incarnation of erotics and aesthetics.

In the next chapter I turn to some literature written about masturbation and focus on the work of three disparate writers, Paul Bonnetain, a forgotten French naturalist writer who wrote a lurid novel about the dangers of masturbation, entitled *Charlot s'amuse*; Michel Tournier, whose work I have also dealt with in *The Shock of Men*; and Philip Roth, who, in *Portnoy's Complaint*, has given us the best modern fable about the forbidden activity in question.

In the last chapter, I have assembled several works that focus on the representation of the male body during certain points of the gay liberation movement in France and the subsequent celebration of the male body, ending with the inscription of the male body in the literature of AIDS. The first is a study of the rhetoric of liberation in the work of Guy Hocquenghem. The second is a study of some of the work of Hervé Guibert before his AIDS diagnosis. The last two parts of the chapter deal with the representation of the body of the philosopher in a reading of Foucault and his critics, and finally, the representation of the AIDS-infected body in some contemporary French narratives. In its own way, that final chapter is a counterweight to the chapter on Poe. If in the chapter on Poe I propose a figuration of the subject of masochism, for which the power game is almost tangential, in the last chapter, I propose the construction of a sadistic subject for whom action means independence and not the abuse of power.

π

PI: *principium individuationis*, "the notion of that identity *which at death is or is not lost forever*," the "perfect identity."

—Edgar Allan Poe

I. Of Stereotomy

In the Introduction I discussed the problems with which the reader of the male body may be faced in trying to understand how that body has disappeared twice: once behind a symbolic transformation of the vulnerable or sentient body into a phallic power, and a second disappearance behind a system of numbering, counting, and accounting that insists on singularity, countability, and integrality, a system that therefore discounts other ways of approaching a subjectivity that may or may not fit neatly into such a grid. In this chapter, I would like to focus on one of Edgar Allan Poe's short stories, "The Pit and the Pendulum," because I think it is an exemplary work for exhuming this double disappearance. Poe's tale asks and answers questions relating to the constitution of the individual as a subject. It provides an accounting of how we can understand what an individual is and what the limits of that individual may be.

Additionally, though Poe's work is framed by a historical context of the Inquisition, the writing bears only an accidental relation to that specific historical moment. With the exception of that initial throwing into the pit and the final rescue, there is no real effect of the Inquisition on the content of the tale. Any repressive regime and any rescuing hand would do just as well as those of the Inquisition and its enemies. Poe's break from social and historical context allows the individuality ostensibly to be contained by a single body not determined by genealogy, family, social context, or historical moment. It allows a reading of the body that is not framed *a priori* by the laws of reproduction. Here as elsewhere, Poe radically poses the problem of his character, for by and large, his characters are almost always profoundly alone with themselves. This is true in the majority of the tales and in many of the famous poems, including "The Raven." Moreover, while Poe's dead are more often than not women, his characters, at least the living ones, are always profoundly men. Poe thus affords an exceptional opportunity to examine the *mise-en-scène* of the male body.

One can imagine a reading of "The Pit and the Pendulum" that falls wholly within the realm of the logic of identity. Such a reading would entomb the victim permanently, for it is so predictable: its vision is of an abuse of power, of a glorification of that abuse through our scopophilic gaze. We love to read the description of the torture of another individual; our pleasure comes not only from some *Schadenfreude*, but also from our reveling in the knowledge that it is not we who are the victims. We are not being sacrificed; we are not the subjected other.

And yet, for all that, such a reading is deceptive. Here there is no mystery: the narrative form of the tale tells us, without a doubt, that the victim is not in hell, will not die, but will survive. Does part of our pleasure in reading this tale also come from his survival? This is certainly possible, and yet, the bloodlust and *Schadenfreude* of a system of sacrificial violence, as René Girard would term it, or of a system of carno-phallogocentrism, as Jacques Derrida would term it, comes from our comfort in the knowledge that the system is closed by the bloodletting. In other words, it does no good to have a body count and to say, at the end, well, it was all a game. Narrative itself— the most formal aspects of narrative such as tense and person—vitiates the model of carno-phallogocentric sacrifice and victimage.

And I think Poe does so not only because of the formal structure that narrative provides is in the end only a vehicle for this deconstruction of the "scene of writhing," but also because he is aware that the positivist/realist model is seconded by this irrational model, a model of partial sums, of partial theories (again, to go back to a term I proposed in *Flaubert and Sons*), of parts lying somewhere between one and its other. Read from the point of view of the subject as a subject determining his own action and logic, of determining his own viability, and not as the subject of some sadistic and therefore different other, "The Pit and the Pendulum" is the tale of a writing against the principle of identity.

Now there is a caution to be taken when reading Poe within such a poststructuralist perspective—a mode in which I would include my own reading. And that problem is the looming presence of a French debate (really, a set of readings over time) that focused on "The Purloined Letter." I would like to read Edgar Allan Poe's "The Pit and the Pendulum" not by Americanizing a French Poe nor by Gallicizing an American Poe. My goal is modest: I want to understand the first word of the story, "I." This is the speaker, the suffered, the subject, or simply the instance of the one saying "I" at that moment, as Emile Benveniste would have it—or the one writing "I." As we already have seen, the formal qualities of a first-person narrative, however it may be defined, put that spoken "I" into a completed and survived past, and make the problematic of the written "I" different from the problem of the contents of the story. In any case, I would assume that this "I" is the integral, fictional name for some irrational subject. The first-person singular pronoun is made a fiction, or presents itself as a fiction, for it purports to name some unknown, and perhaps unknowable past identity, whose survival we already know, yet whose very same survival we must refuse to know for now. The "I" is a fiction because it says that at the same time—to put it into words familiar to all poststructuralist readers of Poe—the letter always reaches its destination and the letter never reaches its destination. In this case the letter is "I."

Beyond that, I would like to figure out what other constraints have been placed on that "I" by two institutional contexts. In fact, I am twice prevented from reading or from finding out that I cannot read. The recent institutional context for Poe studies is the French line focusing on Lacan's reading and its aftermath and the equally important, though seldom discussed, generic context: a historical, literary context that relates to a specific subgenre of literature of torture. So before approaching "The Pit and the Pendulum," I am bound, like the unfortunate protagonist of the story. To get to him, to find out what and how he means, I must make two detours. The first will look at several implications of the institutionalization of the debate following Jacques Lacan's study of "The Purloined Letter." The second will be through a small corpus of works to see what general insights can be gleaned from literature about the kind of torture seen in "The Pit and the Pendulum."

According to the dictionary, the word I have used as a title for this section, "stereotomy," is the art of cutting solids, and specifically the art of stone-cutting: Poe's detective, Dupin, says to the narrator, "perceiving your lips move, I could not doubt that you murmured the word 'stereotomy,' a term very affectedly applied to this species of pavement" (404). But if only it were that simple: as long as the parts of Poe's tales add up to wholes, things are all right. For example, in a detective story like "The Murders in the Rue Morgue," traces of an absence talk; they are threads of some unknown presence found elsewhere. Even the nontraces speak. Toward the beginning of the story, Dupin invents the signs of the thoughts of his friend, the narrator, without there being an act of presence, an index; there is rather a series of non-indications that leads both the narrator and Dupin to the same conclusion (401–4), a method that Nancy Harrowitz relates to what C. S. Peirce describes as abduction, only coincidentally, but in an *unheimlich* fashion, a word that can be applied to so many of Poe's narratives.

Yet abduction also seems strangely the right word for describing both the process of imposing the logic of orthogonal stereotomy on a chaos of disparate elements and the displacement of a woman. In fact, when it is a question of women, Poe's tales bring the pieces back into place. The idea of separation is related to men, just as the *topoi* of sudden death and recapturing are related to the woman as other. In "The Tell-Tale Heart," for example, the old man must be separated from his eye. This heart, which keeps on beating in the mind of the narrator, and thus rejoins the clocks of other stories beating a time of death, is also separated from him. But in a tale like "Berenice"—like many others in which the heroine dies a natural death—the separation of the body occurs in order to bring the female body back to the narrator, to rejoin her pieces to him. Fixated on "the white and ghastly *spectrum* of her teeth" (230), the narrator becomes monomaniacally obsessed with them, just like the narrator of "The Tell-Tale Heart" becomes fixated on the eye of the old man. After Berenice dies in the throes of an epileptic seizure, and after her burial, the narrator, in a parallel syncope—for he does not know what happens—finds himself to be the possessor of her teeth: "there rolled out some instruments of dental surgery, intermingled with thirty-two small, white and ivory-looking substances that were scattered to and fro about the floor" (233).

And yet to accept this idea of recuperation as a *sine qua non* is evidence of a more fundamental problem in Poe's writing. What is identity for him, or what could it be? When there is so much disappearance, death, destruction, when there are so many instances of decomposition, of being used up, when there are dances that move toward death, what could the identity of the individual be for Poe? I would hypothesize that from the very beginning the extreme scenario for Poe is found in a work where there is no visible trace of the ideology of abduction and recuperation, and where, singularly, stereotomy would not solve the problem but prevent the very existence of the story: the tale in question, is, of course, "The Pit and the Pendulum." Even before approaching that work, I would like to dwell for a little while on the question of identity itself. What does it mean to ask that question, to ask what identity may be, to ask when we know there is no answer?

The question of identity that is at the heart of the radical experiment that is known as European thought, the figuration of that identity, at least since Aristotle and the Greek tragedians, lies at the heart of the praxes of that experiment. In every literary work it is the question of fundamental importance. We know, or we think we know, that a resolution to the problem of identity is the ground on which the literary work is constructed, that the differentiation of the persons in the grammatical sense as well as the differentiation of the characters within any given work are fundamental to any paradigm of interpretation and understanding. As I have already suggested in the introductory chapter, the account of this differentiation into various identities is a clear-cut tally; without leaning too heavily on the philosophical, I would simply point out that these would be the beings at the heart of Being, *étants* participating in the *Être*, various *Seienden* in the *Sein*. More germane to what I have already been talking about is the fact that this differentiation is done along rational, integral lines. Beings are individuals, countable members of a set, a number of units to be ticked off in the roster of determining identity. Identity is therefore always figured as male. I have also suggested that this model of integral numbers is not the only one available to us. I would go on to hypothesize that just as the mechanisms of realist writing are coming into being, simultaneous with, I would add, both the figures of positivism and the first attempt at the development of a scientific socialism, at least one competing model arises simultaneous with those events. It seems to me no coincidence that these models of human thought, arising at the same time as photography, all have similar constructs. First of all, reality is discretely representable. Even when there are approximations to reality, such as that offered by language, there is an alternative found in another means of representation to the same end: the photograph, for example, or the Balzacian *captatio benevolentiae*. This latter, a rhetorical device used in various forms within realism, but especially by Balzac, is a plea, or a ploy to capture the reader's will. In capturing the reader's good will Balzac seeks to capture the images constructed within the reader's mind as figures used to fill in gaps or ruptures that are foisted on the act of representation by the comparatively weaker vehicle of language. To approximate the photographic simulacrum Balzac combines a technique of detailed description with an appeal to a cache of images in the reader's mind.

Along with realist writing, which I do not pretend to treat in this book except as it serves as the paradigm in which Guy de Maupassant will write, come positivism and scientific socialism. Again, there is a continuity of representational logic, a logic of reason. So in addition to the fact that reality is discretely representable, in these systems there is a logic of consequence that relates present to past, in a knowable and epistemologically reversible fashion, and relates present to future in the same way. Given the complete knowledge of a moment and understanding its representability means that we can re-present the past and predict future representations of any moment after this one. The logic of socialism as well as the logic of positivism is an integral logic, performing in the counting house.

Situated in another world and agonizingly feeling the belatedness of all representation, Poe is caught between the truth of the model into which he has come to write and the competing truth of his melancholic model that says solving codes and finding clues leads to no reconstruction other than that of a simulacrum. What good does it do to find a murderer, to find a treasure, if there is no concomitant rediscovery of the truth of being? And so Poe posits not only a *principium individuationis*, discussed by John Irwin in *American Hieroglyphics* (108, 121), but also an irrational deconstruction of reason and its numbers. The *principium individuationis* marks the unit, defines the self and its own concept of eternal, discrete identity. That identity is the unshakable logic of the three detective tales, the distillation, I would say, of the system of logic that founds the ratiocinative mode within realism, or as the ultimate paranoia of realism. It is, as David Bell points out in his excellent article on "Marie Rogêt," the realm of probability as well, in which numbers, like the very words I have just discussed, have a predictive value: words used as clues are metonymies of a probability table.

At the same time, reason has its other or several others. One would be what is commonly thought of as the irrational, but as Poe shows in "The Murders in the Rue Morgue," that irrational is doubled by the rational, the reasonable, and the probable. So this language which is not a language "spoken" by the murderer, who is not a murderer in that a murderer has to be human and capable of reason, is redoubled by the rational language of Dupin, just as the irrational of the nonmurderer, the killer of the story, is redoubled by human reason. Another of these others is the pure madness figured by the absence of the dialogical in various Poe stories: there is an unchallenged narrative constructed from a single point of view. Consider the unreason, the madness that structures the discourse of works like "The Cask of Amontillado," "William Wilson," and "The Black Cat." And there is, at least as a shadow of the light of reason, a reason of melancholia, as figured in works like "Ligeia" and "Morella," among others.

But there is another other to reason: a completely sane, though almost impossible figure that neither explains nor can be explained by reason. It is the figure of the pure irrational, in the arithmetic sense: that which is neither one nor two, that which by its very nature, if nature is even the right word, is always already caught up in a between. We have traditionally read this between as a game of power, as a structuring of power, phallic power, as I have suggested in the first chapter; it is the story of subjection and subjugation, the inscription of the sadomasochistic couple, in the most unerotic realm of *potestas* imaginable. And thus it has been somehow considered an aberration, a figure that is created through the refusal of the norms of human reason. But wait: on whose account does one assume that reason must prevail, that the model of behavior is the Aristotelian schema of identity that is the ontological and epistemological translation of a moral and ethical golden rule? The rules are the same, obeying the same logic, beating time by the same clock that counts out the seconds equally to us all. For Poe, though, there is another model, a more shadowy one, to be sure, that is the other to the reasons and logic of reason, neither preceding it nor following it, a tractable otherness fitting squarely within the realm of the nonphallic.

As Joseph Kronick notes, "Poe has long been the other of American literature" (22). Perhaps more than any other American writer, Poe has had as many defenders and detractors as he has had critics. His fortunes have varied; his influence has been felt more overseas than at home. In figuring the indeterminate, in writing about that space between life and death, in giving a perlocutionary force to a character *in articulo mortis*, in short, in writing in that space between, Poe has become the figure of that indeterminacy, the incarnation, even in his death, of that irrational no man's land: "Tel qu'en lui-même l'éternité le change." Over the course of time, Poe has become that other Poe, not merely the Poe writing of horror and despair, but the Poe who can never comfortably fit within a literary canon. It is difficult to wrest him from his heritage, and specifically from Baudelaire's invention of Poe as a French writer. In the end, one wonders if such a task is worth the effort. Is not the interest of Poe precisely in this indeterminacy, an author found somewhere between North America and Europe, or, *pace* Jacques Lacan, between Baltimore, where Poe is buried, and Paris, where he was reborn?

It would seem natural then to deconstruct all of Poe, to follow the French line, the logic of French thought—and we should never forget that Poe's detective is French—to read any one of a number of his works in this middle area. I shall look at the famous reading of Poe's "Purloined Letter" shortly, and *concesso non dato*, let us still for the moment suppose that it is possible that the Lacan-Derrida readings are appropriate to Poe's work. Let us at least take that as a working hypothesis. One might very well assume that such a reading or approach is suitable to some or all of Poe's other narratives. Would it work for the tale in question, "The Pit and the Pendulum"? At least one critic, Doug Robinson, has made such an attempt. While noting that Poe is often seen as the great precursor, "via the French line of Baudelaire-Mallarmé-Valéry-Lacan-Derrida," Robinson says that "Poe's work is full of intriguing alternatives to the binary options of deconstruction" (66). And though the critic has duly warned the reader of the dangers of such binarism, he winds up falling into the pit of the French line of binary oppositions, or its New Haven variety, the numbers game that crops up in Barbara Johnson's reading of "The Purloined Letter": Robinson proposes a deconstruction of the tale as "an allegory of reading." For Robinson, the narrator, deep in the pit, "had but two choices, absolute absence or rescue into presence" (71). Now even if this is not necessarily the only deconstruction of the tale that one might imagine, its error, for lack of a better word, is its shining exemplarity. One may choose a work in which writing is a theme, in which therefore there is a naturalness to the idea of the work as an allegory of reading—the *Recherche* passage chosen by Paul de Man in the book of the same name, the "Purloined Letter" chosen by Lacan in his insistence on the signifier, and thus in his own allegory of writing, if not reading, or any one of a number of Poe works: *The Gold Bug* comes to mind as does John Irwin's approach to Poe, entitled, appropriately enough, *American Hieroglyphics*.

The problem is that "The Pit and the Pendulum" is not *a priori* an allegory of reading, of writing, or anything of the sort. Is Poe's tale a Hobson's choice? Or has "the French line" forced us always to read Poe according to the reason of binary logic and/or deconstruction? My initial answer is no, for Jacques Derrida himself is never trapped in this binary logic. One solution to the Poe problem has been to posit a moment that frames that logic: a metatextual frame, the exigencies of verisimilitude, or an overarching irony. Thus Robinson sees Poe as ironic and R. D. Gooder (123) sees a tale like "Valdemar" as a "hoax," with the "attention to detail" there mainly for reasons of verisimilitude. Still, even if the allegory is ironized, it remains steadfastly present and most readers of Poe seem to have been caught in the vise of binary logic.

While we understand Lacan's predilection for a work like "The Purloined Letter," with its underlining of the insistence of the signifier, we can imagine that instead of "The Purloined Letter," Lacan had chosen to read or to rewrite another Poe tale, perhaps "The Tell-Tale Heart," "The Fall of the House of Usher," or even "The Pit and the Pendulum," all likely objects of psychoanalysis. In choosing "The Purloined Letter," Lacan opted to make the theme of the insistence of the signifier part of the theoretical structuring of the framework of Poe. It is this insistence as theme that has been so often forgotten by almost everyone except for Derrida.

Let us look at the reception of this uncannily insistent seminar. Lacan read "The Purloined Letter," spoke about it in 1955, and published his "Seminar on 'The Purloined Letter'" in 1957. Much later, Jacques Derrida's article, "The Purveyor of Truth" appeared in 1975, and was followed by Barbara Johnson's clever study of the two, "The Frame of Reference," three years after that.[1] Sarah Kofman (91n) refers the reader to Lacan, Derrida, Johnson, and "for a critique of B. Johnson's text," Marian Hobson, "Deconstruction, Empiricism, and the Postal Services." And John Irwin has summed up the whole debate in a brilliant article about reading and exemplarity, "Mysteries We Reread, Mysteries of Rereading." I shall not take time to go over all this familiar ground, except insofar as it touches on the strange connection between the allegory of reading and its relation to integrality.

None of these readings was done in a vacuum, and the debate is one of the most politicized in all of modern critical theory. This series of works has fueled an ongoing debate between the institutions of deconstruction and psychoanalysis, even if Derrida and Lacan have always shown nothing but the highest esteem for Freud. It has also challenged us in our reading. Can we read Poe as if Lacan had not read him? Is it in our interest to do so? Can we stop playing the minister or the queen in "The Purloined Letter" in order to play another part, though not that of Dupin, who always already reads for us? The role I shall eventually suggest, that of the narrator-victim in "The Pit and the Pendulum," may seem extreme—aberrant, masochistic, eccentric—to some. But, for now, I ask for patience.

The questions are not frivolous for (as Irene Harvey points out in her study of Poe) Lacan, Derrida, and Johnson all engage the notion of exemplarity, and Harvey suggests that it is time to deconstruct exemplarity itself (Muller and Richardson, 266). The set of readings has made an example of "The Purloined Letter"; reading Poe has made the tale exemplary. So Poe himself in being exemplary has been purloined for other uses, to be used, thus, as an example for other people, other readers. Two observations on the purloining of Poe's letters: first, as "The Purloined Letter" has lately been taken as an example, we cannot read Poe without echoes of the debate. There must be a trace of that set of readings in any subsequent one. But I think the second consequence is even more important. Through no fault of their own, Lacan and Derrida have given us readings in which we have tacitly accepted the adding and subtracting of units and unities and the fragmentation of a unit into component parts. Exemplarity means seeing that *one* letter as present or absent, one or zero. Exemplarity means numbering, counting, and accounting. We have come to rely so extensively on the numbering system of exemplarity—its ones, twos, and threes endlessly sought and found, its doublings discovered, its dyads and triads monumentally erected—that we actually have come to believe in a sense of unity fetishized as presence.

Unity = presence. A strange consequence, to be sure, an impossible purloining of being and beings. Where is it written that unity may or should be fetishized as presence? Are the pieces of fiction necessarily fragments of some whole? Do the images of some ego, superego, and id add up to a whole? Does not the very natureless nature of deconstruction imply the eternal otherness from the self, the irreducible difference that cannot be co-opted into a system of wholes and its parts? Certainly Lacan's argument about inmixing and intersubjectivity lends itself more readily to the ideology of wholes and parts than does the Derridean model of the letter that may or may not reach its addressee, and for which receipt there is no definite probability. But the institutionalization of the argument has led to a counting off of numbers, rational frames, correspondences, and signs of logical countdowns toward understanding.

John Irwin's excellent article on Poe, "Mysteries We Reread," provides so thorough a summary of the first three works in the Poe debate that it is unnecessary to repeat the arguments one more time. Significantly, before getting into the meat of the three pieces, he points out that there is a thread of numbers and geometry that runs through the story and through the readings (1170). Irwin shows that Derrida also gets into the numbers game and, in fact, Irwin follows him in his critique of Lacan. Specifically, for Derrida and Irwin the structure of the tale is quadrangular, and that quadrangulation is a criticism of Lacan, who structures the work according to threes, for it is not only the letter that insists, but also, and more importantly, the Oedipal triangle, countable in three, just like the ego, id, and superego. Lacan is thus brought to refuse the twos of doubling, an activity that is the basis for detective work, as the detective doubles the actions of the criminal.[2] In her own reading, Barbara Johnson sees both Lacan and Derrida as being caught in a numbers game. Following Johnson, Irwin notes that the two Jacques are caught in a game of even and odd, as "Derrida and Lacan end up as reciprocal opposites, as specular doubles of one another: Derrida asserts the oddness of evenness, while Lacan affirms the evenness of oddness" (1175). Johnson wants to get around the numbers game or go beyond the numbers game, for to get involved means to be caught in an opposition of odd and even. And still, Irwin notes that "Johnson's essay is at odds with itself, as she is the first to acknowledge" (1176). Indeed, one might consider Johnson's final words, at least as they appear in print; they are an endnote to a statement in the penultimate paragraph of the body of the work: "What we call a random series is, in fact, already an *interpretation*, not a given; it is not a materialization of chance itself, but only of something which obeys our conception of the laws of probability" (Muller and Richardson, 251n). Perhaps there is no nonnumerical position. Perhaps we are doomed to count everything out. And yet we know that such a ticking off of the numbers, such a ticking away of ambiguity (or of the irrational that appears somewhere before probability is realized), is exactly what is refused in "The Pit and the Pendulum." Despite the swinging of the mechanism, despite the clock that counts toward death, the victim survives; he escapes the supposed inevitability of the escapement. So we already know that we must clock him differently: a letter does and does not reach its destination; a victim is and is not killed by a relentless blade; Schrödinger's cat both is and is not dead.

Nevertheless, the debate has been and will continue to be informative. As odd as it may seem to someone who knows that the story was around for a hundred years before it became this object of massive inquiry, there is no way even to look at it without remembering the numbers game. The discourse of the numbers game now has an institutional force: it has become the example by which academics read Poe, and the institutional force that makes an example of Poe. To a certain extent, Poe has become imprisoned in the institutionalization of the numbers game, so that he too has become, like the narrator in "The Pit and the Pendulum," a prisoner within the walls of a very sophisticated machine.

Irwin's second insight is that the way around the imprisonment of the numbers game is to review numbering itself. He notes that self-conscious thought cannot be "absolutely even with itself" and is "essentially at odds with itself." It is a small leap of faith and not a leap into the pit that brings this reflection on self-conscious thought to the literary artifact. The literary work cannot be absolutely even with itself and is essentially at odds with itself; the even/odd game has no comfortable solution and the reader is always odd man out, as the expression goes. The solution is to be found elsewhere in "The Pit and the Pendulum": the mathematical solution is not the stuff of grade-school arithmetic, or as Kafka remarks in his novella "In the Penal Colony" of the same matter, "it's no calligraphy for school children" (121). And Poe himself starts "The Man of the Crowd" this way: "It was well said of a certain German book that 'er lasst sich nicht lesen'— it does not permit itself to be read" (388). Poe protects his writing from our eyes, protects its deciphering by making it far harder to read than we might at first expect. This is far more difficult than the cipher of "The Gold Bug."

An infinite number of numbers exist between two integers, an abyss of uncountable numbers. The figure for the work is not one, two, or three, but an irrational number. And the "exemplary" irrational number is between Lacan's three and Derrida's four: π. π marks this tale, filled as it is with the abyss of the infinite, the circles of hell, the circularity of reason. π marks this tale by making the figure of the irrational, the figure between, the only number that counts. Neither self nor other, neither three nor four, strange reversal and simultaneous confirmation of the *principium individuationis*, π figures the details of "The Pit and the Pendulum," as it too, marks its own impossibility as a tale.

"The Pit and the Pendulum" is exemplary in that it is impossible that it be exemplary. For the story is like that irrational number, never completely self-reflexive, never completely capturable. This Poe tale *par excellence* does not demand the doubling, trebling, and quadrupling of "The Purloined Letter" and its theoretical postscripts; it insists on the irrational immediacy found between two integers, between the annihilation of the subject at point zero and the completion of the subject at a unitary, integral position. In its own unrepeatable way, this story shows that every literary work rehearses the literary *supplice* as the generalized scene of writing. If we have come to see the reflective moment in many self-conscious literary works as the scene of writing itself—the letter in "The Purloined Letter" being a case in point—"The Pit and the Pendulum" presents us with a far more tantalizing solution. The scene of writing does not depend on the representation of what we normally consider writing for its self-reflexivity. No matter how useful that scene of writing may be in our understanding of the textual dynamics, it is not necessarily the solution of the literary work. Rather, if we return to a generalized concept of writing first announced by Derrida in *De la grammatologie* in 1967, we see that the scene of writing does not depend on the "vulgar" representation of that act. And though it may give us clues, it is not the only path taken. Despite the absence of pens, paper, ink, and a writing desk, "The Pit and the Pendulum" is no less the generalized scene of writing in the sense that Derrida understands it.

II. Supplice

Having read the tale, the reader returns to reinscribe the beginning, to understand exactly where the tale occurs, how it means. For the announcement of sickness at the beginning of the story stops the reader: "I was sick," Poe's narrator starts. If one is interested in understanding to what extent the body in question may or may not be whole or integral, it is necessary to pause. What does it mean to be sick, to have the body or mind somehow in a state of incompletion or dysfunctionality? Moreover, what does it mean to write about it?

We expect a sickness, but having read the story, we know that it is not the case: it is a tale about torture, about an induced sickness unto death, a movement toward the death of a victim, always defined as a victim, always subjugated, who is watched as he suffers. The gaze of the torturers is the same gaze as that of scopophilia, is the same gaze, ultimately, as the medical gaze of discernment and differentiation between sick and healthy. The difference is that in the latter, the gaze focuses on one organ, part, or member. The gaze of torture is a remarking of the suffering of a whole being, even if the torture is applied at a local level. The scopophilic gaze is somewhere between the two, somewhere between the *Schadenfreude* of the whole and the fetishism of the part.

What does it mean to have these gazes remarked in literature, or more exactly, how has literature formed a corpus around the idea of pain? The literature of pain has various forms by no means mutually exclusive: the record of a true illness, works about sexual sadomasochism, and works that reflect or describe political torture. I shall leave the first two aside, for the announced sickness here, as well as any sexual pleasure derived from pain, is a by-product; I shall concentrate on the third.

There are two kinds of torture. The first is that of torture itself, the pain inflicted on a victim in order to extract information. As Elaine Scarry says in *The Body in Pain*, "Torture consists of a primary physical act, the infliction of pain, and a primary verbal act, the interrogation. The first rarely occurs without the second" (28). Torture is found in a system of verbal exchange in which this linguistic economy is posited on the base of physical violence. Its dynamic and literature are of politics and exchange; of master and victim; and of actions, words, and ejaculations. In torture, one cannot go to the extreme if the act is to be successful, for death means the end of the linguistic exchange. As soon as there is no more verbal exchange, as soon as torture has either been too successful or gone too far, the physical action becomes *supplice*, the supplement to its original meaning.

Distinct from the economy of torture and its inscription within a process of exchange, there is a second kind of torture and a second kind of literature of torture. These deal with what French calls *supplice*, which is any kind of torture that happens after judgment. Historically, supplice was considered as expiation and martyrdom, but it undergoes a change in the era preceding the literature of supplice. As a certain modernity develops in the eighteenth century, supplice loses its cosmological prop and its ontological justification. The death penalty is the final, vestigial sign of this order of cosmological punishment, the wrath of God or his vicars on earth, yet supplice as such disappeared about a century and a half ago in the West. The disappearance of supplice is the enactment of the prohibition of "cruel and unusual punishment." As Michel Foucault remarks in *Surveiller et punir* of the reforms of the post-Enlightenment, "Among so many modifications, I shall insist on one: the disappearance of supplices" (13).

In the literature of supplice, the narratives relate the long agony of pain inflicted, not to extract information, but to punish. Saints' martyrdoms and narratives of the *autos-da-fe* of the Inquisition come to mind, as does the satirical criticism of the auto-da-fe in Voltaire's *Candide*. Distinct, at least on the surface, from narratives of sexual sadomasochism, this literature of supplice is a small corpus with, to my knowledge, only three modern canonic narratives: Edgar Allan Poe's "The Pit and the Pendulum," Octave Mirbeau's novel *The Garden of Supplices*, and Franz Kafka's "In the Penal Colony." Add to that a few lesser-known stories such as "Torture by Hope," by Villiers de l'Isle Adam, and various dungeon scenes from earlier Gothic or horror novels, or even historical novels like Walter Scott's *Anne of Geierstein*, and the set is fairly complete. Indeed, the small number of works in this set makes intertextuality an inevitability. Donald Ringe (281–83) notes the influence of one of Scott's Waverley Novels, *Anne of Geierstein*, on "The Pit and the Pendulum." Specifically, along with the family name of Arnheim, there is a dungeon scene in chapter 15 of the novel in which the play of light and dark as well as various other descriptions are clearly an influence on Poe. What distinguishes the episode from Poe's invention is both its episodic nature and also the fact that, emblematically, in *Anne of Geierstein*, the trial episode happens *after* the torture scene. Poe's insight was to show that the writing of supplice occurs not *before* the law, for there is no longer truth *before* the law, but that it always occurs at a point subsequent to the law. I would add to my list of the three major narratives the category of snuff films, whose existence is often put in doubt perhaps because we believe a literal enactment of supplice is impossible, even though we believe torture for political ends is an everyday occurrence and we more or less accept the existence of the fictional representation of sadomasochism even in its "snuff" form.

Supplice is the act of punishing a condemned individual who is viewed as a criminal by the powers that be. Supplice occurs after torture, after judgment, and after sentencing; it occurs between judgment and death. Supplice is more than the continuation of torture. Supplice is simultaneously the act of punishment, the act of undergoing punishment, and the record of pain felt by the subject. As Kafka shows in his story "In the Penal Colony," supplice is the double inscription in one locus: the inscription of the punishment and the record or registration of that inscription. But as far as the body is concerned, supplice is simultaneously the act of the presentation of the body, the representation of that presentation, and the record of that act of representation: signifier and referent are joined mercilessly. In supplice, there is no economy of exchange, and as opposed to torture, in which the response, or the representation of the presentation of the pain, must be heard, this record is silent. In torture, there are two possible responses: information or "I will not talk"; the former is given in exchange, the latter, as supplementary expense. But in supplice, as Kafka demonstrates, the language or sounds elicited by the act of inscription are moot. The screams are muffled by the fact that they are not a message in a system of communication; they say nothing that is not already known. Moreover, the screams cannot make known to the other, be he the torturer or the observer, what exactly is being undergone: they cannot represent.

Supplice is also supplication: what precedes the physical act and what is said before the law is enacted. Supplice is a verbal genuflection that does not participate in exchange. Real exchange is followed by clemency; the physical supplice must not take place in its full-fledged form; it must not be itself. Effective supplication may detour supplice into nonsupplice, making it enter into an exchange system. True supplice consists of three parts: supplication that is not considered, pain that is not reflected, and action that has no subject.

Though I am using the gender-neutral language that has become the benchmark of contemporary criticism, I would remind the reader that the literature in question—Poe, Mirbeau, Villiers, Kafka—always has a male victim. There is a literature of supplice with female victims, but it is always predicated on sexual sadomasochism. Beyond supplice on the economic and social side is torture and on the side of the subject in his presence to himself or herself is sadism, sexual pleasure that depends on the total, violent subjugation of the other, even unto death. Sadism involves desubjectifying the other as a human being until all contracts are eliminated. Sadism is the work of an individual joined to the absolute word of the subject-actor. Again, I am not engaging the psychoanalytics of sadism, but the literary depiction. This absolute word at the literary level would be seen as the rationalist discourse that approximates primal nature, as opposed to secondary nature where the sadist, too, is a victim. On the other hand, torture is work by the depersonalized State or pseudo-State acting as authority; it acts, asks, and insists that the subject continue to speak and that there always be communication. Supplice is situated in the vague area between the subject and the nonsubject, between the particular and the general, where action and word are linked without the pleasure of the individual or the saving of the community. Supplice is "pure" supplementarity that does nothing, changes nothing, and exchanges nothing.

One of the most interesting offshoots of this disappearance is the appearance of a literature of supplice in which the supplice is not an episode in a novel reflecting some external reality, but the imaginary construct that is the very focus of the writing. In retrospect, who would be surprised that Poe invented sustained literary supplice? Poe was also the inventor of the detective story and of the literary work *in articulo mortis*, "The Facts in the Case of M. Valdemar." These are not three inventions but one: the three discourses are the same. In fact, in "Der Flaneur," Walter Benjamin (545) remarks Baudelaire's and his own belief in a method that unites these different genres. Instead of letting the body talk and showing the identity of a system in its reproduction, Poe shows three discourses that make absence speak and show that the system is never identical to itself. In one case, it is the nonexistence of supplice as such, its disappearance from the real world, reinforced by the setting of the Inquisition, whose otherness is underlined; these are the givens of literary supplice. Poe makes the nonexistent speak: the nonpresent and the representable separate from the real. In the detailing of the clues in "The Murders

in the Rue Morgue," for example, the index is not an identity of one
thing with another; it is rather the absence of identity that counts:
the language overheard is neither Spanish, nor French, nor Russian,
nor Italian, etc. (415–16). Like "The Pit and the Pendulum," this tale
also echoes *Anne of Geierstein*: "Curiosity was further excited by the
circumstance that they spoke to each other in a language which was
certainly neither German, Italian, nor French" (18). And at the end,
there is not even a criminal, just an animal. This is, in fact, like so
many of the features already mentioned, somewhat of a leitmotiv in
Poe. In *American Hieroglyphics*, Irwin notes: "The irrational animal in
man is, of course, a frequent culprit in Poe's double stories—from
the perverse self of 'William Wilson' to the savage ape of 'The Murders in the Rue Morgue'" (125). We will have to nuance this remark
as we look at the rats in "The Pit and the Pendulum," defined not as
some irrational animal in man, but as an irrational swarm to which
the subject is complexly linked. And finally, consider the "strange
case" of "Valdemar," in which it is not presence that speaks. Here the
body is already dead, already waiting to be buried, and already potentially the putrefaction with which the story ends. Like so many of
Poe's other narratives of decomposition, including "The Fall of the
House of Usher," and especially the narrative of dismemberment,
"The Tell-Tale Heart," the body in these stories is always already in
the process of decomposing, even before the law of language rein-
scribes that body within the representation of decomposition: "I
made up my mind to take the life of the old man, and thus rid myself
of the eye for ever" (555).

   In all three cases, writing occupies the locus once occupied by the
victim of supplice. Writing occurs on or at the body. It is the same
spot occupied by the truly innocent victim in the scapegoat mechanism, whose innocence assured the system of identity in which the
Law proclaims the possibility of whiteness, innocence, and purity.
The literary locus replaces the tautology of creation and the invention of the same with the analysis of difference that is based on absence. But in the nineteenth century there is no real, absolute innocence: everything takes place in language, and the individual, invented in the eighteenth century, has quickly become a statistical
simulacrum of that ideal, as actuaries, chance, and statistics come
onto the horizon. So there is now only the "presumption of inno-

cence." Innocence is a construct that takes fiction itself as a fiction: the erasure of language as an intervention. For there to be innocence and purity, there must not be language. Yet, always there, language cannot be avoided and its presence is at the price of the individual's innocence.

In the world of Marx, Quêtelet, and Adam Smith, there is no need for a real, integral body that would be the equivalent of the law.³ Numbers exist elsewhere, in statistical abstraction, in the general equivalent of money that is always the inexact translation of the labor of one and all. With the disappearance of supplice and the dominance of capitalism, the role of the subjected body has changed. The individual's body is invented as an interchangeable, potential corpse. Overall, there is a general equivalence that demands neither identity nor presence to operate. What was identity is now translation.

Literary supplice is denuded writing, a fiction that reveals the very nature of fiction, which is the presumption of presence. If there is a body, it is in language, it is the subject subjected to blows and to the language that replaces the blows. Even when buried, the late subject is not bolstered by any martyrdom or mythology of innocence. The body is created in language that serves as a crypt for, in, and before the law. Unable to be equal before the law (equal to whom, to what?) since there is neither identity nor perfect reflection, the unified subject disappears from the real world. In literature, the imaginary body and language coexist: literary supplice will be less of a reflection on the practice of such torture than it will be a reflection of the unequal repartition of the subject. Literary encryptment—encoding and burial—shows the desired body that has disappeared from the real world along with the desiring body, the code, and its translation. Poe nostalgically insists that the body be wrapped, entombed, mummified, and buried: "The Black Cat," "The Cask of Amontillado," "The Tell-Tale Heart," "The Premature Burial," "The Fall of the House of Usher." But there is always something that insists on being heard; Poe's tales, and especially "The Pit and the Pendulum," reflect modern supplice: the confrontation between the self and the other to which it is unequally bound.

The setting of the punishment that is not one and the supplice that asks for no act of contrition nor any return of innocence show the impossibility of regulating, rectifying, and righting the system and its law. And as the plot shows, the victim is saved. Later, in other versions, it will be much the same. In Mirbeau, the system produces dissipation; in Kafka, the machine is destroyed and consumes the one who had once been the bearer of the law. Thus, what might have appeared for various reasons to have been the excesses of Poe, the telling of an extravagantly Romantic, fantastic Gothic tale, is both real and modern: the recognition of the reign of a writing that typologizes even as it demands the singular, a writing that needs its own exemplarity to coexist with a denial of the possibility of exemplarity. Thus I cannot agree with the assessment of the tale given by Tobin Siebers: "Such a story [of the horror of one's own death] would be Poe's 'The Pit and the Pendulum,' although even Poe did not dare to portray violence straightforwardly: the victim of the violence is so delirious and self-parodic that his suffering seems unreal, and the genuine violence of the Inquisition is softened by Poe's ironic touch" (100). We need to read the story literally, for much is at stake in the way we count, the numbering of bodies, and the singularity of the body itself.

"The Pit and the Pendulum" is all too true, all too much the representation of the exemplarity of this subject, an exemplarity that, elsewhere, in "The Premature Burial," Poe neatly ties to *Schadenfreude*. Considering tales of woe and death, Poe says, "We thrill, for example, with the most intense of 'pleasurable pain'" (666). The almost parenthetic "for example," given to the reader as if by chance, puts the victim forth—the victim who becomes, I believe, the figure of the universal subject in literature to come. It is the birth of the corporation man, the origin of the Kafkaesque subject, not only that of the story already mentioned, but that of *The Castle* as well; it is the origin of Hašek's Schweik, of Céline's antiheroes, and even of the protagonists of Dreiser, Hardy, and Zola. In short, if realism portrays a protagonist like Julien Sorel or Emma Bovary who succeeds and then dies, the figure given birth by this tale—that is, the antihero in general—is one whose victory or survival is at best a Pyrrhic victory.

III. The Voice of the Subject

"I was sick," Poe starts, and again, I can go no further, for I am not sure how to parse that sentence or the paragraph that follows. In his discussion of the voice of verbs, the great linguist Emile Benveniste takes an example from the Hindu grammarian Panini. Benveniste distinguishes between "he sacrifices (for another)" and "he sacrifices (for himself)." While the first example is in the active voice, where there is "a process accomplished beginning with and outside the subject," the second example is of a verb in the middle voice, where "the verb indicates a process whose subject is the seat [of the action]: the subject is interior to the process" (172). This self-sacrifice is not identical to the *voice* of self-sacrifice, for to accomplish the sacrifice, there must be another: the sacrifice must not be the sacrifice *of* oneself, but simply a sacrifice *for* oneself. And yet, this possibility of self-sacrifice is only excludable in a latter-day logic that appears when a system of the representation of sacrifice is established, as René Girard shows in his masterful work *La Violence et le sacré* (110–23).

In the logic of Aristotelian identity, we are obliged to distinguish between the sacrifice *of* oneself and the sacrifice *for* oneself, a breach in which the logic of representation is found. This distinction works only for several verbs, such as "sacrifice," a distinction that distances this verb from the rule given about the middle voice in which the subject is interior to the process. In other words, for Benveniste's other examples, there is no distinction between the action for oneself and the action of the subject interior to the process. Sacrifice is different from the rule; in this distinction the space in which representation occurs is in the real and in history.

In the literary supplice of "The Pit and the Pendulum," the subject is within the process of the middle voice. The innerness of the subject is not complete, for the literary logic that is Poe's, which is also a logic of representation, demands a faithfulness of the literary work to itself. In a story narrated in the first person, this means, as I have already indicated, that the narrator will survive the narrative. Indeed, the death of the narrator before the story is told is a mark of irony. In *Le Rouge et le Noir*, Stendhal gives us a small example in his discussion of the guillotining of Danton: "Count Altamira used to tell me that on the eve of his death, Danton would say, in his vulgar way: 'How odd, the verb "to guillotine" cannot be conjugated in all its tenses; one can say "I shall be guillotined, you shall be guillotined," but one does not say "I have been guillotined"'" (1:677). Despite Stendhal's ironic parsing of the Reign of Terror, it is still grammatically correct to say "I have been guillotined"; what is not correct is to say it literally or literarily. Other examples of dead narrators are equally ironic, including, most famously, Machado de Assis's novel *Epitaph of a Small Winner*, and in another genre, the Billy Wilder movie *Sunset Boulevard*. This movie plays ironically on the impossibility of enunciation throughout: the star, Norma Desmond (Gloria Swanson, herself a star of silent movies), was a star of the silent screen; her chauffeur-husband, Max, is played by Erich von Stroheim, himself a noted director of silent films; her cardplaying friends are also played by silent-screen actors, including Anna Q. Nilsson and Buster Keaton. Poe's belatedness, however, is not this ironic one, but melancholic instead.

On the literary level, the narrator must survive his narration and cannot be killed intradiegetically. This is true even though every narrator dies at the very instant that the story ends: he or she shall have been guillotined in the closure of the narrative. Poe's story is a first-person narrative and is thus a kind of trick in the writing. It forces a certain literary logic that determines the salvation of the narrator, yet it changes nothing in the story. Poe's writing is the voice of the subject within the process, the voice that is simultaneously the subject in the action of transforming himself and the voice of the whistling blade of the pendulum.

The subject is not simply the narrator-victim but is his voice united to and seconded by the blade, the voice of the pendulum that determines the voice of the subject. The voice of the pendulum orients action and narration; it determines the voice of the subject always in the process of inventing himself and the tale as well. The narrator is neither united nor complete in and of himself, but depends on the other voice to exist and to be enunciated. Telling itself and sacrificing itself in the middle voice, the voice of narration in "The Pit and the Pendulum" is fractal and partial. Its sense is found in the amalgamation of textual voices: narration, self-sacrifice, and the story; the sum of the voices of the assailed, subjected subject, the whistle of the pendulum, the rats that gnaw, the tongues of fire that heat the cell just before the end. And the only silence comes from the two authorities that are unified subjects: one is the Inquisition, which speaks in a booming, thundering voice at times, and at others in a silence from lips forming words to be read but not heard. The other is the physical subject at the end of the story that returns to a logic of fragments, synecdoches, and wholes: the support of the arm offered by, or which is, General Lasalle, a physical presence that ends the complication of the subject telling a tale in the middle voice.

IV. The Subject Undone

This subject knows itself to be imaginary. The fiction presented the reader from the beginning is announced as such, for every reader knows that the narrator will survive what he tells and that every horror is fictional. The subject of narration, subject at the same time to the textual machine, will have incorporated the facticity of the plot in the very act of narration and in the recognition of the narratable imaginary. The fragmentation of body and a division of subjects at the very beginning of the tale is testimony to the breakdown of the standard model of communication. The dispersed subject in the field of narration acts so that, as the subject evolves, the narrative and communicational model evolves in a simultaneous fashion.

The deep structure of the standard communicational model depends on a verbal system in which active verbs dominate both passive and middle verbs. Passive verbs can be considered as the negative, contrary, or opposite of their active counterparts; it is a neat binary opposition. Middle verbs, however, do not have a role in this model. They relate both to the subject and to the object in a complicated fashion in which the subject in action is not identical to itself. The subject is not the one who acts but the one who changes in acting. We cannot yet measure the effect of the suppression of this modality in general, though we can suppose that the history of literary modernity would be that of the reinvention of one or several middle-voiced models that refuse the dominance of the active/passive system to put the middle in place.

Poe proposes a decomposed subject that occurs in an unknown spot:

I was sick—sick unto death with that long agony; and when they at length unbound me, and I was permitted to sit, I felt that my senses were leaving me. The sentence—the dread sentence of death—was the last of distinct accentuation which reached my ears. After that, the sound of the inquisitorial

voices seemed merged in one dreamy indeterminate hum. It conveyed to my
soul the idea of *revolution*—perhaps from its association in fancy with the
burr of a mill-wheel. (491)

The sick subject is in the process of slowly decomposing and becoming less than an integral whole. And why not? More than creation, this decomposition can signal the effect of the new communicational model; with every word and sentence, the agony of transformation underlines the change occurring at the level of the subject
always in the process of moving toward a nonbeing which would not
be the opposite of Being. In other words, the decomposition of the
subject, visible in works like "The Black Cat," "Valdemar," "The Fall
of the House of Usher," and "The Tell-Tale Heart," sets the model
of representation and communication on its head by refusing to put
writing under the literally protective aegis of action and passivity in
word or in deed.

The existence of this agony is the act of narration: the approach
of death is told, as the very title of "The Tell-Tale Heart" announces.
The heart beats and literally tells the tale of death and destruction,
as the clock will beat the time of death in "The Masque of the Red
Death." This heartbeat is not the sound of an action moving toward
a goal, but a slight declination toward nonexistence. Thus in "The
Pit and the Pendulum," the legal sentence is simultaneously the narrated sentence. In its enunciation the legal sentence breaks the law,
interrupts the constant donation of the law; for once announced, it
cannot be repeated. As Derrida remarks in "Devant la loi," the law
itself becomes fantastic: "If the law is fantastic, if its original site and
its taking-place have the status of a fable, we understand that *das
Gesetz* remains essentially inaccessible, even though the law is presented or promised. . . . the story becomes the impossible story of the
impossible. The story of the forbidden is a forbidden story"
(117–18). The voice of authority changes, diminishes, and is modified in its enunciation, just like the voice of the subject subjected to
the machine. After that there is no more distinct voice. The meaning
of communication is to dissipate into nondirected indeterminacy.

And the geometry is already changing: the communicational system turns into a circle, the geometric figure of π, the irrational number par excellence, the number between Lacan's three and Derrida's

four, the irrational number that measures the circle. The voice comes from nowhere, the voices are indistinctly put in a circle, as Coleridge says, "like voices in a swound." The dizzying circularity of the voices, set aright in Coleridgean Romanticism, cannot occur in Poe's work. Here, the ambiguity of the subject in the process of changing is always occurring: no clear distinction can be made between sleep and waking, between the conscious and the unconscious, or between reason and unreason. The writing occurs in the spot in which the subject changes: "I had swooned; but still will not say that all of consciousness was lost" (492). And the circle that offers no point of origin tends toward an ever more complicated destruction:

I saw the lips of the black-robed judges. They appeared to me white—whiter than the sheet upon which I trace these words—and thin even to grotesqueness; thin with the intensity of their expression of firmness—of immovable resolution—of stern contempt of human torture. I saw that the decrees of what to me was Fate, were still issuing from those lips. I saw them writhe with a deadly locution. I saw them fashion the syllables of my name; and I shuddered because no sound succeeded. (491)

In decomposing, the authority tends toward the destruction of any model that might fix meaning. Lips speaking silently or almost silently are a recurring image in Poe. As we have already indicated, Dupin, in the "Rue Morgue," believes he perceives the lips of the narrator move (404). In "Morella," the narrator reads "the phrases and expressions of the dead on the lips of the loved and the living" (238); in "Ligeia," the narrator hears a "vague sound" and then perceives "a tremor upon the lips" (274) of the supposed corpse. And in "William Wilson," the title character, as opposed to the narrator of the same name, has no speaking voice, but a "singular whisper" (344). The most striking example, along with that of "The Pit and the Pendulum," is that of "The Premature Burial": "I endeavored to shriek; and my lips and my parched tongue moved convulsively together in the attempt—but no voice issued from the cavernous lungs" (677). The cutting up of the human, the displacement of the voice, in Poe turns into a reversal of ventriloquism, or an upending of authority in a transgression of the model of authority to which we have become accustomed.

Michel Chion's concept of the disembodied voice, taken up by

Slavoj Žižek in his reading of film with and against Lacan, is what Chion calls the "acousmatic" voice, a voice heard but whose provenance is not known. The acousmatic being, what Chion calls the "acousmeter," may stay invisible, unknown, or may become subject to a "disacousmatization," by which the one who speaks is shown (28–29). But in Poe, the source of the voice is visible while the sound of the voice is not audible, or, in the melancholic version, it is only barely so. Now I have indicated above that for me there are two different kinds of models at work in Poe: the recuperative model that is defined by the presence, albeit dead or dying in most cases, of the woman in the tale, a tale built ultimately on melancholy and often on monomania; and a nonrecuperative, non-integrated model, of which "The Pit and the Pendulum" is the most stellar example. So the acousmatic voice returned to its origin is wholly reversed in this nonrecuperative model: there is law, but it is never knowable, because the source can only silently name the name that we do not know. It performs the law, but cannot speak with authority, for the system, as we shall see, is most perversely other: the act-of-faith, the supposed cleansing of the soul performed by an individual, is actually performed on him or her. It is not an action in the middle voice, but an act of aggression. In "The Pit and the Pendulum," the tables are turned when all is said and done: it really is a tale told in the middle voice.

Here are white lips from which words visibly but silently flow, mixtures of death and syllables that name; they contrast with the straight lines that are the belatedness of writing. Within nonwriting, death, disjunction, absence, and change run free. This writing that traces words on a white sheet will always be involved in the straight, active model, while reality, which does not assert its presence, is an eternal death sentence. Faced with Western phonocentrism, Poe makes writing readably pictocentric, while rendering the voice mute. Poe allows an image to surge up, breaking through language, which is bound to the phallocentric model of power. Sometimes visible and sometimes not, this silence is at the heart of Poe's discourse of supplice. For him, the words that should have meant life indicate, but never in a foreseeable fashion, the death sentence. Against the impurity of the voice is the supposed purity of sound: "And then there stole into my fancy, like a rich musical note, the thought of what sweet rest there must be in the grave" (491). The possibility of salvation through purity exists for just a moment, but this music too is an insistent one, a repetition in which silence and buzzing are confused. The music becomes an *Ohrwurm*, an earwig that is both the animal and an insistent, obsessional melody: "is not he whose brain grows bewildered with the meaning of some musical cadence which has never before arrested his attention" (492).[4] The voice is bound by the opposition, even in its dialectical version, of life and death: a living human being has a voice, though often a distorted one; the dead ostensibly have no sound. The voice therefore is sullied by the imposition of this division, and all of Poe's examples quoted challenge that imposition of voice on human existence and disappearance. Not so with sound, which is not limited by, or limiting of, scenarios of life and death.

Parallel to these voices, sounds, and agonies that are simultaneously audible and silent, the end of the story brings the reader out of the revolutionary communicational model of the middle voice to return the reader to the right path. Again, this end is predicted by the first word that assures the last. To end then, Poe offers voices that have once again become human, the music has returned to being an appealing call, a fanfare of presence; the distinction between subject and object has returned to the *recto* of narration: "There was a discordant hum of human voices! There was a loud blast as of many trumpets! There was a harsh grating as of a thousand thunders! The fiery walls rushed back! An outstretched arm caught my own as I fell, fainting, into the abyss. It was that of General Lasalle. The French army had entered Toledo. The Inquisition was in the hands of its enemies" (505). The narrator-victim is in the general's arm; the Inquisition is "in the hands of its enemies." The direct, right voices have the power to break the space of supplice to reconstitute a space sustained by the laws of this world, all of which work in consort. The laws of the physical universe, one in which space no longer collapses, are represented by the outstretched arm of General Lasalle: the stretching out counters the closing in that had been the condition of space heretofore, and the general, whose name means "the room," marks the space with a righting of the coordinates. This rectification of the disposition of physical space is seconded by the application of moral law, in the form of the defeat of the Inquisition, the end of the *autos-da-fe*, the remarking of an individual as a free, singular being.

And the third law is literary: this is where the story ends, this is where there is an act of closure. In other words, this is where we get beyond circles and circularity, beyond supplice and the middle voice. For one of the problems of a circular space that is both abysmal and abyssal, a circular literary space in which no subject can say "I am," is the impossibility of saying "this is a metaphor," the impossibility of distinguishing between figural and representational language. The problem for the narration of an event in this space of the middle-voiced verb is that no signifier guarantees writing; at every moment, there is a difference. Transforming its subject at every instant, writing is as metaphoric as it is not. With law and order reestablished, the human voice renews its rights to presence, is defined as a presence, and allows comparison to occur; the figure is reborn in the writing "as of a thousand thunders." Now that the danger of confusion between subjects has disappeared, the possibility of saying that such a sound is discordant has been reestablished; in the end, the immutability of the subject and the hypothetical possibility of distinguishing have returned.

V. The Space of the Abyss

Thus the framing of the story is a destruction and reconstitution of the communicational model of activity and passivity. Between these two moments, the unfolding of the tale occurs in a space in which the whole field is simultaneously subject and object, voice and silence, action and reaction. From this framing through reason comes a space in which the subject undergoing change is integrated into the space that he occupies, though without being able to define himself through that space or determine himself through his voice. Through the framing, Poe shows us the composition and the decomposition of this space, yet the middle space of transformation is not subject to the laws of rectilinear space. Far from it: the framing shows its own fictional nature and the nature of the fiction-making process; the framing is not determined by a transcendental law, but by a law of genre: the literary structure says "omega" while still saying "alpha."

The space of the writing develops in the frame and it will soon be seen to be the space of supplice. By destroying the traditional space of representation through the recognizable, though no less powerful, fictional framework, Poe opens his writing to the abyss. In Poe's work in general, the abyss is the sign of the infinite and of God, and is marked by incomprehensibility itself. Such is the quotation from Glanville given as an epigraph to "A Descent into the Maelström": "The ways of God in Nature, as in Providence, are not as *our* ways; nor are the models that we frame any way commensurate to the vastness, profundity, and unsearchableness of His works, *which have a depth in them greater than the well of Democritus*" (432). Thus God would be the meaning of the system, but the system does not function to offer or to give meaning, for the frame no longer exists. The power and the unmeasurable meaning of God depend on the impossibility of seeking them out if man is the measure. With the framework destroyed in "The Pit and the Pendulum," there cannot be a moment in which man recognizes that impossibility. The God who would have been beyond measure no longer exists, for there is no point beyond which measure has ceased to work. Instead of the recuperation of meaning, there is a fall into negativity; deprived of referents, the signs spin dizzyingly. Without the recognition of the subject faced with the abyss that was engulfing him, there can be no transcendental meaning, as in "A Descent into the Maëlstrom." In "The Pit and the Pendulum," the abyss is the fall into non-identity. Without a subject, and without the recognition of the possibility of reflection on the signifier and the signified of the abyss, the dispersed subject falls as a shower of signs into pure negativity.

In this fall, there is no consciousness of the self, for there is no longer any self: "the state of seeming nothingness into which my soul had lapsed" (492). The abyss will produce the composite subject of the supplicant joined to the machine in what Mark Seltzer calls "the body-machine complex" (103). Seltzer studies what he calls the "problem of the body in machine culture" (3), as he concentrates on turn-of-the-century literature. Without taking anything away from this insightful work, I wonder what place there might be for an examination of the question of the body-machine complex when the naturalist depiction of the body-machine in a sort of *Wiederspiegelung* is not present. Put another way, just as we have wondered if there is the necessity for the actual "mimetic" representation of a scene of writing to have a "scene of writing" in a work, I would posit that the body-machine complex exists in Poe in works other than those, like this one, in which the actual mechanism is shown. Neither Poe's story nor that of Kafka many decades later seems to need the support of either a societal mechanism or a direct, naturalist, mimetic representation to enact the scenario of the body-machine complex. Now the subject can offer only a liquid, intermittent state of nonsubjectivity: "After this I call to mind flatness and dampness; and then all is *madness*—the madness of a memory which busies itself among forbidden things" (493). The possibility of retrospectively calling—"I call to mind"—the mark of fiction, cannot explain the total destruction of the space of representation. When the space of representation is replaced by the abyss, neither the objects nor the subjects are solid. How can one represent what no longer exists? The supplice machine rediscovers the third dimension.

As this nothingness is not the sublime nothingness associated with God, there is a false abyss at whose bottom the subject begins to be reconstituted, though it is encrypted in a locus that cannot be recognized unless denied. There is recognition, not of some self, but of parts: sound, movement, heart, blood, and touch. And after the announced madness come thought and the search for truth: "Then, very suddenly, *thought*, and shuddering terror, and earnest endeavor to comprehend my true state" (493). Madness and thought run side by side in this world; without a solid base, without a body, and without the possibility of signifying, the one who speaks, recognizes, or even writes after the fact cannot distinguish between these states. In such a case, what could truth be? Truth is effectively retrospective: truth is what was. The present is impenetrable, blinding, deafening, and decomposing:

So far I had not opened my eyes. I felt that I lay upon my back, unbound. I reached out my hand, and it fell heavily for many minutes, while I strove to imagine where and *what* I could be. I longed, yet dared not to employ my vision. I dreaded the first glance at objects around me. It was not that I feared to look upon things horrible, but that I grew aghast lest there should be *nothing* to see. At length, with a wild desperation at heart, I quickly unclosed my eyes. My worst thoughts, then, were confirmed. The blackness of eternal night encompassed me. I struggled for breath. The intensity of the darkness seemed to oppress and stifle me. The atmosphere was intolerably close. (493)

Bereft of all true senses and feelings, the subject that is no longer one is pushed toward zero. Moreover, he will have become a "what," neither subject, object, nor thing, but the reduction and absence of possibilities. This detachment has nothing to do with the perception of pain, nor with desire. In fact he continues to "suffer," "long," "struggle," and to feel "desperation." Supine, without being grammatically supine, he has become a congeries of subjectless verbs. A prediction of Samuel Beckett's narratives, this passage brings the story ever further downward as the last links of independent subjectivity are destroyed.

VI. Space and Locus

Can space exist without a sentient subject? It is this Kantian question that Poe is now asking his reader. Certainly, it will be answered, space and time will remain transcendental to any given subjectivity. And for the possibility of textuality even to exist, the space must be given a priori even before there is a subject. And yet Poe is in the process of destroying the presuppositions of textual spacing. Remember, Schrödinger's cat may be both alive and dead in the world of quantum mechanics, as its positions of observer and nonobserver are superimposed one upon the other. Only in the world of integers and of binary logic is the cat one or the other.

Schrödinger's cat is a famous thought experiment imagined by the quantum physicist, Erwin Schrödinger. As Douglas Hofstadter explains it, a cat is placed in a prepared box that contains a radium sample and a radiation detector: "The sample has been chosen so that there is a 50-50 probability that within any hour-long period, one decay will occur. On the occurrence of such a decay, a circuit will close, tripping a switch that will break a beaker filled with a deadly liquid, spilling the liquid onto the floor of the box, and killing the cat." After the cat is placed in the box, an hour passes, and someone goes to check on what has transpired: "According to one extreme view of quantum mechanics . . . only *at that moment* will the system be forced to 'jump' into one of the two possible eigenstates—cat alive and cat dead." Thus Schrödinger's cat exemplifies the superposition of two states, one with a dead cat, a nonobserver, and one with a live one, and thus "observer status" (468). Poe's story depends on the nonspace of reference: neither real space nor the space of reality is necessary to the establishment of this literary writing. Thus, textual space cannot exist without a subject to measure it according to his own gauges.

Here and now there is no space for the subject. Precisely, there is no space and there would be no recognition of the space even if there were one. And the "now," the time of the subject, has disappeared as well, for duration occurs in unmeasurable processes, syncopations between consciousness and fainting. Thus there is no assurance that the narrative occurs in one space and time. Yet there seems to be the conception of the limits of the space. What is this space, since there is no subject? This space is as formless as the processes without subjects; it is determined, if at all, by fictional limits:

A fearful idea now suddenly drove the blood in torrents upon my heart, and for a brief period, I once more relapsed into insensibility. Upon recovering, I at once started to my feet, trembling convulsively in every fibre. I thrust my arms wildly above and around me in all directions. I felt nothing, yet dreaded to move a step, lest I should be impeded by the walls of a *tomb*. (494)

To tremble and vibrate in every fiber of his being is to correspond to the image of the formlessness outside as well as to be exterior to that image. The limit exists as "the walls of a tomb"; however, these limits are changing parameters and not absolute limits: in the end they will move to determine the reduction of space, will become compressed, and will imitate the destruction of the subject and his suppression. And yet again, when there is movement, it is not by a subject that can define a point for himself. Space so constructed is like a line, a series of points and of momentary durations linked to one another not only by a movement, but also by unconsciousness; continuity is assured, meaning is not.

The line is not straight. How could there be a straight line if there is no space that guarantees the orthogonal nature of three dimensions? The point moves; it is wrongly thought that measurement is possible; but the point errs: it wanders, and in wandering, it is wrong. This wandering and this wrongness are the very space of narrative itself as well as the physical space it constructs: the locus in which narration takes place is what *forms* the narration. The form taken by what is said depends on the space of the subject, first in syncopated fashion, then in supine duration, now in a point tracing a wandering line. Just as what happens is a wandering line, the voices are unfixed as well: "And now, as I still continued to step cautiously onward, there came thronging upon my recollection a thousand vague rumors of the horrors of Toledo. Of the dungeons there had been strange things narrated—fables I had always deemed them—but yet strange, and too ghastly to repeat, save in a whisper" (494). Disconnected tales replace the humans who have completely disappeared from this space; rumors and detached stories appear to form a throng of partial, disembodied subjects. So in this world of partial subjects, it is possible for a corpus of language to stand in the stead of a real individual, a body, or a subject of knowledge. At the same time, the tales of the dungeons serve to create those dungeons in impossible scenarios of enunciation. For the tales are those of disembodied voices—of characters like the fictional Danton in Stendhal's *Le Rouge et le Noir*, who allows the impossibility of saying "I have been guillotined" as he enunciates that very sentence.

In a sense, then, this key moment in Poe's tale underlines the perspicacity of the author: the repetition of impossible moments of enunciation couple the living subject/listener/reader to the voices of the dead, those who can no longer speak but who continue to do so. And the fables, at the same time, are the voices that form the discourse into which any new subject is inserted: they mark the representation of the supplice in the impossible position of being the inscription and its recognition. These rumors are distinguished from other things said, for they are impossible locutions. We know that the "condemned to death . . . perished usually at the *auto-da-fes*" (494). Thus no one could usually tell the frightening history of death, except from the outside; and from the outside, death is glorified in the act of faith. Like fables, inventions, and lies, stories are not fabulous; their truth exists outside of time and space, and outside of the possibility of anyone enunciating it. The truth can be told, if the telling has no voice, if it proceeds mutely, or if it goes forth in a whisper. The enunciation of the truth can take place only if there is no place from which to tell it.

The constitution of the space is changed by these voices that recall the space; they construct a space of recalled words and give nonphysical bases to the exploration of the space that exists only through that construction: "I followed it up; stepping with all the careful distrust with which certain antique narratives had inspired me" (495).

The space still has no reality outside a verbal or imagined one. The textual space is not defined by becoming the double of a space in the real world: the real world does not exist. The textual space can be constituted with words and only with words. This space from which all decision has been removed is difficult to imagine, irregular in its constitution, and unique: "In the confusion attending my fall, I did not immediately apprehend a somewhat startling circumstance, which yet, in a few seconds afterward, and while I still lay prostrate, arrested my attention. It was this: my chin rested upon the floor of the prison, but my lips, and the upper portion of my head, although seemingly at a less elevation than the chin, touched nothing" (496).

Having started out supine, he has risen, fallen anew, and is now prostrate. From this return or revolution, the limit to the self will have been recognized. But it is not the limit that the reader expected. Since space and place exist only as functions of the subject, there is no subject as such. Thus, the space and place are those of error in which disembodied voices tremble, filter, pass, and vibrate. What applies to space in general is valid for this particular space of the body, for the space occupied by the body does not necessarily resemble real space. Plunged into the imaginary, the imagined body also resembles words, not referential things like "a real body": "And the death just avoided, was of that very character which I had regarded as fabulous and frivolous in the tales respecting the Inquisition" (496). The body becomes narration and even the locus of narration; the fabulous is reintegrated into the imaginary which is the very basis of the narrative's being: to narrate is to exist.

VII. The Partial Subject

Where once there was dark, there is now light; where there were lines and one-dimensional rumors, there is now a three-dimensional space; where there was silence and blindness, there is now feeling: "A deep sleep fell upon me—a sleep like that of death. How long it lasted, of course, I know not; but when, once again, I unclosed my eyes, the objects around me were visible. By a wild, sulphurous lustre, the origin of which I could not at first determine, I was enabled to see the extent and aspect of the prison" (497). But there was no subject at first and there still is none. In the place the subject would occupy in traditional models there is a partial subject that speaks, acts, and writes, though neither with independence nor with rights. More than a Deleuzian desiring machine, less than a constituted subject, the partial subject occupies a part of the locus destined for the subject by the idealist system and its models. When the partial subject begins to talk, a whole linkage is set into motion without the other parts interrupting or staying silent. This partial subject can be heard only through this non-interruption/nonsilence, for it belongs to a set that determines the very form of what it says.

Partial subjectivity is determined by having the body in the machine, a divided subjectivity that no discourse has heretofore imagined. The subject thinks, acts, and talks; he translates these thoughts, actions, and discourses in writing, but no unity ensues. In fact, the unity exists only outside the machine in the somewhat distant, diffuse light of "a wild, sulphurous lustre." The unity is elsewhere, the origin as much of the locus and its signs as of the pain, sorrow, and division of the subject. The subject is not inserted into a passage of discourse, in a simple ideological division of the subject, but is divided by its belatedness, since it comes after the unattainable and unassailable origin. No subject can exist that is not at and from this origin; all those that come after are divided, partial, and subjected. The subject that arrives on the spot is "always already" a victim: "All this I saw indistinctly and by much effort—for my personal condition had been greatly changed during slumber. I now lay upon my back, and at full length, on a species of low framework of wood. To this I was securely bound by a long strap resembling a surcingle. It passed in many convolutions about my limbs and body, leaving at liberty only my head and my left arm" (498).

Attached by a strap to the mechanism, the victim is found in the machine that determines his possible actions, even his words. In short, the machine determines his existence. His body no longer belongs to him and is replaced by the wooden framework that forms, determines, controls, and directs. Like his actions, his words are determined by this wooden frame that permits certain discourses and forbids others. The framework produces the effect of the subject at this moment in space and time, akin to the linguistic, semiotic, and intellectual *episteme* described by Foucault in *Les Mots et les choses* that allows the locus of the subject to occur. Framed equally by the discourses of power and by the mechanism, the subject is constantly subjected to constraints, those of, as Poe himself puts it, "the autocrats of *Place* and *Time*" (457). And so it would seem that the individual is wholly subjected to the model of phallocentric power that I challenged in the introduction to this book. And yet Poe provides the alternative, the unwriting of that model, the unwrapping of the process of victimization. For the strap that fixes him in place is a strap that (un)erringly follows the contours of his body, much as he had followed those of the cell; it can come undone, it can forget to conform. It is his body that determines the strap, his very presence and physicality that order that part of the machine. And moreover, what is woven, wound, and implied has something like the possibility of an unknown and unheard-of textuality. Things will get accomplished, but in an inverted fashion; there will be no orthography, but writing will be accomplished by the left hand, gauchely, an inverse writing that undoes rather than weaving a web.

This inverse writing is a textuality that announces itself as being far from the origin, far from the light that determines the origin in both signaling and hiding it. It is a left-handed writing, unique in its effect of miming the destruction of textuality. It will not seem to be the heliotropic search for the truth, but rather something that tries to evade the truth of the light. And it will be the writing of a subject that resists integration into the machine, who is determined simply by being the rumor of a partial subject. As the subject of writing, the subject seeks to give form to other rumors about the origin and the truth of textual authority. Thus the scene of supplice is a scene of writing *in extremis*. Supplice flirts with the impossibility of writing, but shows writing's nudity along with that of the body it refigures. If the framework implies the voice of the prisoner, it does not do so in a foreseeable fashion. The voice of the victim becomes framed writing precisely because this voice is condemned to repeat sad clichés without subjective individuality counting at all. In repeating pain, this written voice repeats itself to the very end.

It is not that pain is not representable but rather that this pain can be represented only if the act of representation is falsified. In its inability to be formed as a full presence, the inscription of pain determines writing. Nothing is more natural in a denatured world than the aesthetic, the figural representation presenting itself exactly at the moment at which presence disappears in favor of a writing depending on the partial nature of the subject: "Looking upward, I surveyed the ceiling of my prison. It was some thirty or forty feet overhead, and constructed much as the side walls. In one of its panels a very singular figure riveted my whole attention. It was the painted figure of Time as he is commonly represented, save that, in lieu of a scythe, he held what, at a casual glance, I supposed to be the pictured image of a huge pendulum, such as we see on antique clocks" (498). The aesthetic component, the moment at which representation enters the picture, is the moment of recognition of the division and complexity of the subject. The partial subject faces the instance of representation, as if representation—"the painted figure of Time as he is commonly represented"—were the only answer available at that moment. But what exactly is or can be represented here and now? Since the "time is out of joint," there is no express means of determining if time is continuous. Despite the assurances of the victim that he can measure both space and time, we cannot trust his demarcations. He errs in his measure of the cell; at any given moment—but can any moment be given here?—he knows not if an hour, a second, or a day has passed between that moment and the preceding one. As the unity of narrative and verbal tense may or may not hide gaps in the representation of time, the frame of narrative remains unreliable as a frame. Consider another example of the eruption, interruption of time in Poe, in another clock, one also inexorably beating toward death; only in this case, death finally arrives:

It was in this apartment, also, that there stood against the western wall, a gigantic clock of ebony. Its pendulum swung to and fro with a dull, heavy, monotonous clang; and when the minute-hand made the circuit of the face, and the hour was to be stricken, there came from the brazen lungs of the clock a sound which was clear and loud and deep and exceedingly musical, but of so peculiar a note and emphasis that, at each lapse of an hour, the musicians of the orchestra were constrained to pause. ("The Masque of the Red Death," 487)

Time is unrepresentable in a world where the transcendental value of time has no meaning and where no internalized parameter of time determines a subjective measurement of time. In fact, it is not time that is represented, but "Time," the representation of time. The figure of Time repeats a common representation, and in so doing turns it over. Just as the entire scene takes place in a nonreferential world, since supplice no longer exists at the moment at which Poe is writing, time has no referent other than a representation of a catachresis. Moreover, the personification of time underscores the problem of determining who and what constitute a subject in this world. Time personified becomes godlike, but is a *deus absconditus*, gone from the world it has previously ordered. So the painting of time is the painting of an absence, the representation of nothingness. Most importantly, the representation is a trompe-l'oeil, but instead of the usual version of trompe-l'oeil in which a two-dimensional representation seems to be a three-dimensional object, here a three-dimensional object, the pendulum, is believed at first to be two-dimensional, "the pictured image of a huge pendulum, such as we see on antique clocks." Just as Time seems to reproduce the clichéd figure of time, so too this image reproduces another standard cliché of institutionalized, measured, bourgeois art.

But the figure is not a figure, the pendulum is real, an object that has come out of a stereotypical representation to bring an edge to reality. An object moves; when it does so, the idea of representation is left behind: "There was something, however, in the appearance of this machine which caused me to regard it more attentively. While I gazed directly upward at it, (for its position was immediately over my own,) I fancied that I saw it in motion. In an instant afterward the fancy was confirmed. Its sweep was brief and of course slow. I watched it for some minutes, somewhat in fear, but more in wonder" (498–99). The face-off implies a mirror effect: framed by a binding framework that limits movement and speech, the partial subject is faced with the mechanical movement of the pendulum as it slowly sweeps through space. The lack of freedom of the partial subject is contrasted with the typical freedom of the subject in the real world. The relative immobility of representation contrasts with the birth of the object out of representation, the coming to motion of the pendulum as it slowly performs its action. In this world of partial subjects and mechanical objects, the object has more freedom than the subject. Within one framework, there is the possibility of movement; within the other, movement is almost completely stifled. Still, that face-off brings a new dimension to the situation. For at the moment of recognition that the representation is actually an object in this world, the "I" begins to think, react, and imagine—within a restricted field, but in a manner that is no longer completely limited by the constraints of time and place.

Functioning as a possible creator of action, the narrator-victim can now decide if there is a future alternative to the one imagined for him by the Inquisition. This awakening is slow to occur, and Poe saves the event of action for a suitable apex as the climactic episodes begin. During the textual process leading to the moment at which the alternative future is realized, there is a gradual awakening to the implications of a textuality that finds its determination in the rearrangement of the standard system. In this world, the paradigm of self and other as translated into the hierarchy of pronouns has broken down. The "I" has no "you" to address except in the retrospective glance of the writing; and the reader can always choose not to accept the message. Simultaneously, the opposition between self and pure other is not easy to pin down: the individual is part of the machine that includes not only the framework and surcingle that bind him but also the pendulum itself. He is being addressed time and again, by every moment, every movement of the pendulum. As it nears, the pendulum becomes more personified, more vocal, less mechanical. As it nears, it becomes more a part of the possible fulfillment of an inverted, even perverse, vision of the middle voice: not "I sacrifice for myself" but "I am sacrificed for myself."

VIII. The Sound of the Beast

In this world, the only certain space is the gradually diminishing one between the framed subject and the pendulum slowly descending toward him. In the nonalternative world predicted by the voice of the other, the Inquisition, fulfillment and realization will come at the very moment of the sacrifice, the moment of the action: "I am sacrificed for myself" occurs in the middle voice. At that very moment, the various parts of the partial subject would come together to form a whole, if only for an instant. It is the instant of the moment of death that is the completion and fulfillment of the action; in a world of representation where death does not play a role, it is the moment of orgasm or saintly ecstasy, the moment at which the standing out-

side occurs and simultaneously collapses. This moment will not occur in the narrative; the first-person voice guarantees that as it marks
the expected conclusion as being impossible. The impossibility of
that moment is counterbalanced by the presence of the voice of the
partial subject whose unique perspective can be given only by a first-
person narrative.

As the space diminishes and as the parts of the fragmented subject
approach one another in the act of supplice, there is a recognition
that for the subject to be whole again, it must be re-split in the action
of self-sacrifice in the middle voice:

> But what mainly disturbed me, was the idea that it had perceptibly *descended*.
> I now observed—with what horror it is needless to say—that its nether ex-
> tremity was formed of a crescent of glittering steel, about a foot in length
> from horn to horn; the horns upward, and the under edge evidently as keen
> as that of a razor. Like a razor also, it seemed massy and heavy, tapering from
> the edge into a solid and broad structure above. It was appended to a weighty
> rod of brass, and the whole *hissed* as it swung through the air. (499)

The subject is marked by its creation in the simulacrum of writing
that occurs at the same moment as the sacrifice of the subject to the
machine. But the subject is also in competition for the possibility of
making sounds. The writing of the subject contrasts with and sup-
plants, as it must, the hiss of the blade and the eventual gnawing of
the rats. Writing is superimposed on the various partial sounds of the
partial subjects, whose sound is rendered meaningless, as soon as
there is the silent sound of writing.

IX. The Measure of Man

Time, the measure of man in all things, replaces space, which is re-
distributed in this universe. One would expect three-dimensional
space to be ordered orthogonally either relative to or separate from
the point occupied by an individual subject. The measure taken of
space by an individual subject repeats the space that is there without
him: the meter he measures from himself at a zero-point rewrites the
invisible meter posited between two points that is presumed to exist
apart from the act of measurement and apart from the observance of
any given measurer. In "The Pit and the Pendulum," space too is out

of joint. The measure of space is disordered by the very dispersion of the subject: no point can reproduce the abstract sense of measure, because no point is fixed except that of the partial subject, not an origin but a goal that will not be reached. The partial subject can presume to measure the distance between the blade and himself, but every measure is wrong because that distance is always changing imperceptibly enough to allow approximation but perceptibly enough to indicate error. And the one fixed point can serve as an origin for no measure except that of the infinite, the abyss itself. This abyss is calling to the subject to join it, to reduce infinity to zero: "I could no longer doubt the doom prepared for me by monkish ingenuity in torture. My cognizance of the pit had become known to the inquisitorial agents—*the pit*, whose horrors had been destined for so bold a recusant as myself—*the pit*, typical of hell, and regarded by rumor as the Ultima Thule of all their punishments" (499). Again, the usual constellation of figures appears to describe the impossible nature of this pit: impossible tales of an impossible origin and solution, the rumors serve to enunciate the unutterable of hell and the immeasurable of the "Ultima Thule," the last point beyond which there is no other. This last outpost of humanity is the point at which measure of space and time collapses. Since time is also heading toward a zero-point, it too is becoming shorter, as it tropes the distance between the parts of the subject: "Days passed—it might have been that many days passed—ere it swept so closely over me as to fan me with its acrid breath" (500).

As time decreases, the very possibility of humanity seems to decrease as well. As the point of sacrifice seems to near, the point at which the subject becomes whole in his middle-voiced self-sacrifice, there is a competition for being the voice of that sacrifice. Where would that action take place? The blade is given the inspiration, the wholly mechanical position of producing a breath: a sign of life in the real world is the sign of approaching death, the end of time, and the destruction of the partial subject as the whole is simultaneously produced and destroyed. In contrast to the breath of the blade is the ever-diminishing breath of the corporeal subject as he loses his powers of speech: "Long suffering had nearly annihilated all my ordinary powers of mind. I was an imbecile—an idiot" (500).

X. *Action*

The subject is reconstituted only in its own annihilation. In this textual Ultima Thule, the subject can exist as itself if it is in the simultaneous process of disappearing. No speech can occur save that of the recognition of the destruction of the subject. No communicational model serves, because nothing is left to communicate. Survival, for however long, though it really does not matter, is concerned with a discrete number of possible messages, here reduced to zero. In fact, the entire system is the recognition of survival, for at the very point at which the system works, takes action, changes, and makes plot irreversible, the system disappears. The system is intricately bound to the subject; once an action occurs, the whole *dispositif* will disappear.

An action occurs outside the predicted system of events; it destroys the system, while the whole subject is constituted outside the posited model of the simultaneous construction and destruction of the subject in the middle-voiced sacrifice. Any action predicated on the standard model of the subject in action is doomed to fail, because there is no subject identical to a subject of action: "Could I have broken the fastenings above the elbow, I would have seized and attempted to arrest the pendulum. I might as well have attempted to arrest an avalanche" (501). The rats, however, are another matter; they stream and swarm everywhere, acting neither in concert nor in isolation, innumerable partial subjects that do the work of man. After the narrator rubs the surcingle with what remains of the food, he lies still, pretending in a sense to have sacrificed himself, yet really having released himself from the sacrificial position through the action that the rats will take:

Observing that I remained without motion, one or two of the boldest [rats] leaped upon the frame-work, and smelt at the surcingle. This seemed the signal for a general rush. Forth from the well they hurried in fresh troops. They clung to the wood—they overran it, and leaped in hundreds upon my person. The measured movement of the pendulum disturbed them not at all. Avoiding its strokes, they busied themselves with the anointed bandage. They pressed—they swarmed upon me in ever accumulating heaps. They writhed upon my throat; their cold lips sought my own. (502–3)

But what or who are rats? Michel Serres would say that they are the parasites necessary to the functioning of the system. Not predicted by a system, not welcome in a system, parasites are essential to any system and can never be kept wholly away. If they are integral to the system, that very necessity brings integrality into question. The function and presence of the rats in this system are worth a second look. From within the system, as parasites, the rats are a repetition of the army of the faithful, the black-shrouded soldiers of God performing the acts of faith. Guerrilla forces of liberation, they are indifferent to the passage of time and the diminution of space. The unpredictability of the rats within the system recalls other extrasystemic activities. Swarming like so many rumors over the desubjectified body, the rats form a corpus for the narration: like the headless and tailless rumors that mysteriously fly out of the cells of the Inquisition and like the narrative itself that streams out of a closed cell of supplice, the rats are the chorus that tells, acts, and does.

Like narrative itself, the rats are the compound subject that is the seat of unity and the organizing means that makes a unity of the partial subject. By a scattered, multiple, desubjectified, and well-nigh random action, the rats produce a subject in the active voice distinct from the middle-voiced subject that had been predicted by the system:

The surcingle hung in ribands from my body. But the stroke of the pendulum already pressed upon my bosom. It had divided the serge of the robe. It had cut through the linen beneath. Twice again it swung, and a sharp sense of pain shot through every nerve. But the moment of escape had arrived. At a wave of my hand my deliverers hurried tumultuously away. With a steady movement—cautious, sidelong, shrinking, and slow—I slid from the embrace of the bandage and beyond the reach of the scimitar. For the moment, at least, *I was free*. (503)

XI. Epilogue

A momentary setback to the freedom we know is coming occurs as the theory of the enshrouded subject-crunchers of the Inquisition again tries to reduce the subject to his own self-sacrifice. Clearly, this is a momentary peripeteia; it does not signal the renewed dangers for the subject as much as it does the destruction of the system, in which,

ironically, the swarming rats have turned into the eyes of a fragmented panopticon blazing away as the system is destroyed in its
own fulfillment and purification:

> As I arose from the attempt, the mystery of the alteration in the chamber
> broke at once upon my understanding. I have observed that, although the
> outlines of the figures upon the walls were sufficiently distinct, yet the col-
> ors seemed blurred and indefinite. These colors had now assumed, and were
> momentarily assuming, a startling and most intense brilliancy, that gave to
> the spectral and fiendish portraitures an aspect that might have thrilled even
> firmer nerves than my own. Demon eyes, of a wild and ghastly vivacity,
> glared upon me in a thousand directions, where none had been visible be-
> fore, and gleamed with the lurid lustre of a fire that I could not force my
> imagination to regard as unreal. (504)

When all is said and done, the victim will be snatched from the
jaws of death, the fire of pit and cell, and the destruction of self-sacrifice. His final writhing and his eventual writing are now the same
thing: "At length for my seared and writhing body there was no
longer an inch of foothold on the firm floor of the prison" (505).
Writing in the extreme will not have the measure, the solid base, or
the certainty of the standard, objective writing of the nineteenth and
twentieth centuries. It will, however, make the most of the writhing
of the subject, his agony, and the impossibility of his wholeness. To
paraphrase Viktor Shklovsky (57), "The Pit and the Pendulum" is the
most typical narrative in modern literature.

Designing Men

Our scribes found an outlet and serenity in the
metaphors of the *phallus*. Converted into a symbol,
the organ is innocently manipulated.

—Jean-Paul Aron and Roger Kempf

Novels abound in kissing scenes, but none that I had
read made any reference to such a thing as erections
on such occasions.

—Yukio Mishima

I was in a show with a couple of male dancers once.
And wherever we went, on the Monday night some
woman used to complain about their tights bulging.

—John Osborne

I. Eve and Abelard

At least since romanticism, and until very recently, the ideas and
ideals of masculine beauty have been marginalized. While there has
been a continuous, albeit changing history of the construction of female beauty, the masculine equivalent has remained in the shadows.
To appear as beautiful, or, more conservatively, as handsome—which
the dictionary defines as "manly, dignified, and impressive"—is to be
suspected of femininity, delicacy, effeminacy, marginality, foppery, or
dandyism, the criticism changing according to the era and its political climes. The point is this: in any period during the last three centuries or so, masculine beauty has, in the West, at least until the advent of film, been by and large consigned to a realm in which its
presence was suspect, whether it be the two simpering marquis of
Molière's play *Le Misanthrope*, Beau Brummel, or Oscar Wilde. And
even as he is writing a defense of the dandy in an act of lèse-majesté,
or at least lèse-bourgeoisie, Baudelaire warns the reader that this
cold embodiment of male beauty is part of a decline of civilization.

As he writes in *Le Peintre de la vie moderne*, "Dandyism is a setting sun" (712). Male beauty is stylized and the sign of a decadent civilization, or it is effeminate and a sign of a problem at some local point within the civilization. To be safe, just as the word "handsome" indicates, the attributes of masculine beauty, whatever they may be, are invariably immediately translated into the world of the manly, into what is impressive. Again, the English language gets it right: a man is handsome just as a sum of money can be handsome: bigger *is* better. These attributes become cathected onto the body of power so that masculine beauty, instead of being part of an aesthetic, becomes the index of a reinforced ideology of power and phallocentrism. For not only does beauty cede to the structures of the handsome, beauty is also simply forgotten. Sign of the feminine within the masculine, beauty needs to disappear from the constructions of the man, of manliness, and indeed of masculinity as a whole. To feminine beauty and delicacy correspond the constructions of power: a man is built by his deeds, a woman by her attributes.

So in a first moment, while thinking about this marginalization of masculine beauty as a set of masculine attributes, we are called to make a contrast between that which has disappeared, and the full, continuous history of presence of an aesthetic of feminine beauty. Now it is evident, even in this project of comparison, that the construction of feminine beauty, at least within the same period, is precisely a construct within the realm of phallocentric ideology. And that is precisely the point. A manipulation of the discourse of the feminine aesthetic is simultaneously a wielding of power over the feminine that runs counter to the feminine itself and what inherent power it may have. The social construction of the feminine through the imposition of the masculine means that both an essentialist concept of the feminine and a social construction of the feminine by women are by and large marginalized and that both versions of feminine discourse are always already subject to the masculine. The construction of the aesthetic of the feminine and the repeated inscription of that aesthetic onto the sites of the woman's body make her body automatically subject both to the writing on it and to the structures of a phallocentric ideology that tells the feminine it cannot exist without discourses of phallocentric power informing it. Inscribing the feminine aesthetic means writing that aesthetic and including in that writing the construction of the feminine body as a product of that discourse: men are born, but women are made.

Certainly, in fantastic literature, the nineteenth century has a leitmotiv of the construction and destruction of the woman. The positive version, albeit a diabolical one, can be found in works by Hoffman and Villiers de l'Isle-Adam: like Mary Shelley's *monster*, a woman is constructed by a man out of a few spare parts lying around. The negative version of the same story, which would amount to the destruction of the woman, is framed as the loss of feminine beauty—her "essence," as it were—the destruction of her femininity. In the first phases of bourgeois narrative, men die battling the elements or the forces of society itself; women die because they have lost their beauty. Among the myriad versions of this story in the eighteenth century are *Candide* or *Les Liaisons dangereuses*, and the more extreme nineteenth century offers Poe and Baudelaire, just to name two. The myth is ours, for nothing could be simpler than this game of producing and destroying women or a woman.

Everyone knows how to design a woman. Women are generic; the parts are interchangeable; one slides smoothly from individual to species, gender, genre, genus, and back again. Even nursery rhymes tell us the story: little boys are made of countable, if not to say detachable, things, metonymies of their always castrated penises: "whales and snails and puppy dog tails." Little girls, however, are made of indiscrete amounts of stuff: "sugar and spice and everything nice." No quantities are given, nor do they need to be. It is the easiest thing in the world to create a woman by adding unnamed quantities of the right ingredients. By the end of the nineteenth century, designing a woman has become streamlined. Take the right ingredients, unmeasured, overflowing amounts of the component parts, and then, with a bit of substance and smoke or electromagnetic forces, one can produce a new woman. To make the design real, one needs only a bit of literary knowledge. As Villiers de l'Isle-Adam writes in *L'Eve future*: "I shall endow this Shade with all the songs of Antonia by Hoffman, the storyteller, all the impassioned mystery of *Ligeias*, of Edgar Poe, all the burning seductions of the *Venus* of Wagner, the powerful musician!" (112).

If the designer is unsure, then, he need only delve a bit into the fund of literary production that has explained its feminine creations throughout time. All that is necessary is a "dissection"—the word is a title of a chapter of the novel just quoted, *L'Eve future*—in order to anatomize women, the woman, a woman. And having performed such a dissection, the inventor is ready to build a new and improved version of the original. Not even the most hidden part is neglected in literary descriptions of women. As Naomi Schor notes in *Breaking the Chain*: "the female body is, to borrow Roger Kempf's expression, 'the literary body' par excellence" (57). To design a woman, one has only to follow a certain model for assembling the pieces. With the assurance of a penetrating gaze, no other knowledge is necessary. Nowhere is this clearer than in a work by Villiers's contemporary Guy de Maupassant. In a somewhat neglected novel by Maupassant, *Mont-Oriol*, the woman is designed and drawn—or drawn and quartered—with nothing more than a three-leaded pencil as a tool:

> The doctor made her lie down on a couch, then, taking out a three-leaded pencil from his pocket—one black, one red, one blue—he began to examine his new client by auscultation and percussion, while covering her gown with little colored marks noting each observation.
>
> After a quarter of an hour of this work, she resembled a geographic map that indicated the continents, seas, capes, rivers, kingdoms, and cities, and bore the name of all these earthly divisions, for the doctor wrote, on every line of demarcation, two or three Latin words that were understandable only to him. . . .
>
> Then examining his notes on the gown from head to toe, reading them as an Egyptologist would decipher hieroglyphics, he transcribed them into his notebook. (489–90)

The special pencil becomes a tool of power in the capable hands of the doctor, who subjects Mme Andermatt to a triple violation. Subjected to the penetrating gaze of the male other, the woman is also subject to this anatomy session, where she is written over as if she were nothing but a blank piece of paper waiting for male dominance. This is the power of the one capable of writing that also decides who and what she is. At a figural level, Mme Andermatt, compared to the earth herself, is therefore allied to all that is fecund, all that is source and origin. Yet at the same time, that very earth is always subjected to rewriting by the male cartographer. And if that

were not enough, she is reduced to a map of herself. She is no longer
human; the words, notes, signs, and symbols that float over her
scantily-clad body can be translated to the scientific notebook held
by the doctor as he enters his notes that amount to a retelling of his
grammatico-geographic rape of her body.

That women have been constantly subjected to this novelistic gaze
comes as no shock to any reader with the slightest awareness of the
contemporary critical scene. In fact, the subjectedness of women is
their reduction to a generic "woman," as if each were identical to her
own practico-inert image or the *pour autrui* determined by male
dominance. The simultaneous subjugation, reduction, and the inscription thereof is one of the main figures of feminist criticism of
the novel. Over the last two decades, the repression of women's
voices, figures of feminine writing, and female authors disfigured by
a world in which the concepts of male dominance and masculine discourse endlessly have the upper hand have become common subjects
of study.

So there are two continuities in the representation of gender, but
they are not at all commensurate. On the one hand, there is a continuous representation of masculine power; on the other hand, a continuous representation of feminine construction and beauty. And the
latter category is quite problematic in and of itself, for the construction of the feminine and the construction of feminine beauty, ideologically intertwined as they are, mark the insistence of a phallocentric model for representation. Feminine beauty is constructed from
within the masculine. At the same time, if the discourse of feminine
power has been endlessly repressed with few exceptions, the same
cannot be said for the representation of masculine beauty. Certainly,
there has been a loss and forgetting, occurring not as a result of this
reading of the feminine, but as a consequence of not reading the full
panoply of the masculine. Indeed, one of the great insights of feminism is not some repressed reading of the masculine; quite to the
contrary, feminism has put into question what it means to write as a
man. Feminism re-members reading masculinity. Feminism has
brought into the foreground of our reading the functions of gender
in literature by focusing our attention on a series of figures of the
feminine that have been disfigured by the dominance of masculine
discourse. Specifically, it has reminded us that it is the gaze, the

defining mode of operation of masculist discourse, that constructs
the "woman" as textual object, prevents the woman from being herself—from "being," from "Being," from having a "self" separate from
or prior to the sociovisual construct imposed by the male gaze and
its/his discourse

Still the gaze is there, and it is a distorting effect without which
the feminine presence might remain invisible: you have only one
lens, and it is a phallocentric one that distorts. If you refuse that lens,
you shall remain in the dark. Feminism has lit that darkness and
shown that there are other, far less distorting lenses, mediating de-
vices that do not thrust the woman under a distorting telescope, mi-
croscope, or kaleidoscope. The distortion, however, much as one
might now decry it, serves a singular purpose: it is the tool that forbids total repression. No matter how distorting, no matter how inaccurate, the phallocentric gaze keeps the figure of the woman disfigured, raped, even blurred. The feminine voice is disfigured, forced
to parade as a man's voice: George Eliot, George Sand, the Brontë
sisters writing with male pseudonyms. Or else, the female voice is
garbed as some figure determined by the male gaze: the acceptable
levels or objects of feminine inquiry, like the Austenian novel of
manners, or, as an object, the anatomization of the feminine, whose
summary and reinscription can be found in the description of the
medical examination of *Mont-Oriol*.

It might seem odd then for me to make the statement that comparable work has not been done on the disfigurement of the masculine figure. More precisely and more radically, I would say that the
beauty of the masculine figure has been marginalized, disfigured, and
otherwise distorted in much of nineteenth-century narrative. As distorting and as dehumanizing as the gynecological examination may
be, and I think that medical figure accurately describes the attitude
of the nineteenth century vis-à-vis the "woman," there is no comparable andrology. Male characters in the nineteenth-century novel are
basically a bunch of Ken dolls, sexless simulacra of men: Barbie may
be a caricature, but at least she has breasts, and at least in a few instances (Courbet, Zola), she has genitalia as well. Not to put too fine
a point on it, I am making the following suggestion: the representation of male beauty as a positive attribute is distorted or absent
through much of eighteenth- and nineteenth-century narrative. In

its place is a representation of the translation of that beauty into the handsomeness of power, the translation necessary in fact for realist narrative to prove itself, to be successful, to accomplish the production and distribution of power it sets out to describe. And yet male beauty is not wholly absent. It appears here and there in nineteenth-century narrative, and will reappear in full force in a position in which it cannot always operate a translation: in the early part of the twentieth century, film itself, a new medium exercising its own parameters, and needing masculine beauty (as opposed to power as such) to entice its feminine viewers to come back, will provide a clear representation of masculine beauty. And this beauty is often an odd recapitulation of the masculine beauty needed in novels three-quarters of a century earlier: it is a discourse of feminine beauty in men's clothing that animates the descriptions of Eugène de Rastignac on the one hand or Rudolph Valentino on the other.

Now the representation of masculine beauty—or really, of masculine physicality unrelated to a representation of power—was not always absent from the modern arts. Indeed, there was a period in mainstream modern Western art in which the exact opposite of the representation of power existed in all its insistence on the physical vulnerability of the male, with an insistence on the presentation of male genitalia. In fact it is only in the early nineteenth century that the penis ceases to be represented, an anomaly that we shall engage shortly. After the Middle Ages, the carnivalesque insists on the physical, as Bakhtin points out in his study of Rabelais, who endlessly writes descriptions ranging from the flooding of the good citizens of Paris by a stream of urine to the best method for wiping one's ass. Rabelais certainly makes the physical present to the reader; at the same time, numerous instances of this representation already point to a game of power. Indeed, as the carnivalesque itself can be conceived as the representation of a reversal of power, one may speculate that this occurs within the systems of the representation of power itself. So such scenes in Rabelais's work, much as they begin to create for us a world that starts to resemble the modern one, negotiate the path between the erotic and the phallic, between the physicality of the body in its humanness and the symbolic translation of the body into the phallic.

A stellar example of representations of the vulnerable male body, perhaps less well-known than is Rabelais to a student of literature, is in Italian Renaissance painting, specifically in the representations of Jesus. In his brilliant work *The Sexuality of Christ in Renaissance Art and in Modern Oblivion*, Leo Steinberg demonstrates the absolute centrality of the representation of the genitals, often veiled, and in that veiling erect, of Jesus as Christ. Hands (Mary's, Jesus') both cover and indicate the penis to mark it as the very focal point of the humanness, and therefore the vulnerability and mortality, of Jesus as Christ. Steinberg points out that this focal point and its attendant thematics of vulnerable humanness has been forgotten by history. Far from being the sign of potency, paternity, and therefore the indication of immortality, the representation of the penis is a sign of mortality, of fleeting pleasure, of death itself. No wonder then that the signs of *jouissance* in that most genitally inspired of writers, the Marquis de Sade, are inevitably also the signs of the reign of the transitory and of death. Beyond that, it is a simple but often forgotten truth that, despite the limit-breaking nature of Sade's works, in this matter Sade is merely the last of a long line of authors that includes Rabelais and Voltaire, to name just two. The figure of narration in the eighteenth century, whether it be in *Clarissa*, in *Les Liaisons dangereuses*, or in *Tristram Shandy*, not to mention in Rousseau's *Confessions*, written in a related vein, is that of writing occurring wherever the penis leads.

In French literature, the point of suppression or even the act of repression of the penis seems to occur in four early nineteenth-century works: two novels called *Olivier*, one by the Duchesse de Duras and the other by Thibaut de Latouche; the more famous *Aloys* by the infamous Astolphe de Custine; and Stendhal's *Armance*. As Aron and Kempf (82) point out, each of these novels deals with the theme of impotence, "that bizarre thing that threatens male honor without wounding consideration for him." A bit later than those four, Balzac's *Louis Lambert* also has a subtext of impotence and in fact, in the most literal application of the philosophico-religious byword at the heart of Lambert's philosophy, "Et verbum caro factum est" (11:639) threatens to move from word to deed: "He believed himself impotent. I began to watch him with the attention that a mother has for her child, and fortunately discovered him at the very moment that he was going to perform the operation on himself that Origen believed was the reason for his talent" (11:679). Balzac's allusion to Origen repeats a line in his earlier *La Peau de chagrin*: "In order to struggle better with the cruel power whose challenge he had accepted, he became chaste as had Origen, by castrating his imagination" (10:217). Identical in Balzac's novel to the will to create the phallus, castration is the will to power; it is only through the removal of masculine pleasure, physicality, and beauty, and the submission of that physical presence to the law of the phallus, that a hero may inevitably succeed: Eugène de Rastignac, challenging Paris, will succeed precisely because he submits to the law of the phallus by cuckolding another, by taking the vagina that belongs to another man away from him.

Now I am maintaining that the law of the phallus, which includes both the exchange and the domination of the feminine, means participating in a model heterosexual economy. Aron and Kempf (82) see this impotence as a disguise for something unprintable: male homosexuality (*pédérastie*). As they rightly point out, while male homosexuality barely makes an appearance in the nineteenth-century novel, the single most important exception, and certainly not a negligible one, being Balzac's Vautrin, female homosexuality, from Balzac on, and including Baudelaire, Zola, and Maupassant among others, exists in an episodic set of presentations (90–92). Hence, they conclude, there is a systematic repression of male homosexuality as the dark, unspeakable side of human sexuality. Or at least this is the case in the realm of fictional narrative, for in scientific discourse, as they have pointed out and as Foucault noted extensively in his *Histoire de la sexualité*, there is an explosion of discourses on sexuality, and especially its "perversions"—excessive masturbation, hysteria, and pederasty—and the cures for these perversions. And with that extensive volume of theorizations, scientific studies, and biopolitical tracts, it becomes difficult, if not to say impossible, to talk of an act of repression.

Certainly Aron and Kempf are right, but too conservative: it is not that there is a suppression or a Freudian repression *per se* of male homosexuality in nineteenth-century narrative, but a suppression of male sexuality and its visible sign in the penis itself. The writings about impotence are not so much a sign of unspeakable homosexuality but of an act of complete castration. The early nineteenth century makes a Faustian pact with the devil: narrative will be granted absolute power if the penis disappears in favor of a symbolic phallus. This gives the law, determines meaning, and decides on exchange: what better incarnation of the capitalist model that will be the economic system of the age? What better figure than the modern city, with its extraordinary power that has taken on mythic and yet invisible and impersonal qualities? And what better way, one might add, for controlling the unknowns of women, their desires, and their power? Later incarnations of the phallus, the so-called phallic symbols, signs of an ineffable symbol, are safe and effective. In the process of symbolization, the very humanness of the penis, the sense of the penile symbol in Renaissance painting, disappears in favor of the safer and far more powerful signs of the power of "inphallibility." And who knows if the direct physical representation of the organ of pleasure is not itself an act of dangerous representation: the erection of the penis may lead to a breakdown of the categories of desire. Indeed, as Leo Bersani has suggested in his article "Is the Rectum a Grave?," the fear of homosexuality may itself be a cover for a deeper fear, the fear of becoming, feeling, or representing female desire within the phallocentric order. Exorcizing the penis in favor of the masculist phallus keeps the world safe from the fascinations of male desire.

A traditional Freudian interpretation would see this exchange as a means of warding off castration anxiety, for the disappearance of the penis occurs in favor of the phallus, which cannot be castrated: in Daniel Sibony's felicitous expression, "the uncastratable other." But at the same time, if we believe in the idea of castration anxiety, the very belief means that the castration has "always already" occurred. Certainly, in Lacan's return to Freud, much is to be made of the distinction between the penis and the phallus. In "La Signification du phallus," Lacan attempts to answer the question of the mystery of the phallus. He casts the question relative to what he perceives as a fundamental Kantian antinomy, as he asks why man [Mensch] must assume the attributes of "his" sex relative to a threat, indeed, to a removal [privation] (685). This threat/removal is the double figure of castration anxiety of the Freudian male and the infamous Penisneid of the Freudian female. Contemporary feminism has rightly criticized the idea of Penisneid as an imposed structure of phallocentrism, not the least of whose figures is the forgetting of the equally plausible structure of womb-envy. Castration anxiety is, however, another matter.

Again, understood as a textual figure as opposed to a psychoanalytical abstraction, castration anxiety can explain various manifestations of nascent nineteenth-century narrative. It deals with the horror of castration that every woman supposedly represents to every man: the engulfing of the male organ during sex always retains a slight echo of the fear of castration by the *vagina dentata*. An exchange, then, of the castratable penis for the all-powerful phallus is a net gain of power. Along with the examples from some of Balzac's early entries in *La Comédie humaine*, one might consider the famous exchange in Goethe's *Faust* between Mephistopheles and Faust. With great economy, Goethe says in a few lines what takes Vautrin/ Herrera several pages in his conversations with Rastignac and Lucien in some of Balzac's other works:

Faust: The little thing! . . . It grows in my hand! . . . .
Mephistopheles: It leads you to women. (ll. 6259–64)

If the male is "always already" symbolically castrated because of ever-present castration anxiety, the exchange seems a valid one. For the phallus, the locus of power, the Signifier that speaks and knows at the position of the Other, marks the possibility of a purely phallic discourse, that is, an unbounded narrative. And if the phallus maintains its invisibility and its power at a transcendental pole, it has operated an effective exchange of the invisibility that accompanies the defining moment of the recurring symptom of castration anxiety—sexual intercourse—for an invisibility of the panopticon, the world of the all-powerful gaze. Thus, in the nineteenth-century novel, the woman is eternally subject to the gaze of the male who, at every moment, has replaced his own vulnerability with the panoptical gaze that visually incarnates his power.

II. Ken Dolls

In this second part, I am interested in exploring the intersection of this disappearance of the penis with the teleology of this chapter, for the last part of it will be devoted not to the reappearance of the penis in the nineteenth-century novel, for it really does not reappear, but to the appearance of its place: the return of penile symbols instead of phallic symbols. To do this I shall examine a work that seems to me best to exemplify the change in the orientations of desire: Guy de Maupassant's 1885 novel *Bel-Ami*, a *roman d'apprentissage* that illustrates the changing categories of desire in the era between traditional realism and modernism. And in the next chapter, I shall deal with a forgotten work by Paul Bonnetain, *Charlot s'amuse*, more or less contemporary (1883) with Maupassant's canonic novel. Yet before we can understand the return of the penis, we must go further back into a prehistory of the rise of characters of modest origins in the literature of the century and look at the descriptions of some of the earlier heroes of *romans d'apprentissage* to see at least what the origin of the undesigned man may be. To do so is obviously to repeat the gesture sketched out by Edison in *L'Eve future*: to write the present by rereading the past. The *bévue* in such an action is obvious, for it is the "blindness" or "misreading" that became a watchword of the critical practices fostered at Yale in the 1970's (Bloom, de Man). By providing a genealogy for Bel-Ami, or even for *Bel-Ami*, we are forcing him into a mold that is perhaps not his, that could not in fact be his. Maupassant provides one genealogy for designing Bel-Ami that is completely different, and perhaps it would be right to look briefly at that one, before examining Maupassant's predecessors.

Maupassant casts Georges Duroy as the heir to the models proposed in mediocre popular fiction for the unheroic, amoral hero who makes his way in the world:

Although dressed in a sixty-franc suit, he kept a certain rowdy elegance, a bit common though real. Big, well-proportioned, blond, a chestnut blond that was slightly reddish, with a turned up moustache that seemed to foam on his lip, light blue eyes pierced by tiny pupils, naturally curly hair with a part right in the middle of his head, he resembled the bad egg [*mauvais sujet*] of popular novels. (198)

The editor of the Pléiade edition (1348) notes, "According to the typology of the genre, the 'bad egg' [*mauvais sujet*] was always seductive and somewhat handsome, and had the airs of a non-commissioned officer 'back in civilian life.'" Yet in no way does the career of this subject compare to the bathos created by the "mauvais sujet" in other novels. Duroy succeeds, through his seductive powers, through his talent to be in the right place, through his learning curve; no tears, few heartbreaks, little underhandedness to speak of: even his reorganization of the money his wife inherits, however little he may merit such an inheritance, does not leave her destitute, as would be the case in a popular novel. Georges seduces, but the seduction is never tainted by the polarization of honesty and dishonesty of the popular novel, nor even the intense machinations of Zola's *Rougon-Macquart*. Georges has not usurped other men's phalluses, but only "their" vaginas, with his penis. Georges succeeds because the very description of his body represents the act of male sexual pleasure, the top half of his body the aroused penis, the lower half miming a frequent male sexual position: "He walked the way he walked when he was wearing the uniform of the hussars, his chest thrust out [*la poitrine bombée*], his legs slightly apart [*un peu entrouvertes*] as if he had just gotten off a horse" (197). Incarnation of desire, and desire in action, Georges Duroy will figure a success of pleasure through the redistribution, through his very being, of quotients of joy. We will return to such descriptions of Duroy, but only after having looked at the descriptions involved in other *romans d'apprentissage*. Through such a comparison, we can gauge the difference of Duroy.

Specifically, I am interested in the descriptions of the leading characters in two of the best-known novels in this category: *Le Rouge et le Noir* and *Illusions perdues*. Some justification needs to be made for these choices: why *Le Rouge et le Noir* instead of *La Chartreuse*; why *Illusions perdues* instead of *Le Père Goriot*? The elements present in the books chosen, and missing to some extent in the ones not chosen, are those found in *Bel-Ami*. These are two in number: first, the chronicle of a success of a character of modest origins within the pages. So Eugène de Rastignac's success, though intimated in *Le Père Goriot*, does not occur until later; similarly, Fabrice is not at all of modest origins. On the other hand, Lucien Chardon is of a modest background, though in part noble; he has to rebaptize himself, much as Georges Duroy will do, though certainly with more right to the renaming than Maupassant's figure; we should remember too that Julien Sorel is ultimately rebaptized and ennobled in the process (Schor 53). Secondly, each of the three main characters has much to do with writing: Lucien writes poetry; Julien has memorized books and becomes, in the second half, the secretary to M. de la Mole;

Georges Duroy writes for newspapers. And again, this second salient feature is figured in the process of rebaptism: each is good with words and knows how to use them to effect. The story of all three novels is the same: a goodlooking man of modest origins trades on his looks to gain the power of using words to great advantage.

First, then, let us consider Julien Sorel, who is so engrossed in his reading that he forgets that he is part of an all-male family. When we first are made aware of him, we are told that he has a thin waist (232); when we first see him, he is in tears. When he is described, the description is what we would expect of a protagonist who follows shortly after the "weak" Octave of the earlier *Armance*. Julien has purple cheeks and lowered eyes. He has "irregular, but delicate features" and is "svelte" and "well-shaped" (233). Julien will hardly be a man like his brothers and his father; of that we can be certain. In addition to being of a different class and stature, he will not be oafish or coarse like them; his physical attributes will be a plus in helping him pass in society. Whether he will succeed and at what price are things not yet clear from the description. It is clear that Julien has no right to a complete body, nothing to indicate that there is a male power within him, other than that of the phallic trade-off. And it can certainly be argued that Julien's power and success occur as he mimes the position of the phallus, in the part of the novel that occurs between the scene with Mme de Rênal and her cousin in the garden, when he takes the hand of Mme de Rênal (267), and the counterrevolutionary conspiracy of M. de la Mole and his friends, when Julien is asked to serve as living paper for a message (569–81). In the first, he takes action, possesses through his gaze and disdains the feminine: "the little he dared understand of the kind words of the two friends displeased him as being meaningless, weak, in a word, *feminine*" (271). In the latter, no longer master of his own words, he loses all power to control what he does with his tongue, mind, and heart.

In *Illusions perdues*, there are two male protagonists, Lucien de Rubempré, the poet, and David Séchard, the printer, who is arguably the figure of the author seeing himself as the powerful organizer of the written word and not its slave. At first sight, David seems the epitome of masculine strength: "His large bust was flanked by strong shoulders in harmony with the fullness of all his parts [*toutes ses formes*]. His face, dark-complected, colored, heavy, supported by a big neck, and enveloped by an abundant forest of black hair at first glance resembled that of the canons sung by Boileau" (5:144). At first glance, David seems the epitome of masculine virtues. He has a large neck and strong shoulders, and has the abundant hair of a truly masculine man. But even in that first glance something is missing: aside from the vague "toutes ses formes," David has no body below his bust. Bereft of his body, he is "at first glance" already emasculated, as he is compared to a man of the cloth, that is, someone in a cassock who has taken a vow of chastity. Compare the description of Eugène de Rastignac in *Le Père Goriot*, a character who is made of a head and clothing:

> Eugène de Rastignac had a southern face, white skin, black hair, blue eyes. . . . If he was thrifty in his dress, if on ordinary days he finally wore out last year's clothing, he could nevertheless go out from time to time dressed like an elegant young man. He usually wore an old frock coat, a bad waistcoat, the evil, faded, badly knotted black tie of the *Student*, pants to match, and resoled boots. (3:60)

In contrast, Vautrin has a body, described here, and exposed later, as his shirt is removed and his very real body is remarked (3:213). That is the body disguised in the cassock of the Abbé Herrera, and not some emptiness. If we return to *Illusions perdues*, at second glance the situation becomes even more precise:

> But a second examination revealed to you, in the furrows of the thick lips [*les sillons des lèvres épaisses*], in the cleft chin [*la fossette du menton*], in the shape of the broad nose split by a tormented facial plane [*méplat*], especially in the eyes! the continuous fire of a singular love, the wisdom of the thinker, the burning melancholy of a mind that could take in the two extremes of the horizon while penetrating all the turnings [*sinuosités*], and which was easily disgusted by ideal pleasures on which he would bring to bear the clarities of analysis. (5:144–45)

David's face, with its furrowed thick lips and its irregular split along the chiseled features of a nose, the organ that stands outs in the face, and now "split," with its cleft in the chin, is a series of displaced descriptions of female genitalia. Indeed, the situation is even underlined etymologically. As J. N. Adams points out, in Latin the standard word for male genitals was *mentula* (9–13). I would speculate that the diminutive "-ette" in *fossette* coupled with *menton* echoes this *mentula* but feminizes it and hollows it out. David's face is the result of the exchange of penis for phallus; there is no hidden innerness as there would be with "real" female organs, but rather the marks of the "having been cut away" that establishes the phallus instead of the penis, but not in its stead. Thus David is disgusted by "jouissances" and is equally able to "penetrate" every recess.

And what of Lucien? If David is the incarnation of the phallic symbol, which means both power and lack, both narrative potency and sexual impotence, Lucien is the "always already" feminized victim of Balzac's narrative strategy: "His face was distinguished by lines of classical beauty; he had a Greek nose and forehead, the velvety whiteness of women, eyes that were so blue they were black, eyes full of love, whose white could challenge in freshness that of a child" (5:145). At first glance, Lucien is somewhere between the female with her vulnerable, penetrable sexuality and the child's asexuality. Lucien's face already bears the indication of femininity, with its velvety whiteness. If David is described through the complete ellipsis of his body, Lucien is described as a woman: "Looking at his feet, a man would have been even more tempted to take him for a young lady in disguise, since, like most fine, if not to say astute, men, his hips were well-formed like those of a woman. This index, which is rarely wrong, was true in Lucien's case" (5:145). Though one might be tempted to see him as a figure in travesty, as is the case for Zambinella in "Sarrasine," the travesty is that Lucien is disguised as a being-with-a-penis when, in fact, he has neither penis nor phallus. A man—a "real" man, a man with a penis, and a man with heterosexual desires—might momentarily be deceived into thinking that Lucien is a possible conquest, since he appears to be a young lady. But the penetrating reading offered by the position of the phallus tells us otherwise. Lucien has neither, and is doomed to fail.[1]

III. Bel-Ami

Georges Duroy is the incarnation of this missing penis. This means that within the framework of a phallic system, a phallocentric system, Georges is in a sense a mark of sexual ambiguity, because he marks the male organ of pleasure without associating it (or without it being associated) with the ideology that translates and removes that organ in the process of creating the phallic model of dominance and power. Indeed, in her article "The Harlot's Apprentice," Mary Donaldson-Evans discusses *Bel-Ami* in terms of the "unstable *sexual* identity" of the main character, whom she sees as having "a serious gender identification problem" (617). Were Duroy not necessarily in conflict with the ideological system that surrounds him both textually and socially, there would be no gender identification problem at all, for he is wholly, consciously male and heterosexual. However, in that I posit Georges as having a penis instead of a phallus, and in that the ideological construct of phallocentric discourse necessarily posits the absence of a phallus as a problem, as weakness, as femininity, I would say that Georges does not fully occupy the traditional phallic role assigned to the male.

The women in the novel, all immediately attracted to him as if by some hypnotic or magnetic pull, are struck by his beauty, even though we already know that his beauty is in the realm of the vulgar. Still, his ability to be an instant cynosure is never put into question and is succinctly stated at the very beginning: "As he bore himself well, by nature and as a former non-commissioned officer, he stuck out his chest [*il cambra sa taille*], twirled his moustache with a gesture that was both military and familiar, and shot a quick glance all around at the remaining diners, one of those looks that handsome young men give that spread out like blows from a sparrow-hawk" (197). What can we say about this description? Certainly the next page, which contains the description of Georges as the "mauvais sujet," will reduce this beauty to a typology of vulgarity that Maupassant seems to tell us is not worth a second look. For to his eternal literary chagrin, Georges is the image of a character in a penny dreadful or a popular romantic novel: his elegance is ironically described as being "a bit common." What he has is the mask of another character combined with his own impenetrability: his very small pupils do not let in the gaze of the other. For if the masculist gaze has been seen to be an encompassing one that anatomizes the body of the woman, the gaze also penetrates and hypnotizes through eye-to-eye contact. Though we are not yet sure what gaze could anatomize him, we are sure that his eyes cannot be subject to the penetrating regard of the other. His own gaze is the sharp farsightedness of a sparrow-hawk. With his gaze he encompasses and entrances all he sees.

Yet even without his gaze, he remains the center of attention, a cynosure. Certainly his good looks attract the gaze of the crowd, but elsewhere only a glance is needed. The streetwalker's come-on line takes on a meaning as it becomes true: "With empty pockets and boiling blood, he lit up when meeting the corner street-walkers who murmur: 'Will you come with me handsome [*joli garçon*]?'" (198). In a sense, of course, he is like them, ready to trade on his looks for money, and in distinction to the upright bourgeoisie filled with disdain, Georges does not look askance at these women: "They were women, women of love. He did not disdain them with the inborn disdain of family men" (199). But we are moving even further from the ritualized exchange, because the physical presence of Georges introduces a content into the come-on line. If, by and large, the line is usually empty of meaning, a vapid come-on meant to flatter, albeit theatrically, in Georges's case he is indeed a "joli garçon." Though his beauty does not compete with their allure, the act of prostitution itself becomes detheatricalized as like meets like and as content is returned to an economy that already illustrates, at a local level, the retranslation of phallic order into an expense of pleasure.

The narrative stops full participation in the theatrical model of phallic power by giving real content to an empty line. Our understanding does not come until later, when Georges goes to the theater and sees a trapeze artist getting ready to perform. Here as elsewhere in the novel, Maupassant makes great use of the construction of reflections, of specular images, by describing scenes with mirrors, or in this case, a theatricalization of the life of the audience member. This is a specular image, with the theater saying what cannot be said in the detheatricalized narrative. The trapeze artist has muscles, a body, and goes beyond being the Ken doll to which male characters had been reduced: "Under his tights, you could see the outline of his arm and leg muscles; he thrust out his chest to hide his stomach that stuck out too much; his face looked like that of a male hairdresser, for a careful part divided his hair into two equal parts, right in the middle of his head" (207).

This trapeze artist is the image of Georges himself, who also has a part right in the middle of his hair; this image is an ironic repetition of the typical male eye-rape of the female. Certainly it is a distorted image, with the puffed-up chest that contrasts with Georges's well-built frame while reminding us of an earlier description of Georges's thrust-out chest. Moreover, the trapeze artist's belly destroys the line of the muscles of the torso and legs. But the identical part is the denuding of the body, the point that reveals the naked skin beneath. It is as if the part in one's hair were the *aletheia* of the head, the nonobject that reveals, allows the gaze, and shows the naked truth of the body and its guises. So it is a metaphoric link that marks for us other hair on the body, especially since much of the rest of the description emphasizes the very apparent legs of the trapeze artist: "Then he jumped to the ground, saluted anew, and went next to the scenery, as he showed his leg muscles with every step" (207). Legs lead up, and the very well-defined figure of the trapeze artist's body leads us to consider that his genitals are certainly outlined by the rather revealing outfit. They are there to be seen, they have been laid bare for us to see, they reveal that male desire has a form that is separate from power.

Georges's gaze is a gaze that penetrates, and in return he receives a gaze that sees him as a man, not as an individual who has somehow appropriated part of the power structure for himself, given up his penis for a phallus, but rather as someone who has a penis. The vision of the trapeze-artist's curves leads necessarily to another gaze, one that recognizes anatomy, despite clothing, despite propriety. There is the recognition that Georges is like the trapeze artist, undistorted, but with a body that can function for pleasure without *necessarily* participating in a power game. Gone are the favors and merchandises of the exchange of women as chattel; present instead is a man whose sexuality is as present, both really and metaphorically, as that of the character who sees him:

Duroy was no longer listening. One of those women, leaning on her elbows in her box, was looking at him. She was a big brunette with flesh whitened by powder, black eyes that were lengthened and emphasized with eye-liner and framed with enormous false eyelashes. Her rather large cleavage stretched the dark silk of her dress; her painted lips, red like a wound, gave her something bestial, burning, outrageous, yet which still excited desire. (208)

The reader might have no problem in making the rather facile metaphoric leap from the woman's painted lips to the stereotypical image of her genitals. The violence of the image that compares the woman's mouth explicitly and her genitals implicitly to a gash underlines not only the penetrating gaze of male dominance by the narrator, but also the nonwoundedness of the character at whom she is looking: Georges. In fact, Georges Duroy is one of the rare characters in the nineteenth-century novel not to have been visited by the muse of castration anxiety. Even without the usual signs of power, influence, the ubiquitous phallic signifier of money, he is fine; Rachel, the demi-mondaine, is ready to go with him for far less than her usual asking price: "I have only one louis in my pocket" (210), Georges tells her. What he does have in his pocket, as Mae West would have said, makes him happy to see her and vice versa. And the game of the empty pockets is one that will serve much later as well; he is not a man of asexual power, but a man who knows what he has to fill his clothing, and it is far from being money: "In a second, he turned all his pockets inside out in his pants, vest, and jacket" (274–75). If his clothes fit right, the money will come, not from a power game, but from desire itself.

As Rachel says at their next encounter, "You don't know, I have dreamt of you twice since the other day" (247). His desire can produce desire even among the meretricious; clearly he is cut from a cloth different from the typical client that establishes an exchange-system based on money and phallic power. Georges is desire, its incarnation made very literal flesh, and far from the usual emasculated male characters that are always said to "please women." Georges's image of himself, his realization that he need not be anything but a man wearing form-fitting clothing, is not immediately understood. The day after his first encounter with Rachel, his ill-fitting clothing seems to strike a sour note, at least until there is a realization that it is saying and signifying the same thing. For to attract, his body must be seen; he must be able to show that he is a person of pleasure: "His pants, a bit too wide, badly outlined his leg, seemed to wrap around his ankle, seemed to have that crumpled look that used clothing has when it covers limbs by chance" (210).

The problem is that he is subjecting his own self to the same anatomizing gaze that he would use on a woman. The gaze is multiple, disjointed, and fragmenting. And it is only under those circumstances that he worries about the inappropriate fit of the trousers. For he cannot see himself as a whole and he does not know what he might be looking at: "he was wearing a suit for the first time in his life" (210). In that he cannot see or figure or reflect on his whole self, he concentrates on the effect of each part instead of on the cynosuric presence of the whole, of which the readers are already aware. The parts form no unit, no integral whole; in his own mind, because he is anatomized *like a woman*, he is grotesque: "Having only his shaving mirror, he could not contemplate his whole image, and as he could see the various parts of his extemporized outfit only rather badly, he exaggerated the imperfections and worried about the idea of being grotesque" (211). The image of disintegration or of nonintegration of the self lingers far into the novel: "And he suddenly had a singular need to get up to look at himself in the mirror. He relit his candle. When he saw his face reflected in the polished glass, he barely recognized himself and he thought that he had never seen himself" (314). At every turn that doubt may arise; it does so until he is finally convinced that he can be fully reflected in this pleasure system. Rewriting Eugène de Rastignac's challenge to society in the very last lines of Balzac's *Le Père Goriot*, Maupassant makes the image of the subject of pleasure the final image of his novel: "He slowly descended the steps of the high stoop between two rows of spectators. But he did not see them: his thoughts went back, and before his eyes dazzled by the brilliant sun floated the image of Mme de Marelle in front of the mirror, as she readjusted the little curls at her temples, always undone as she got out of bed" (480).

But now let us return to those earlier moments. What does it mean to be seen like a woman, anatomized, divided, segmented, drawn into pieces by a three-leaded pencil? For Georges it means the dissociation of the parts of his body from himself; there is no Lacanian mirror stage for him. He has no idea what his entirety is, though the readers have already witnessed it. It is one thing to be laid bare as a whole individual; it is a come-on for the promise of things as yet unsaid. It is another to be reduced by the gaze of another, or that same gaze that one uses to undress the woman, to have that come back, to splinter the self into pieces, as if the self too were nothing more than a collection of flaccid parts. In those circumstances, the penis would be just another organ, nothing more than something hidden or not, next to the badly draped leg. When the whole being is made present, when the gaze can no longer splinter, the entirety is deemed good: "And now, looking carefully at himself, he realized that the whole outfit was truly satisfying" (211). It is as if he himself had become an ambulatory instrument of pleasure, ready to satisfy. In truth, the truth is out, he will become the "bel-ami" of the title, protean in nature, able to change names, seductive, pleasure-giving, in short, a well-dressed penis.

IV. "Erection Is Said Only of Monuments"—Flaubert

Aware of his newfound power, Georges does not know that new rules come with it, and perhaps will not learn this until the fully integrated image of pleasure is created at the end of the novel; so he still tries to use power in the traditional way. In other words, he attempts to play the old phallic game of authoritative discourse in which the *parole* of the individual ego is generalized to be a powerful, phallocentric discourse whose truth comes not from the adequation of word and thing, but from the adequation of *parole* and *langue*. In the generalized phallocentric discourse of the nineteenth century, the words of any individual ego that has bought into that phallic structure are taken as a system of general equivalences. In that, quite obviously, there is a mirror of the system of exchange itself in which there is a generalized equivalent in the form of the transcendental signifier, be it money, phallus, or their mutual translation in the *langue* of power. This interrelationship is masterfully studied by Jean-Joseph Goux in *Marx, Freud. Economie et symbolique* and *Les Iconoclastes*. Yet Georges's difference is precisely that he does not have a phallus but a penis. And trying to be like everyone else just leaves him looking blank: "Then he sought the beginning of the first sentence. He remained head in hands, focussing on the blank square spread in front of him" (223). It is no wonder that Maupassant is recalling another recent writers' block in which the characters, obviously penisless, are phallusless as well; the lack of phallic power is the story of their lives. I am thinking of course of Flaubert's last novel, *Bouvard et Pécuchet*, in which all modes of learning and knowledge are demoniacally ironized and parodied:

Or they double-locked the door. Bouvard cleaned off the table, put paper in front of him, dipped his pen in the inkwell, and stared at the ceiling, while Pécuchet, in the armchair, meditated, legs straight out and head down. Sometimes they felt a shudder, something like the wind of an idea; but just as they seized it, it had already disappeared. (2:836)

Flaubert's irony is all-consuming, and he even ironizes the phallocentric system itself by describing the ubiquity of phallic symbols: "In olden days, towers, pyramids, candles, milestones, and even trees indicated phalluses, and for Bouvard and Pécuchet, everything became a phallus" (2:810). But it is slightly different for Maupassant's protagonist, who is not found in a context in which a deconstruction of erudition is the order of the day. His position is a hybrid between the social world of Stendhal's protagonists and the epistemological boxes of Flaubert's last work. Like Julien Sorel who does not know what to say when he first meets Mme de Rênal or when he is in the drawing room at the Hôtel de la Môle, Georges is caught by the blank, set awhirl in a maelstrom. And like Bouvard and Pécuchet before him, Georges stares and waits for the very same inspiration from without, as if some divine afflatus would come and inflate his metaphoric phallus to produce the powerful words he needs to conquer. But Georges is quite literally impotent and he cannot compete: "He vaguely felt thoughts come to him; he might have said them, but he could not put them into writing. And his impotence [*impuissance*] made him feverish, he got up anew, hands moist with sweat, blood rushing to his head" (224).

How odd that the usual phallic games of dominance do not work, especially given the fact that the story he is telling is precisely one of phallic dominance, a story about abuses of power in a colonial system. And after all, when he was a participant in that very colonial system, he was abusive like all the others with whom he consorted: "And he recalled his two years in Africa and the way in which he ransomed the Arabs in the little outposts in the South. . . . the Arab being considered somewhat as the soldier's natural prey" (200). The superposition of the phallic order of the white male on another heterogenous, yet phallocentric order within the framework of colonialism reinforces the rigidity of that European phallocentric structure: all systems must bow to it, and everyone else, women and colonized alike, becomes the phallusless other that is the "natural prey" of the system. And Georges was a successful participant in the game of bilateral oppositions of white versus nonwhite, of captor versus prey, of moneyed versus poor. It would thus seem natural for him to be able mimetically to reproduce in writing that power game that once was his. In so doing, he would be the successful purveyor of the phallic writing, the recipe for which he would have mastered.

But now all that is available to him is received language, tales of another world that cannot directly promote him in this one. Purveying the phallic writing is not within his capacities, and not even an act of what is popularly called "mental masturbation" or a more violent act of sadism can erect the phallus he so ardently though wrongheadedly desires: "His innate Norman consciousness, rubbed [*frottée*] by the daily practice of garrison life, swollen [*distendue*] by the examples of marauding in Africa, illicit perks, suspect tricks, whipped [*fouettée*] as well by the ideas of honor that run in the army . . . " (225). No matter how hard he tries, reinserted into this world in which Maupassant proposes a path other than phallocentric dominance, Georges Duroy cannot erect himself the way he could as a soldier abusing a colonized victim. It is therefore not enough to be able to reproduce an event mimetically to give it the power of phallocentric discourse. Nor is it enough to have participated in a power game. And not even the "rubbed," "swollen," and "whipped" consciousness can rise above the impotence. Georges is caught in a model in which desire must be both the power broker and the power: "the desire to succeed [*arriver*] reigned as master" (225), yet it is a master structured by desire and not by raw, brute power. Balzac's concept of *arrivisme* will not work, even if Georges writes his own novel so laden with the phallic symbolism of popular dream analysis as to be transparent:

He had started unknowingly to daydream, as he did every evening. He imagined a magnificent love story which would bring him in one fell swoop to realize his hopes. He would marry the daughter of a banker or a nobleman whom he'd met in the street and conquered at first sight.

He was awakened from his dream by the strident whistle of a locomotive, which, having come out all alone from its tunnel like a rabbit from its hole and going full speed along the rails, headed toward the garage where it would rest. (225)

Whereas Rachel dreams twice and says no more, Georges idly day-
dreams his fantasy but is forced to pull out to go into the garage that
is the storehouse for machines at rest.

Georges discovers that there is another way to write that does not
depend on phallic power. It is, to make a pun, a *jeu de dames*: a game
of women, a game by women; it is the multiple moves of checkers
where all the players are potentially equal instead of the chess game
of a castrated king and a phallic queen. The writer's blank that had
earlier been a block to activity is now just a pause before plunging
anew, dipping one's quill anew in the inkwell; it is the ink that counts,
not the straightness of the quill. Maupassant shows us Mme
Forestier, the woman behind the man, the real writer for Forestier
who then does the same for Georges Duroy: "With two fingers she
manipulated a goose-quill agilely; in front of her was a half-written
sheet of large paper, interrupted by the young man's arrival" (228).
Maupassant has already made us aware that it is the abundance and
disseminability of the liquid that is foremost, as solids begin, even
early on, to give way to their own liquidity. But unlike Flaubert, for
whom the solid/liquid metamorphosis is a sign of eternal miasmic
decomposition, as I have noted in *Rendering French Realism*, Maupassant always makes the liquid the sign of positive nonphallic desire.
Associated with women, liquid imagery counters the too facile notion of phallic penetration that is the mark of success in other written works. Here liquid or its atomization into vapor marks the space
of activity: "Mme de Marelle had turned to him several times, and
the diamond in her ear trembled incessantly as if the fine drop of water would separate and fall" (218). The hardest solid deliquesces in a
world wherein phallic symbols have no exchange value. As Mme de
Marelle says of her earrings, "You would think they were dew,
wouldn't you?" (218). And the softest solid is pure erotica: "The oys-
ters from Ostende were brought in; they were cute and plump, like
little ears encased in shells, and they melted between the palate and
tongue like salty candy" (256).

In her study *Woman's Revenge*, Mary Donaldson-Evans discusses
the "power of penetration," which she sees present in Duroy, but
which dissipates through the "invasion of male by female" in Maupassant's later works (40–41). I would maintain, however, that
Duroy's penetration is of a different order than the typical penetra-

tion scheme of narrative, and that the idea of penetration is already
a two-way street. Now penetration is not for assault, but for looks
laden with desire: "She thanked him with a look, one of those clear
women's looks that penetrate to the heart" (218). Penetration is for
immersion in a voluptuousness of surroundings undergoing perpetual liquefaction: "Entering the living room, he once again felt he was
penetrating a greenhouse. Large palms opened their elegant fronds
in each corner of the room, climbed to the ceiling, then widened into
fountains [*jets d'eau*]" (219). Penetration means no more and no less
than the unnameable nonphallic dissemination of desire throughout
a space: "The air was cool, penetrated by a vague, sweet perfume,
that could have been defined, but could not have been named" (219).
Significantly, a return of the traces of the phallic model means impenetrability, following on the heels of George's phallocentric penetration, expressed in his silent braggadocio:

He looked at the serious, respectable face of M. de Marelle, with a desire to
laugh on his lips, and thought: "I'm cuckolding you, old man, I'm cuckolding you." And an intimate, sordid [*vicieuse*] satisfaction penetrated him . . .
Mme de Marelle entered suddenly, and having covered them with a smiling
and impenetrable glance, she went toward Duroy. (305)

Yet it is as if the model were being ironically quoted in this restag-
ing of cuckoldry, significantly in an onstage remark, as opposed to
the generally accepted *bienséance* of offscreen affairs never directly
represented, even to oneself, that are a major part of Balzac's economy of pleasure. Maupassant brings the mention of the forbidden to
center stage, shows the nonviability of the model of power, and reinforces the model of pleasure. And when in fact a model of penetration resembles the Balzacian one—that is, when there is a reminder of the economy of power—there is a discreet turning away.
Georges Duroy does not mind thinking that he may cuckold someone else by giving pleasure to the wife of that other; he does mind
that someone may think he is the victim of the same economy, even
if the older man, the Comte de Vaudrec, knew Mme Duroy long before Georges did. Now that he is married to Madeleine, and she inherits from the Comte de Vaudrec, "he now avoided the penetrating
look of his wife" (429).

The method takes a while to learn, but eventually, Georges internalizes it as his own. At first, he returns to bad habits: "He continued the adventure started by Mme Forestier, accumulating details, the surprising twists, and overblown descriptions of a serialized novel, with a schoolboy's bad style and the cliches of a noncommissioned officer" (246). Yet he will eventually master the writing style that he is taught in the scene that initiates him to a new kind of writing game. In fact, by the last part of the novel he has it down so well that he can fake it: "And Du Roy went to rummage through the collection of *La Vie française* to find his first article: 'Recollections of an African Hunter,' and which, unbaptized, reworked, and modified, would do splendidly from A to Z" (402). This writing will eventually be matched by Georges's simulated for Mme Walter: he masters not only the idea of pleasure for its own sake but also learns, at least metaphorically, how to fake an orgasm.

What exactly is this writing? First of all, it is writing taught by a woman. Eternally bereft of a phallus, though in the Lacanian model she can clearly be the phallus, she has only one protection against the gaze of penetration, and that is desire itself. It is this nonphallic writing that Georges must learn. Writing, and by that I mean, metonymically, being successful and getting where one is going, depends on the nonphallic nature of the production of writing. Before Mallarmé's disappearing cigar in "Toute l'âme résumée," writing is signified by the destruction of the phallic symbol and its replacement with a multiply woven bit of writing:

She arose and began to walk about, after having lit another cigarette, and she dictated as she blew wisps of smoke that initially came out straight from a little round hole from her pursed lips; the wisps widened and evaporated, leaving here and there in the air gray lines, a sort of transparent fog, a cloud like a spider's web. Sometimes, with her open hand, she erased these light and more persistent traces; sometimes she also cut them with a slicing motion of her index finger and then, with deep attention, watched the two halves of the imperceptible vapor slowly disappear. (231)

Writing is woven of different filaments, imperceptible disseminated atoms that form wreaths and figures. Woven like the threads of a spider's web, the writing is done in a vaporous round of activity, not a penetration by a phallus that organizes the space, but an ever-widening dissemination whose center is constantly in the process of changing. If the source is unique, it is wholly without merit, a narrow hole that has no channel or canal-like pretensions. And even the endgame of writing, the final bit that depends, as it must, on a cut, is not the "little death" one has come to expect, but rather a slow disappearance, a fading (out) of voices.

As one might expect, Roland Barthes discussed this fading as the very model of enunciation in classical writing: "The best way to imagine classical plurality is to listen to the text as a sparkling exchange of multiple voices, on different wavelengths, grabbed from time to time by a brusque fading, whose breach [*trouée*] allows enunciation to migrate from one point of view to another" (49). Yet Barthes's object is the writing of castration, "Sarrasine," the tale without a phallus. And we should wonder about the generalization of the model of plurality from such a work, which is part of the textuality of suppressing the penis in favor of the phallus. And yet using such a work is not as far off as all that, for like *Louis Lambert*, Balzac's other writing of castration, "Sarrasine" is an early work written before Balzac becomes "Balzac," that is, before Balzac fully considers the ramifications of the trick of the recurring character and the will-to-totalization that is the project or idea of *La Comédie humaine*. Balzac shows us how to eliminate the fadings to give the feeling of continuous, omnipresent, and omnipotent phallic narration; it is that against which Flaubert will write, as he lip-synchs the same narration in *Madame Bovary* and shows the world the extent of the simulation.

One might draw a conclusion *a contrario*: the myth of nineteenth-century narrative is that it cuts out those fadings, since phalluses must always remain erect, and that the plurality of voices inherited from the eighteenth century, and specifically from the epistolary novel, is mythologized as the unified, phallocentric discourse of omniscience. Nineteenth-century narrative is a series of splices that pretend to be a continuous take. If we follow a path from Stendhal through Balzac, Flaubert, and, I am suggesting, Maupassant, we see that just as the techniques of realism are cohering to make a more seamless whole of narrative, the phallic model is in fact on the decline. Indeed, the irony is that the phallic model becomes propped up in a narrative *Anlehnung* just as its efficacy is being put into question by repeated assaults on the concepts of otherness and wholeness on which it depends. The novel of disillusion of which Lukács writes so effectively is but one example, or one way of naming, the gradual receding of a phallocentric model in favor of a model that considers the pull of desire within language, the surging of desire from within the structures of representation. Proust and—to use a heterogeneous example—Mallarmé don't just "happen": as revolutionary as their works may seem—and indeed they are revolutionary—the way has been prepared for quite a while before their individual explosions.

In *Bel-Ami*, writing or, for that matter, being, in the sense of being successful, is a *jeu de dames*. Indeed, in *Woman's Revenge*, Mary Donaldson-Evans quite rightly points to Duroy as the model of the *homme-fille* of Maupassant's writings and especially of the story of the same name (124). These shifting generic boundaries are subject to a ludic dance in the novel. Having a penis instead of a phallus means being momentarily "it" in a game of erotic tag, the position of giving pleasure or not giving pleasure, perhaps endlessly renewed, certainly endlessly replaced. The game involves the aptly named Mme de Marelle, Madame Hopscotch. This is a game in which there is momentary control over a local space as opposed to a global one: just like checkers, hopscotch is a local game, whose goal is to return home after having successfully completed a prescribed circuit. Having "it" or being "it" [*le chat*] means a game of tag, aptly named *chat perché* in French, where the game is in the chase and not in the moment of tag (253–54). Significantly, the words *chat* and *chatte* (which is, parenthetically, also French slang for "pussy") become the favored terms of endearment in the novel: "But no, my *chat*, it's no concern of yours, it's I who wants to do this little madcap thing" (267); even the simulated love between Georges and Mme Walter follows the same pattern, as her "mon chat" (416) is echoed in his "ma chatte" a few pages later (419). The movement from spot to spot and from situation to situation, while disseminating some imperceptible *odor di uomo*, occurs in that very same space in which phallic penetration would once have occurred. It is a game of ruses and tricks, of teases and momentary flashes of desire, far from the conquering discourses of phallocentrism: "It was the moment for clever hints, veils lifted by words as skirts are lifted, the moment for language games, smart, disguised boldness, the moment for every sort of immodest hypocrisy in a sentence that shows undressed images with cryptic expressions [*des expressions couvertes*]" (258). It is a verbal joust that finds its physical parallel some pages later in a game of footsie initiated not by a man, but by Mme de Marelle (297).

No one would doubt that the novel will follow a planned trajectory: any reader of the first part knows that Georges's rise will be successful, even despite certain chicaneries; he will become the renamed figure, Georges du Roy de Cantel (346), with all its attendant graces, honors, and rights (Prince 218). His double renaming—with this *nom à particule* and with the nickname of "Bel-Ami"—can only signal the success of the character in the novel.[2] Significantly and ironically, the success of the nickname is ensured by a powerful Jew, M. Walter, who says "I baptize you Bel-Ami like everyone else" (401). With this inversion of the powers of the old guard, the story signs its own truthful success. If a Jew can be in the position of baptizing, then the powers that be, the powers that rely precisely on the symbolic value of the phallus, are no longer needed. And Georges (402) will soon have the power to "unbaptize" writing and therefore reuse it where he will. Significantly, this unorthodox baptism by a Jew occurs at the end of a long episode (368–402) in which Georges is jestingly renamed "Forestier"—that is, the name of Madeleine's dead husband. Again, this episode is part of a system in which the economy of exchange is determined by the exchange of women, and by the position of the phallus. But this game, which casts Georges as nothing more than the *sosie* of the dead man, can have no productive value for Georges, for he must operate, not by filling the shoes of another, although that does happen, but by giving pleasure in his own right. Finally named for himself, he becomes immediately renamed by all and sundry, women and men alike, as "Bel-Ami," the figure of pleasure for all to enjoy. Instead of being the usurper, mimetically vying with the other, he is mimetically repeating his own position of pleasure: "He smiled, sat down, and took her between his open thighs just as he had done with Mme Walter shortly before" (418).

That the phallic symbol can finally be abandoned is clear as the now successful Georges du Roy de Cantel leaves the symbolic phallus at the door. No need, he says, for the magic walking stick that Mme de Girardin thought gave Balzac his powers to penetrate the recesses of women's boudoirs. That magic walking stick has become a symbol that everyone knows is a symbol, but which has no intrinsic power: "It's that religion is used like an *en-tout-cas*. If the weather is nice, it's a cane, if it's sunny, it is a parasol, if it rains, it's an umbrella, and, if you don't go out, you leave it in the hall" (394).

V. Rubbing Out the Phallus

A final word then. We know that the penis reappears, quietly, pleasurably, and locally itself in the twentieth century in works like *The Immoralist* and *Swann's Way*, where desire begins to work anew on the level of the individual; where there is no aspiration to complete power, be it narrative or other; and where, because these two in specific are "homosexual" texts, there is no requirement for the most phallic of institutions, nineteenth-century bourgeois marriage. If these works start the twentieth century, the nineteenth century ends with another, Octave Mirbeau's *Le Jardin des supplices*, and that one, quite literally, kills the phallus. You would have to be a madman, Mirbeau seems to be saying, to think that your penis entitled you to magic powers, all the women in the world, unlimited wealth, and so on.[3] Madmen need to be punished; and the punishment must fit the crime:

> The madman—he didn't seem mad—was spread out on a very low table, his limbs and body tied down by solid cords . . . his mouth gagged . . . so he could neither move nor scream. A woman, neither beautiful nor young, with a serious mask, completely dressed in black, her naked arm encircled with a large gold ring, knelt next to the madman. . . . She grabbed his rod . . . and she officiated. . . . Oh! my dear! . . . my dear! If you had seen it! . . . It took four hours . . . four hours, think of it! . . . four hours of fearsome, knowledgeable caresses, during which the woman's hand did not slow down for a minute, during which her face stayed cold and cheerless! . . . The patient expired in a spurt of blood that splashed all over the face of the tormenter. (166–67)

Significantly, in one of the final scenes in the novel the phallus has become "The Seven-Rodded Idol" (264), unmovable, inanimate, powerless, for women to offer flowers to and caress. And beyond that, after that, the presence of the phallus and the suppression of the penis in writing can never be the same.

The Writer's Hand

As I came back, I saw Uriah Heep shutting up the
office; and feeling friendly towards everybody, went
in and spoke to him, and at parting, gave him my
hand. But oh, what a clammy hand his was! as ghostly
to the touch as to the sight! I rubbed mine afterwards,
to warm it, *and to rub his off.*

—Charles Dickens

Who are you when you masturbate?

—Leo Bersani

A quasi-subversive organization founded recently in
Prague encourages its members to invent obstacles to
overcome while masturbating. The organization is
called Masturbation and Its Discontents—MAID for
short. The first task set by the English chapter is to
complete masturbation while reciting Milton's "Il
Penseroso" to no less than three listeners. The feat is
first accomplished in Durham by a male, aged fifty-
seven, who ejaculates at the line "While the bee with
honied thigh."

—Harry Mathews

The set of nonpornographic literary works depicting masturbation is
discontinuous. No anxiety of influence, no intertextuality, and no
canon appear. Here and there, one finds furtive references, passing
episodes, fleeting indications, and rare direct depictions, but no continuity. Rereading post-Enlightenment literature brings to light half-
hidden episodes whose nature had been ignored. Masturbatory se-
quences, erotics, and structures appear that had been disguised in a
more publicly acceptable and more abstruse language. The discontinuity that keeps these works as separate islands is a metatextual reinforcement of the presumed solitary nature of the event itself. Clearly,

any poetics of the subject must include both the covert representation and the fragmentary nature of the set of representations. Though discontinuous, the episodes of the fragmentary representation of masturbation in Western narrative recall underlying paradigms: the danger of reading, the subsumption of sex in literature by official discourses that control meaning, the intermittent reappearance of masturbation in the modern novel, the advent of looking at masturbation with a dispassionate eye, and the search for the voice of masturbation that speaks for itself without fear of contradiction. This voice, of course, will not be found, and in its stead is a rhetoric about masturbation and the discursive impossibility of the act. Recognizing that there is no capturable, pure voice of masturbation will be the recognition as well that masturbation, even in its solitude and intimacy, posits the other, an other that may very well turn out to be the self.

Masturbation is a singular activity. It is no news that the mechanics of masturbation and literary writing, as least that literary writing defined as the praxis of dead white European males, resemble one another. Insofar as the relation of writing and masturbation is concerned, rather than seek some theoretical ground, which, as I hope to show in this study, must necessarily remain shaky, it might prove useful to follow a series of interrelated readings as they refer to the simultaneous joys of writing, reading, and sexuality. The interweaving of two sets of figures, one sexual, one autoreferentially literary, provides a motor that produces a literary work and the means by which to read it.[1] And again, my use of the word "he" reflects the creation of the inscription of masturbation by white male writers. White males are not alone in writing masturbatory writings, but their means of writing against the dominant forms of literature are necessarily different from others in subaltern positions.

A singular activity occurs with the agent in isolation, separate from any community and divorced from any absolute knowledge. He moves one hand along a vaguely cylindrical object until a liquid is released. No other is necessarily there to receive the liquid; the dried traces of that liquid may or may not be noticed at a subsequent point. However patent, generalizing, or exclusionary that analogy may appear, reviewing it helps distinguish masturbation poetically from other sexual praxes and discursively from the languages that veil it. If

masturbation considered medically is one of many pathological behaviors, if considered economically it is in a smaller set that includes
prostitution, literarily, it stands alone. Literally alone.

So if a certain number of activities may be precluded by the act of
writing, masturbation remains the one that is both most similar and
most dangerous: writing *ex nihilo* about masturbation may make the
analogy a homology. And although the scientific discourse operates
under a fiction of believing and positing its own purity, I am still separating such discourse, which pretends to find its distinct "object" in
masturbation, from a literary discourse that dangerously takes masturbation as its "subject." Masturbation and writing are thus linked
and divided by the fear of that writing, which may metamorphose
into the sin of self-abuse, and by the similarity that makes simul-
taneity impossible. To write is to let masturbation go, not to abandon
the self, but rather to reinforce the self, as the trace and in the wake
of the moving hand: it is to abandon the ecstatic position of sexual
bliss. More accurately, to write one's masturbation, the action must
stop. To continue to masturbate means to leave the action as unnar-
ratable and unnarrated in the present tense, only to turn that action
into its accomplishment, its fall, its finitude, and its death in the past
tense.

In its most radical form, which is also the form most proper to it,
masturbation is autoeroticism. No other hand or eye enters the
game, no other subject is in the space of activity. The agent may envisage, ideate, fantasize the presence of the other; he may keep the
other at a distance as voyeurism and masturbation reinforce one another. Yet when another is present as a subject, the agent is aware of
the awareness of another; immediately it becomes a question of sexual interaction, exhibitionism, and touching (even mimed at a distance), in short, sexual congress. And then the language of masturbation is far less problematic. Parts of an exchange system, gifts or
trade, language and masturbation as symbolic activities find a mutual
interchangeableness.

I shall focus on how masturbation is voiced through the regula-
tory mechanisms of discourse, the parameters of literary invention,
and the insistence of the impossible fulfillment of the desire for masturbation to write itself. In short, I shall attempt to approach a fragmentary poetics of masturbation as it is figured in several realist and

modern novels. To see the details of this poetics, I shall concentrate on works of three authors: after a brief discussion of Dickens to set the stage, I shall focus on a novel of Paul Bonnetain, a little-known French naturalist writer who dedicated a whole book to the subject, plus works of Michel Tournier and Philip Roth. I shall also periodically allude to the imposition of an alien rhetoric in textual formulations that redouble masturbation: the various gazes and discourses that seem to underscore the danger of the solitude of the solitary vice. The presence of these modes of representation, no matter how lurid or violent, will seem then to take away the singularity of masturbation: its solitude and its bliss. But first it is necessary to move even further back to see what is at stake when the nineteenth century begins to take on masturbation as a topic for various modes of representation.

By the eighteenth century, the representation of masturbation was already becoming problematic because of competing views on the role of masturbation within the representational structure. Certainly, this was the period during which, as Michel Foucault put it, "the war on onanism" (*Volonté* 138) began. This was an all-out war against the sin of self-pollution on the part of the scientific community, and among the many examples of tracts, there were two outstanding works representative of the "scientific" warnings against the dangers of masturbation: *Onania or the heinous sin of self pollution*, published in 1710, and Samuel-Auguste Tissot's well-known and influential book *L'Onanisme*, published in 1760. And yet to write about it means invoking the figure of the masturbating individual, means somehow representing the act even if that representation never actually occurs. A scientific treatise would describe the dissipation and antisocial behavior caused by masturbation, but would never become a how-to manual.

Literature too has a blank in the representation. With the exception of pornographic writing, whose catalog of sexual possibilities was wide-ranging and explicit, the literary work tends to admit the same blank in representation as the scientific treatise, and focuses on the recreation of the act at a distance. Literary endeavor turns masturbation into a spectral activity that remains present, here and there, but which, like much else relating to the representation of the male body in particular, can never be represented head-on. With a nod to

Rousseau, Jean Marie Goulemot has studied the interrelation of masturbation and eighteenth-century pornography. For Goulemot, the literary work provokes, teases, and excites the reader to abandon herself or himself, to let her/himself go; in wild abandon, the free hand seeks the ex-static subject's genitals. Through diegesis and mimesis, the work spurs the reader to masturbate, an action seen as a metonymic *mise-en-abîme* of copulation, lovemaking, lewdness, and general debauchery described in the "dangerous" novel. Rousseau (40) writes of those books one reads with one hand; ever virtuous, he did not glance at one of those "dangerous books" until he was over thirty (Derrida, *Grammatologie* 203–34).

By the nineteenth century, the gulf widens between the two forms of representation. As is often the case with the representation of acts at a distance, the titillating excitement produced by a certain brand of eighteenth-century libertine literature tended to fade. The possibility of literary representation of male masturbation in the nineteenth century invariably turned into the impossibility, or at least the distortion, of direct representation; but this was not the same for scientific language, which arrogated that space of representation to itself. For the scientific nineteenth century, the discourse about masturbation is one of many discourses of sexuality that seek to control, manipulate, or define an entire field and entire power grid. Indeed, Michel Foucault's entire oeuvre treats the development of discursive praxes as the fields in which any specific instance of discourse might take place. In *The History of Sexuality*, he stresses the development of the discourses of biopolitics, those official discourses that sought to regulate the individual through a series of prescriptions, admonitions, and recommendations. The discourses of biopolitics involved the identification of the individual with his (and not "his or her") political self as a citizen. The individual was to act so as best to fulfill the functions of a member of society. Specifically, in his well-known arguments against a simplistic repressive hypothesis, developed at length in the first volume of *Histoire de la sexualité, La Volonté de savoir*, Foucault argues that sex and sexuality are not repressed as such in the nineteenth century, for the nineteenth century never stops talking about sex. And with such extensive discourse, there cannot be repression. Rather, the nineteenth century's discourses on sex seek to channel sex productively and to categorize behavior in a multiplicity of possibilities. For Foucault, the nineteenth century began to accept heterogeneity: "The nineteenth century and ours have been instead the age of multiplication: a dispersion of sexualities, a reinforcement of their disparate forms, a multiple implantation of 'perversions'" (*Volonté* 51). One of the classic examples Foucault uses is the genesis of the homosexual, who, in the discourses addressing the subject in the nineteenth century, changes from a set of penal discourses relating to the generally forbidden act of sodomy, to the development of a discourse that takes the homosexual or invert as an individual with a history and background.

By the nineteenth century, the ideological discourses of power combine in an economic and medical discourse of repression, one of whose most important targets is masturbation. Masturbation is seen as threatening the economic unit at the base of nineteenth-century society, as much of a threat as prostitution itself (Lacqueur 340). Medical science makes masturbation pathological, a sign of the possible decline of civilization. And as Nye notes (164–65), the second half of the nineteenth century develops a close relation between discourses of sexuality and discourses of pathology. However, a distinction is made between social and literary discourse. Whereas the discourses of economic stability and medical pathology were perceived as being capable of maintaining a safe distance from the heinous activity, in the literary model there was a fear that the action might infect the work itself.

What indeed could literature say or represent? What damnable scenes were there, what negative models were there at midcentury? When we look, we see no one but shadowy spectral figures who seem to be masturbating in the shadows thrown by candles dripping their melted tallow onto the floor. A century before Philip Roth's Alexander Portnoy raised the act of masturbation to a poetics worthy of description in the pages of the *New York Times Book Review*, the most well-known literary masturbator was undoubtedly Charles Dickens's Uriah Heep, the incarnation, if that is the correct word, of the obsequious, the concrete representation of all that is "umble," and ultimately the hypocritical transformation of the "umbleness" into economic social climbing, disreputable transactions, and failure. Long before he becomes prisoner number 27 jailed for a bank fraud, and long before we might think he is being punished for the moral evil that accompanies his felony, Uriah Heep is the misshapen model of moral depravity, one of the dreaded masturbators of which the nineteenth century will make so much. Along with Charley Bates, called Master Bates, in *Oliver Twist* and, as William Cohen points out in his excellent article on the figures of masturbation in *Great Expectations*, that very novel's own Pip, Uriah Heep is one of Dickens's masterful figures of self-abuse.

Needless to say, because of the censorious nature of Victorian poetics, we do not see him commit his heinous act, and, certainly, since there is no representation of the act as such, I am only hypothesizing that Dickens is creating the signs for all of us to read. As Cohen asks: "How can we make these silences speak? Precisely through the rhetoric of unspeakability" (221). Uriah Heep is constructed as an eccentrically shaped character whose physical presence, thin and attenuated, is remarkable from the outset as a distinct (in)human shape:

[The face] belonged to a red-haired person—a youth of fifteen, as I take it now, but looking much older—whose hair was cropped as close as the closest stubble; who had hardly any eyebrows, and no eyelashes, and eyes of a red-brown, so unsheltered and unshaded, that I remember wondering how he went to sleep. He was high-shouldered and bony; dressed in decent black, with a white wisp of a neckcloth; buttoned up to the throat; and had a long, lank, skeleton hand, which particularly attracted my attention, as he stood at the pony's head, rubbing his chin with it, and looking up at us in the chaise. (275)

With a reddish-tinged skull sticking out at the end of a long body, with a wisp of a neckcloth encircling a neck like a withdrawn foreskin, Uriah Heep looks like an erect penis. Barely touched by hair, as befits a mere adolescent of fifteen, this man-penis stands erect, as an equally lank hand rubs his chin. One of Uriah's main actions, at various times, is this repetitive rubbing, but his hands are not restricted to touching that part of his own being. It is as if the whole of his being is a touchable object for these hands, themselves the copy of the body as a whole, the specular *mise-en-abîme* of the masturbatable body: "It was no fancy of mine about his hands, I observed; for he frequently ground the palms against each other as if to squeeze them dry and warm, besides often wiping them, in a stealthy way, on his pocket-handkerchief" (291). At any given moment, this erection in a state of nascent excitement can give way to a repetitive reinscription of excitement itself, and every part of that body, endlessly caught in repetition compulsion of the act of masturbation, is signed as the excited erection of the inveterate masturbator: "As I watched him reading on again, after this rapturous exclamation, and following the lines with his forefinger, I observed that his nostrils, which were thin and pointed, with sharp dints in them, had a singular and most uncomfortable way of expanding and contracting themselves" (290–91). It is even in the act of naming—a leitmotiv of great importance in this novel for the protagonist himself—that Uriah manifestly springs to attention: "'Oh, how pleasant to be called Uriah, spontaneously!' he cried; and gave himself a jerk, like a convulsive fish" (440). The very recognition by David Copperfield of Uriah as Uriah, the recognition that this is the great masturbator himself, is enough to make Uriah's entire body jerk and flail. And as Heep, seemingly victorious in his plotting, raises his sniveling and hypocrisy to new heights, he continues to act the role of the serpentine member moving in and out of empty space: "writhing himself into the silence like a Conger-eel" (682). Indeed Dickens's careful comparisons of Uriah Heep to those two aquatic animals, a fish and an eel, underlines the darting movement of masturbation, as if Heep becomes totally and completely the masturbating hand/penis combination, moving back and forth in spasmodic motions.

There is a double metamorphosis or interchangeability at work here. The first is on an onomastic or intertextual level. The reader will recall that the Biblical Uriah for whom Dickens's character is ironically named is more an innocent victim than a moral reprobate. In II Samuel (11:3–21), having espied Bathsheba, David lies with her, thereby cuckolding her husband Uriah. Finding Uriah an inconvenient embarrassment, David has him carry his own death-warrant to David's general Joab: Uriah carries a letter saying that he should be sent to the front lines, where he is promptly killed. Dickens's ironic twist is to take the letter of death and turn it into Victorian capitalism's accounting books and frauds and to take the supernumery male member of the innocent Biblical Uriah and to make his useless seed the sign of guilty depravity in Uriah Heep. The interchange of nonauthorized positions that starts with the very act of naming Uriah, that moves him from the Biblical cuckold, more to be pitied than censured, to the Victorian masturbator, is visited on his body as well, for we see the possibility of an interchange of body parts that makes us focus on the scene of masturbation rather than on the specific nature of the members. Prey to a capitalist system of exchange and definition, the unfortunate Uriah masturbates by his very position in society. Uriah Heep's hands and head, his fingers and nostrils, are the interchangeable parts of this scenario of masturbation. In one way or another, the various parts are all interchangeable metonyms and synecdoches for the hands of masturbation. The male member itself, which must stay completely invisible in a literary work such as this, is part of that "rhetoric of unspeakability" mentioned by Cohen. This invisibility comes at a price, for the signs of that masturbation, invisible as to the penis, are ever more visible on the hands. Uriah Heep's hands are not solely the betrayal of his slimy soul and his moral depravity, though they are certainly that. His hand is variously described as feeling like a fish (293) and a frog (437). But also, and just as important, his hands are a betrayal of his slimy activity: "It was such an uncomfortable hand, that, when I went to my room, it was still cold and wet upon my memory" (282). The lingering traces of Heep's depravity imprint his own hand, and slimily infect the hand of another. David's moral superiority will help him avoid becoming a dreaded masturbator, but the threat is there.

For Uriah's hand, and more specifically the hand with which he writes and reads, is the telltale member, where the penis can neither be seen nor speak. It is his hand that plays all the roles in this simulacrum and repetition of masturbation to the state of orgasm and ejaculation: "But, seeing a light in the little round office, and immediately feeling myself attracted towards Uriah Heep, who had a sort of fascination for me, I went in there instead. I found Uriah reading a great fat book, with such demonstrative attention, that his lank forefinger followed up every line as he read, and made clammy tracks along the page (or so I fully believed) like a snail" (290). Proust will later use the same image of the snail's trail to describe the visible presence of the ejaculate in a space that has no literary language for the poetics of masturbation. Here Dickens's protagonist and narrator, somewhat uncomprehending, yet fully recognizant of his own less than charitable feelings toward Uriah Heep, chooses words to underline the disgust or distaste that his right-thinking readers should feel at this unnameable act being performed right before their own voyeuristic eyes. Whereas Proust will reinsert the description into nature itself—the analogy is made to a snail's trail found on a leaf—Dickens has Heep sully the space of writing, which must remain pure if writing is to be effective. Indeed, in a move that resembles nothing less than a deconstruction of the moral imperative attached to novelistic writing in the Victorian age, which brings the desire for edification into the forefront of the objectives of prose, Dickens, here better than in anywhere else I can think of in his work, brings the traces of an ambiguous past to center stage. Yes, the work will edify, and it will do so, in part, at the expense of representing or presenting unsavory models: Dickens cannot show Uriah Heep masturbating. At the same time, the traces of that activity find their way into the heart of writing itself, as wraithlike reminders of the activity that cannot be seen for itself.

Dickens's use of the male body of Uriah Heep is as a phantasmagoric collection of parts, never complete, never fully present, never completely visible. It is more hidden than obvious, more invisible than manifest. Those parts that are there seem to burn all the more brightly, as if every present part were a member of a caricature that emphasized the presence through an engorged representation: in the person of Uriah Heep, the visible body parts are made to resemble nothing less than the absent, erect, attenuated, engorged member.

The question then is this: does Dickens, for example, in giving us the adolescent onanist incarnate, participate in the expansion of discourses about representation, or does he somehow participate in an act of repression? The question is too easily asked, because it elides history and a praxis of representation. Foucault points out, for example, that the homosexual becomes an individual with a history and a background; yet he does not really recognize that this individual does not become a directly represented literary figure, again, within the context of a generally accepted normative praxis, until far later. If the 1870's give us the word "homosexual," it is not really until Gide's writings and, *a fortiori*, Proust's *Sodome et Gomorrhe*, that the literary representation occurs with any coherence. So too we might say that Dickens cannot represent the masturbator directly with the discourses available to him, discourses that describe masturbation

only in the act of repressing it. Dickens needs *not* to repress Uriah
Heep precisely to show the consequences of such heinous activity. It
is not until later, much later, that literature intermittently represents
the masturbator as an individual. Dickens's representation is neither
repressive nor discursively expansive, but is a function of the literary
means available. I would argue then that the shadowy, discontinuous
representation of masturbation, intermittent at best like that of the
male body in general, continuing simultaneous with the nineteenth
century's discourses about the dangers of onanism, provides a figure
necessary to maintaining the representation of the praxis in a permanent twilight state.

A similar if less immediate situation can be found in the magiste-
rial chapter of *Moby-Dick* entitled "A Squeeze of the Hand." This
time it is a question of both masturbation of the self and of the other
in a daylong orgasm that takes over Ishmael, body and soul. Again,
as is the case with Dickens's Uriah Heep, the vocabulary slips and
slides over the diverse objects, not necessarily through some displacement, but because of a lack of proper place: there is no locus for
talking about masturbation. Melville offers the reader a frolicking,
meltingly sensual, effervescently liquid back room:

Squeeze! Squeeze! Squeeze! All the morning long; I squeezed that sperm till
I myself almost melted into it; I squeezed that sperm till a strange sort of insanity came over me; and I found myself unwittingly squeezing my co-
laborers' hands in it, mistaking their hands for the gentle globules. Such an
abounding, affectionate, friendly, loving feeling did this avocation beget; that
at last I was continually squeezing their hands, and looking up into their eyes
sentimentally;—Oh! My dear fellow beings, why should we longer cherish
any social acerbities, or know the slightest ill-humor or envy! Come; let us
squeeze hands all around; nay, let us all squeeze ourselves into each other; let
us squeeze ourselves universally into the very milk and sperm of kindness!
(1239)

Leo Marx links this scene to a wish for the return of the childish
and the pastoral (303–4) and Robert Martin, I think more acutely,
mentions the "impossibility of sustaining the vision of a harmonious
world of mutual sexuality" (83). Indeed, it should not be lost that in
this homoerotic circle-jerk of ecstatic pleasure, Melville does not fail
to remind the reader of the pathological with the word "insanity"
and the moralizing of society with "social acerbities." Moreover, such

frolic leads to dissipation, "since by many prolonged, repeated experiences, I have perceived that in all cases man must eventually lower, or at least shift, his conceit of attainable felicity" (1239). And in the final image of the chapter, as the readers are borne on the metonymic movement of the prose, we are faced with what amounts to a displacement of castration: "If he cuts off one of his own toes, or one of his assistant's, would you be very much astonished? Toes are scarce among veteran blubber-room men" (1241). There is a difference: the possibility of castration is a circumscribed act that is representable within the narrative imaginary; thus displacement can occur. But masturbation is not yet directly representable as such, though both Dickens and Melville point the way: in these cases there is a congeries of body parts and fluids, too disordered to be a Freudian displacement. In these cases, one might think of them as belonging to a rhetoric of anti-catachresis: not something for which the figurative term, like the "leg of a table," has lost all links to the figural, but something for which there is only a figural sprawl of disjointed words, because there is no word. Outside of the pornographic and its attendant ecstasy, the representation of masturbation is still, in mid-century, limited to the discourses of science and ostensibly juridical power. Realism, as here in Dickens and Melville, begins to introduce a linguistic locus into which a language of masturbation can start to be written.

By the end of the nineteenth century, with the extensive medical and scientific discourses devoted to a *scientia sexualis*, it should come as no surprise that literature finally had the means of discussing, in literary terms, various kinds of "pathological" sexualities. We should not think that the scientific presentation is either dispassionate or neutral. Indeed, the nineteenth century transforms the intertwined behaviors of masturbation and dangerous reading into a social interdiction of unhealthy literary works and unhealthy practices. At the end of the nineteenth century, the ingrained prejudice against masturbation has been itself reinforced by a slew of anti-onanistic arguments that have become part of the same general discursive economy as discourses on productivity, on reproduction, and indeed on general class and gender structures. The "common knowledge" about the dangers of onanism is thus seconded by discourses of social engineering, biopolitics, and eugenics that see masturbation, if not as something "dangerous," then certainly as something detrimental to well-being. And yet at the end of the century the accumulated discourses of biopolitics, epitomized in the scientific stance that allows a panoptical gaze, has even found its niche in literature: the revision of realism known as naturalism. And at the same time, the sheer numbers of discourses talking about the matter will not only allow for the return of a more or less direct representation of masturbation in Bonnetain's work, but will finally allow for the puncturing of the scientific, antimasturbatory balloon in Mark Twain's satiric lecture, "Some Thoughts on the Science of Onanism."

Naturalism allows forbidden subjects to be treated as long as the decadence, the degeneration, and the negative exemplarity of the situation can be demonstrated. In the wake of Zola's explicit works *L'Assommoir* (1880) and *Nana* (1882), Paul Bonnetain published a novel in 1883 entitled *Charlot s'amuse* (*Charlie Has Fun*). As is often the case with the more licentious objects of inquiry in naturalist writing, this exposition of masturbation is primarily a visual demonstration. Not subject to reading or analysis as such, masturbation is presented as an object for the panopticon and its vicar, the scientific language of naturalism. And as shall be seen, in this book, masturbation is part of a mutable set of sexual depravities which include homosexual relations and ephebophilia, an addiction to romantic poetry, as well as a general moral decay on the part of all who give themselves over to such practices. The book itself is little known today, though at the time of its publication it was subjected to an obscenity trial much like that of *Madame Bovary* a quarter-century earlier. Bonnetain was acquitted of the obscenity charges, undoubtedly in part because of the fact that, despite the scabrous descriptions of sexual activity, he maintains a moralizing and implicitly condemnatory language throughout the novel. Unlike Flaubert, whose more explicit descriptions are presented in neutral or even flattering language, Bonnetain protects his work, as Zola does, by arming himself with the language of scientific inquiry, but with the language of moralizing righteousness as well, which is not Zola's wont.

This novel is the singular tale of a protagonist who suffers the devastating results of being addicted to self-abuse. Bonnetain, who was also the author of a book called *L'Opium*, took it upon himself, in the lines of naturalistic inquiry, to develop a character portrait of an individual who, like Nana, suffers from the malevolent blood of moral depravity. In that case, Nana's mother's alcoholism is transformed into wantonness and sensuality, into prostitution, and even into lesbianism in the depiction of the relationship with Satin. In the case of Charlie in Bonnetain's novel, he too comes from what we would now call a dysfunctional family, with lasciviousness and obscenity in its blood. His dead father not even cold, his bereaved mother goes out and picks up someone for the night and the two are lost in their "lewd obscenity" (70). Whereas Zola's Gervaise has what we today, and the nineteenth century as well, would consider a kind of dysfunctionality that is more social than sexual, and has basically an honest sexual behavior that would be considered acceptable within the social paradigms of her class, in *Charlot s'amuse*, Charlie's mother already leans toward the sexual depravity that will become monomaniacal in her son. So Charlie's bad habit is an intensification of a kind of sexuality always present to him; whereas it will eventually migrate into different forms of sexual misconduct, his masturbation is already a strong enough nexus and has sufficient identity of its own to maintain his eventual depravity wholly within the realm of the sexual. Depraved sexuality is always and already inscribed on his body, a body of symptoms waiting to happen, a body of predilections for antisocial *volupté*. As he lies in bed in the room adjoining his mother's, he listens to her and her lover of the evening. Lying there, Charlie mechanically and unconsciously mimes the sex act without quite knowing what is going on. Like Emma Bovary waltzing ever and ever more rapidly at the ball, Charlie undergoes a metaphoric version of sex that is counted in his very breathing:

Fever burned his blood; he shivered and his hands shook mechanically. Now he was dreaming that he was imitating the chauffeur. He panted from fatigue; a whistle left his dry, tight lips. Suddenly, his breath accelerated; he sighed. In his head, something was vibrating; rigid, immobile, and spent, he felt a new and mysterious feeling of infinite sweetness born in him.[2] (71–72)

Predisposed by social climate and the genetic traits that determine behavior and disposition, Charlie is already a lost soul. Moreover, his body is already a lost body, marked by the decadence of masturbatory activity, the signs of depravity, the diathesis for onanistic excess. From his mother he inherits a tendency to sexual excess; her own

sexual behavior, which could be described ambiguously as either
nymphomania or prostitution, changes into his onanism and homoeroticism. Again, we notice that as Bonnetain bravely tries to represent masturbation within the techniques afforded by naturalist representation, he must necessarily limit it: masturbation becomes a
specified locus that can certainly relate to other sexual depravities
and antisocial sexual behaviors, but which can no longer be accused
of being the means to all sorts of other antisocial behaviors. It is certainly a tenet of naturalistic representation that specific kinds of degeneration can, especially across generational lines, change into others, and indeed, within the general degeneration portrayed by naturalism in the work of Zola, Maupassant, and Huysmans, all
biopolitical pathologies can spontaneously mutate into others.

Bonnetain ensures, however, that the strength of this act of representation, as much of the masturbatory act itself as of the body performing that act on itself, is not weakened by rampant descriptions
of all sorts of heterogeneous dysfunctional or antisocial behaviors.
Bonnetain maintains the power of his novel (at least on this one line,
for the prose is often less than captivating) by keeping the readers focused on the insistence of the one activity (masturbation) and its
transformation into other sexual pathologies, but not directly into
other moral depravities. For Bonnetain, then, Charlie's masturbation
is linked to other sexual activities, but not to alcoholism or some
other social plague. Thrust into the unhealthy male-only social situation of a Catholic school, Charlie needs only the propitious moment of actualization for his predisposition to masturbation to appear. Here, it is awakened by Frère Origène, implausibly named for
the early Christian and Gnostic who castrated himself to insist on his
purity. Pederast, homosexual, and "ignoble berobed nymphomaniac"
(102), Origène actualizes Charlie's predisposition and teaches him
varieties of self-abuse, masturbation, and pollution. By calling
Origène a "nymphomaniac," a term normally reserved for women,
instead of the expected "satyr," the author shows to what extent the
excesses of this individual and his crime go toward the monstrous
and the indistinguishable and participate in the mutable sexual
pathology already mentioned. Though Bonnetain has prepared us
for the direst effects of genetic degradation (45–46), he still ensures
the novel's viability by condemning the effects of that fatality. Bon-

netain can hardly retain his disapproval as he cloaks his supposedly dispassionate naturalist approach in all the garb of protective scientific discourse:

And the ignoble berobed nymphomaniac instructed him, feeling in his unconscious genetic perversion an atrocious bliss [*jouissance*] in making moral defilement follow manual defilement.

Half an hour later, the crime was unchangeably accomplished; the Ignorantine had a new student to whom the monstrous mysteries of unisexual practices would henceforth be familiar. (102)

One degradation follows another as the horrors of masturbation become the warning signs of total dissolution and even worse depravity, though this does not all happen to poor Charlie at once. In fact, at one point, Charlie does escape from the sin, "monstrous co-onanism" (103), clearly more heinous than those in which he has already been a willing participant, because his teacher asks for no "compensation" in return. On the other hand, Frère Origène knows no limits to his own sexual depravity, and he has turned his entire body into a zone of forbidden pleasure. Indeed, in a poetic moment that combines the dangers of reading and writing with a forbidden sexuality, Frère Origène falls ill: having attempted to use his penholder as a dildo, he has gotten it stuck in his rectum. Bonnetain could find no more concrete an image than this for warning his readers of the dangers of masturbation and reading. At the same time he seems to be protecting the readers from the natural consequences of infection by such a display: this will not happen to their bodies, safe from the infection of sexual depravity. They will protect themselves with the language of disapproval.

Imprisoned in a discourse of depravity and repetition, Charlie has few tranquil moments, and even those bear the warning signs of danger as they recall the perils of reading: "These onanists [Charlie and his friend Lucien] recited Lamartine to each other between two kisses" (185). Generally, though, Charlie's nasty habit drags him so far into the depths of degradation that he even has telltale spots on his clothing (189). As is the case for Gervaise in *L'Assommoir*, a point occurs in the naturalist depiction of depravity where the protective cloak of scientific discourse parts to make the depravity wholly visible to other characters. With the secret pathology out in the open, whether it is Gervaise's alcoholism or Charlie's onanism, the vice once invisible to others is fully illuminated for all to see. Ironically enough, as befits a world in which the discourses of biopolitics have sway, there is no longer any need for the depraved individual to protect him- or herself, for the all-powerful gaze accomplishes just that, once the action is as out in the open as the discourses decrying it.

Everything in Charlie's existence now relates to this depravity. Short stays on the wagon of celibacy are succeeded by even more violent and degrading plummets into self-abuse. So even as his benefactress, with the suggestive name of Mademoiselle de Closberry, is lying *in articulo mortis* (though this is unknown to Charlie), he is out humping the earth, using the planet itself as a substitute for his polluting hand: "he was at *The Pissing Pine-tree*, in the forest, bestially defiling the thick, thatched moss, whose elasticity made his unspeakable pleasure even more delirious" (199). And despite, or perhaps thanks to, the protection of the scientific or even critical language that was prevalent in the early part of the book, Bonnetain seems to take great delight in describing Charlie's onanistic sexual paroxysms depicted in the last third of the novel. With the secret out in the open, literary language can blissfully reassert its own *jouissance* in the act of description. At that moment, the masturbation that had no voice of its own, the activity that was cast into a discursive net that describes it deprecatingly as onanism to be shunned, now finally speaks from within him: "Becoming the little pervert again, he listened to his neurosis speak" (231). But that is one brief moment, and literary excess is tamed as Bonnetain introduces the voice of reason at the level of observable, commonplace truth. Charlie's boss says, point blank, "It's the fault of Rosy Palm [*la veuve Poignet*]" (273). It is no surprise that the dénouement of the book is Charlie's suicide, poetically and impotently accompanied by one last, vain effort:

In a supreme act of self-abasement before dying, he wanted to taste the sweetness of solitary caresses once more, but he spent himself in vain stabs: the alcohol had dulled his senses.

Shit! he said of this last disillusionment and this sudden impotence. (347)

That sudden impotence at the end of *Charlot s'amuse* could be the watchword for the whole novel. Bonnetain cannot escape from the scientific or biopolitical discourses that allowed him to talk about masturbation in the first place. To show it is enough; there is no need, nor any possibility, to let it speak; Bonnetain can do no more than to make it visible. To write about it, he must buy into the discourse of disapproval. There is no possibility of letting masturbation speak for itself, for there is no voice for the offending member. The hand can be chastened, rewritten in a safe, noninfectious discourse. But the other offending member cannot be allowed to have a voice. At least not here, and not now. It is only later, with a belatedness corresponding to the inscription of homosexuality as a repetitive current in literary praxis, that masturbation finds its own literary voice. Indeed, one might suspect that Bonnetain's whole novel is in fact a displacement of the question of homosexuality onto masturbation: as he has been initiated by another man into the heinous acts of self-pollution, Charlie's masturbatory activity is always tied up, at least at its origin, with the praxes of homosexuality.

In any case, the figure of representing masturbation for itself is an intermittent one, as we have already indicated, precisely because of the unrepresentable nature of the subject matter, because of the condemnatory way in which the subject matter is inevitably treated, and because of the ambiguous intertwining of the representation of the material with the representation of homosexuality. If it is bad enough to represent masturbation, to infect another by it would cast both under a cloud of homosexuality. Despite all this, the first half of the twentieth century begins to liberate this once forbidden subject both from the discourses of biopolitics and from the perdition of literary hell. Various authors "naturalize" masturbation as they make it an episode in the development of their characters. There are well-known scenes of masturbation in the works of Proust, Mishima, Cocteau, Isherwood, and Genet, among others, and even if most of these are related to a discourse of homosexuality, the increasing number of scenes within what is now generally accepted as canonical literature necessarily reduces the possibilities of infection and ambiguity. Masturbation is gradually removed from the categories of psychopathia sexualis, and put back into the hands in which it belongs: the hands seeking pleasure in the exploration of the self.

Though it results in a literary decriminalization of masturbation, this renaturalization still does not let masturbation speak in its own voice. Even at midcentury, the explicit depiction of anything more than an episode has to be framed by a format whose singular nonex-emplarity must be obvious, as is the case in Genet's prison fantasies. Elsewhere, if freed from the language of social engineering, mastur-bation still needs to be displaced into metaphor and metonymy. This is a moment of transition between the biopolitical nineteenth cen-tury and the episodic, aestheticized renaturalization of literary mod-ernism and the representation of masturbation by Tournier and Roth in works in which unadorned masturbation attempts to speak for it-self. In this period between the "showing" of naturalism and the uni-vocal, though fragmentary, voice of the postmodern, modernism uses masturbation itself as part of a metaphoric structure: a set of signi-fiers describe the writing as being *like* masturbation.

But before turning to two postwar examples of the representation of masturbation in literature, I would like to linger one last moment on the telltale signs that have heretofore marked the literary work: the hands. We have seen that even more than the male member, it is the hand that is the offending member: the hand that casually glides toward producing bliss by masturbating while one is reading exciting literature, the hand that Uriah Heep endlessly shows as the witness, accomplice, indeed, the agent of his own rubbings, the hand that in-duces Charlie to depravity, as it guides him along the path toward to-tal debauchery. And finally, the hand of the writer, inducing his reader to copy a behavior that is as depraved as it is common. I have said, then, that at least at the point of the crystallization of the biopolitics of masturbation, there seems to be a tight relation be-tween the depiction of masturbation, as a learned activity accom-plished within a homosocial structure, and the antisocial figure of male homosexuality. In other words, though all boys (or almost all) masturbate, to represent it or to teach it means providing a model of mimesis and representation that skates quite close to the ever greater danger of antisocial sexuality, male homosexuality itself.

It is no wonder then that when the hands remain, even if the of-fending male member is completely gone, the same action is per-ceived as an even greater danger. I am thinking of Sherwood Ander-son's story "Hands," which opens his collection *Winesburg, Ohio*. Somewhat better remembered than Bonnetain's *Charlot s'amuse*, this collection of stories is still seldom discussed today. The story "Hands" is about a middle-aged man of forty who "looked sixty-five"

(15), Wing Biddlebaum, "the town mystery" (8) who has lived a quiet life in Winesburg for two decades. Little if anything is known about him, though his hands tell another story: "The slender expressive fingers, forever active, forever striving to conceal themselves in his pockets or behind his back, came forth and became the piston rods of his machinery of expression" (9). Object of curiosity, these hands are finally allowed to tell their story. It seems that, years before, Wing Biddlebaum, then known as Adolph Myers, was a school-teacher in a town in Pennsylvania, one of "those rare, little-understood men . . . not unlike the finer sort of women in their love of men" (13). Needless to say, having "caressed the shoulders of the boys, playing about the tousled heads" (13), Myers is eventually accused of child molestation and run out of town. He winds up in Winesburg, and spends the rest of his life there more or less silently, until the end of his life.

Now while Anderson's character is not by any means a figure of masturbation, I have brought in Wing Biddlebaum as a transitional figure to show how some component parts of the code remain intact even if one of the two central components is excised. That is to say, to remove both masturbation and male homosexuality from the discourses of pathology, literature will have to invent each one of them anew. In a work like "Hands," we see—and I add that Anderson is brave in being sympathetic to his character—that without a whole new discourse, the ambiguous association of masturbation with male homosexuality still remains. If Wing Biddlebaum is the sympathetic scion of Uriah Heep, because of the former's active, present, visible, and signifying hands, he is also the product of a discourse on male homosexuality that sees the two as related depravities. It is not until after the Second World War that both masturbation and homosexuality are consistently found within the realm of normal representations, even if the concept of depravity still peeks through now and again.

A new aesthetic of masturbation soon appears in which masturbation seeks its own voice, not a pale copy of heterosexual intercourse, nor a redoubling of preying, infectious male homosexuality, nor the prey of a biopolitics that maintains its power even while gradually moving masturbation from prohibition to normalization. Nor will masturbation remain the eclipsed vehicle of a metaphoric discourse about textuality. Masturbation will be textually sought for its own sake in a few works that stand out in a short period of time as having engaged the subject overtly: Philip Roth's *Portnoy's Complaint*, Michel Tournier's *Les Météores*, and to a lesser extent, Tournier's earlier novel, *Vendredi ou les limbes du Pacifique*. Even though it does not involve the male body, I would add an example from popular literature, William Peter Blatty's thriller, *The Exorcist*, which was turned into a blockbuster film. *The Exorcist* reduces the activity to a violation of a moral code that anyone, even a nonbeliever, can see; we all luridly spy on Regan's masturbation with a crucifix, and it is at that point that everyone is convinced that she is truly possessed by the devil. In giving herself to a masturbatory sexuality, Regan imitates the position that has only recently been allowed to the male of the species. At the same time, she is miming being penetrated, an activity not allowed the male. As befits a work for mass consumption, there is no ambiguity here, no sign of pleasure, just the horrors of evil. Yet still, for all that, the scene with its reminiscences of artistic and autistic self-stimulation is not so far removed from other versions of the same activity. In fact, *The Exorcist* could profitably be studied for the interrelations of the various acts of masturbation, writing on Regan's body, and the whole litany of prayers, especially the exorcism itself.

Swept along as a part of general postwar sexual liberation, masturbation enters the realm of the discursively acceptable. On one level, its status is particularly unchallengeable. In an era that values the individual as an inviolate monad, the various languages of repression wane in favor of the code of an individual whose language is supposed to be as unalienated as the fictional image of an inviolate ego. A good measure of the sexual liberation of the 1970's takes as its rule the idiomatic use of the self in and as a language and action for which masturbation could be considered the most truthful activity. This occurs in and against a world in which alienation and scission are the products of an imposed, and therefore manipulative, invasive, or terrorizing discourse. And although an escape from repressive discourse is certainly welcome, we still do not know the language of masturbation. Though masturbation may no longer be implicitly or explicitly likened to other steadfast singularities like autism and psy-

chosis, without a discourse it remains an idiot's delight, the transfix-
ion of Saint Theresa or Saint Sebastian, though without the accom-
panying beatitude.

Fittingly, the first important depiction occurs in a world posited
as a *tabula rasa* at the level of the story, but which we know to be an
intertextual redoubling of another work, one of the first modern
novels: *Vendredi ou les limbes du Pacifique*, Michel Tournier's 1967
retelling of the story of Robinson Crusoe. Standing emblematically
in the first few pages is the icon of perfect, solar—or solo—sexuality:
a snake eating its own tail (12). The figure represents an autoerotic,
though immobile, sexuality frozen in the idealness of utopian solar-
ity. This static figure not only foreshadows the supposed, though ultimately false, self-sufficiency that is the basic mytheme of the
Robinson Crusoe story, but also underlines the complete accidental
quality of human relations that go beyond the monad in what is ultimately a haphazard game of chances. So the figure of the nonmas-
turbating, yet still autoerotic, snake sets the narrative in motion for
what will become Tournier's first idealized theory and figuration of
the act of solitary sexuality. Significantly, the same figure will return
at the beginning of Tournier's 1975 novel, *Les Météores*, and indeed,
part of the plot of that book will be a search for that lost innocence.

As Robinson passes through total abjection to renewed "civilization," the poetics of the representation of sexuality in the novel move
away from the initial static idealism symbolized by the *ourobouros* and
toward a mobilization of the autoerotic. For Tournier, masturbation
will speak with the voice of philosophy. Two images of movement,
creation, and stirring to life are announced, mechanical movements
that simulate and predict masturbation: kneading his dough (80)
makes Robinson recall images from his childhood of a shirtless,
flour-covered baker's assistant performing the same activity. And as
Robinson continues to knead, the images continue to sharpen in his
mind of "that great headless body, warm and lascivious, that let itself
go in the kneading bowl under the embraces of a half-naked man"
(81). The bread becomes a body, worked by the hand of another, and
yet the bread is neither wholly other nor wholly the same. Robinson
envisages "a strange marriage" between the baker's assistant and the
loaf of bread, a "marriage" predicated on the homoerotic image of
the shirtless baker. Even if the image of masturbation motions to-

ward heterosexuality, as a marriage is poetically foreseen, the gaze
and language that redouble the event are homoerotic.

Similarly, when the mechanical action is turned on the self, the
same ambiguity between self and other remains, after Robinson
notes that his arm has fallen asleep: "I seized it between the thumb
and index finger of my left hand, and I raise this strange thing, this
mass of enormous, weighty flesh, this fat heavy limb of someone else,
soldered to my body by mistake. I dream of manipulating my whole
body, to be astonished with its weight, to fall into this paradox: *a
thing that is me*" (87). The mechanical movement of producing life
and power has the opposite effect: the realization of the fundamental alterity with which the self is bound. Thus, there is a movement
away from the autoerotic sensuality that might be the figure of this
kneading, for like the image of the bread, it too is strange. Tournier
does not leave us in the lurch for long, for this otherness, glimpsed
here and there, is the Rimbaldian self gone literally *à la dérive*: "If
[this individual] is not he, it is Speranza. Henceforth there is a flying
'I' that lands sometimes on the man and sometimes the island, and
makes me in turn one or the other" (89). And again, homoerotic
commentary redoubles the sexual action.

With these two images that alienate the mechanical action from
the *scene* of autoeroticism while conjuring up the *image* of autoeroticism, Tournier moves toward one of the primal scenes in the book:
Robinson's coupling with the island. On several occasions Robinson
penetrates into the innermost womb of the island itself and has sex
with the island. Against the inklings of homoeroticism that Tournier
has heretofore coupled with the images of autoeroticism, the author
reasserts a model of innocence based on the maternal nature of this
island named Speranza. At first, the images are overtly Oedipal: "the
feminine nature of Speranza took on all the aspects of maternity"
(107). And the first sexual congress does nothing to change that imagery. His seed, a "living yeast" (114) reminiscent of the charged image of the bread, may make Speranza pregnant to produce an "in-
cestuous monster."

To follow this line of reasoning is to accept the male-female ar-
chetype as essential and self-identical; it is therefore to base sexuality, *including masturbation*, on heterosexual coupling. Now without
even having to enter the realm of the performative as described by

Judith Butler among others, we find evidence within the novel itself that the sexual dynamics of the work are not based on some essentialist bipolar model, but on a version in which both homoeroticism and autoeroticism precede heterosexual coupling. Tournier has already offered a version of sexuality that is sublimely different from the bipolar model: the autoerotic, self-sufficient sexuality of the individual closed upon himself and intertwined with homoerotic imagery. So even as Robinson's coupling with the island may lend itself to an interpretation of natural heterosexuality, such an interpretation has to be based on the eschewing of competing models and on the fixing of Robinson's identity as such in the position of the active subject. But Tournier says nothing of the kind, for in that coupling with the island, Robinson is sometimes himself and sometimes the island, he is using the island in an act of autoerotic and homoerotic stimulation. Robinson and the island are not just one but certainly not quite two in this autoerotic frieze. As he will continue to do in subsequent works, Tournier insists on this play of positions as fundamental to his enquiry: it is no exaggeration to say that in playing with the reader Tournier is playing with himself.

Tournier schematizes this play with a narrative alternation between a third-person narrative and Robinson's own first-person diary in the form of a logbook. Whereas the diary shows the difference from and continuity with the present moment by use of the *passé composé*, the narrative uses the preterite (*passé simple*), less the sign of things past than of the narrative fictionality of the event. Through this fiction, masturbation finally becomes simultaneous with writing, though the writing is voyeuristic. To name masturbation, writing must stand outside the action. Stripped of archetypal nostalgia (121, 126), the action is seen for what it is: Robinson uses the whole island in a grand game of *frottage*, a masturbatory activity that does not rely on the hand as the primary instrument of pleasure but which still seems to forbid the engagement of the hand in any other simultaneous activity such as writing. To write about masturbation, one must still be other.

In *Vendredi*, masturbation is nothing in itself, but is the substitute for heterosexual intercourse, even if, at its textual origins, it is coupled with homoerotic imagery. It is not here, however, that Tournier will produce a more radical image of masturbation than as a substitute. So the alternation between self and other is a game of substitutions, the parts of the self performing the activity simultaneously serve as the means of creating the image of the other. Thus in *Vendredi*, the image of sexuality is predicated on a floating image of the self. We can never be sure what is self and other, what is heterosexual, homosexual, or autoerotic: Tournier has peopled this island with a ludic ego that cannot be pinned down to one position. And this ludic ego, who is never who he is, who is thus never masturbating, since he is copulating, and who is never autoerotic, for the island is other in sex, finds absolute safety in this game of "not-me." The final clue comes much later: "insofar as my sexuality is concerned, I am reminded that not once Vendredi woke a sodomite temptation in me" (229). The moving ego has gone far beyond Defoe's Crusoe in reinventing a system of heterosexual dominance so complete that it does not even require a woman. And as for homosexuality, Tournier is still averting his eyes.

Tournier moves toward a more truthful position in *Les Météores* as he accepts masturbation without the excuse of a system of heterosexual dominance: while masturbation is not exclusively homosexual, a heterosexual system, even one that "includes" homosexuality, is not perceived as essential. In *Météores* (1975), Tournier has conveniently organized the material into a short treatise on masturbation, which I have discussed at length in *The Shock of Men*. And though it is just one episode in this novel, it subtends much of the rest of the work. Solitary activity par excellence, masturbation is at the heart of a world of the imagination. It is a protean activity, constantly changing according to the image furnished by the brain. Masturbation is the masterpiece of all the possible activities of the hand: "The brain furnishes an imaginary object to the sexual organ. It is incumbent upon the hand to embody this object. The hand is an actor, plays at being this or that. At will it becomes tongs, hammer, visor, whistle, comb, reckoning system for primitives, alphabet for deaf-mutes, etc. but its master-work is masturbation. There, it becomes a penis or vagina at will" (88).

The naturalness and primacy of this activity are reinforced by Tournier's contention that the hand naturally falls to the genitals whereas contortions are involved for the hand to reach the ear or knees. And moreover, the hand and the sexual organ seem to fit together naturally far more than even another hand fits one's hand, and far more than the male and female members fit each other: "Besides, thanks to its size and configuration, the sexual organ lends itself admirably to manipulation." Again, Tournier is playing the positions. Rather than beginning the discussion, the various uses of the hands seem to be predicated on the imaginary object furnished by the brain to the genitals. One would have expected the imaginary sexual object to come after the statement that the hand's master-work is masturbation. The incarnation of the hand as protean sexual organ conflicts with the model emanating from a homosexual narrator, as does the natural Panglossian complementarity of the hand and the genitals. Only the most narrow heterosexual definition of masturbation as the substitute for sexual intercourse would fit. Thus the hand is a substitute vagina for a heterosexual male who envisages fucking a woman as he jerks off; the hand, or more likely, the fingers, substitutes for a penis dreamt of by a heterosexual woman envisaging being fucked by a man. In a work so intertwined with homosexuality and in which the narrator of this very section is himself unabashedly homosexual, the reader is given pause. Certainly, Alexandre, who is both the narrator and one of the protagonists, cannot imagine that for the homosexual male, the hand serves as either a penis or a vagina; the argument is weaker still as one considers two women: perhaps the hand may seem another pudenda, but the naturalness of the hand as "fitting" the female sexual organ brings even that into question. For the naturalness seems, according to the description of dimension and configuration, to be far more apt for the penis than for this imaginary vagina into which the masturbating hand is thrust as in fist-fucking.

Now Tournier can be notoriously vague about anything relating to the image of a woman given through the figures and eyes of male heterosexuality. Most disquieting is the predication of masturbation on the most banal form of sexual intercourse, heterosexual coupling between a man and a woman. No space is given, for example, to other forms of sexual stimulation for a couple, a panoply of which would insist more decidedly on the protean nature of the activity. Or more accurately, it would be clear to the reader that the activity is both self-sufficient and amorphous, that it is actually a screen of images more than an engagement in an act of communication.

The structure shifts as Alexandre changes his view. Masturbation is no longer a sort of vicarious heterosexual intercourse but a self-sufficient model of homosexual autoeroticism: "The sexual object furnished by the brain and embodied by the hand can vie with the same object—real this time—and outclass it. The man who is masturbating, dreaming of a [*un*] partner, will be bothered [*sera gêné*] by the untimely arrival of this partner, and will prefer to return to his dreams, cheating on him [the partner] with the partner's own image" (89). So it would seem that, at least now, masturbation is related to a homosexual model and not a heterosexual one. Such a supposition seems substantiated elsewhere in the book, for generally, even when speaking of nominally heterosexual twins, Tournier gives primacy to various forms of homosexual activity, including homosexual incest. On the whole, heterosexuality is seen as merely a process of breeding or animal husbandry. Thus heterosexuality is never wholly present unto itself because it always has an eye to the future; homosexuality and masturbation constantly reaffirm their presence, immediacy, and self-fulfillment. Tournier underlines the self-sufficiency of masturbation by using the future tense to contrast with and interrupt the pure immediacy of the present. Once the other is present, masturbation is undercut to become a pale copy of sexual congress. In its true, self-centered nature, masturbation is simultaneously both its own self-sufficiency and a turning away from the other: "True masturbation is solitary and its emblem is the snake eating its own tail." As Camille Paglia remarks, the Egyptian god Khepera "gives birth to the second stage of existence by an act of masturbation" (41). The act of masturbation gives way to an act of autofellatio whose symbol is the snake eating its own tail. For the true masturbator, the other exists only as an internalized image; any other version is a displacement of the truth that allows alienation to enter.

Indeed, the extreme version of this alienation can be found in *La Goutte d'or*, in which Tournier sets one episode at a peep show (187–91). In that novel, masturbation still has a potential space in which to exist, but it is constrained by the dominance of a certain kind of discourse—this novel is about the postcolonial—and also by the economics of desire into which men are forced. And even as the novel itself is a plea for a Barthes-like or Derrida-like version of the free play of the signifier, in this scene at least, the images of desire are not conjured up by the subject engaged in autoerotic free play but are forced on him by the other who dominates the system. In this novel at least, the system of dominance is such that it even forces the body of the subject into other images, other constitutions; it is not the portrait of the protagonist Idriss that comes out of the photo machine, but that of another.

Even within the self-sufficient world proposed in *Les Météores*, the image remains problematic. Confusingly placed among the tools or instruments that a hand can copy, including the *sosie* of a penis or vagina, the original image now seems to be the whole individual. Certainly this makes more sense—but is literature supposed to "make sense"?—on a physical plane for the male homosexual. If, for the homosexual, the hand is imitating a receptacle, it is an anus, a mouth, or another hand. In a heterosexual world, these receptacles would all be substitute vaginas, but here they are both primary and present. At least this seems more likely than the hand "naturally" imitating another penis for *frottage*. On another level, it is simultaneously the whole individual and his penis, a collection of parts and the defining part of the individual, for which the hand substitutes. For if the penis cannot truly be the Panglossian "natural" organ of the other for which the masturbating hand substitutes and could arguably come in last place, it is what defines the male sexual activity as homosexual: the "other" has a penis. Simultaneously the penis of the masturbating individual is itself a substitute for the penis of the other: the defining point of the external sexual relation has been internalized without any alienation because the masturbatory fantasy is a repetition of the same, a coalescence of self and other in a completely self-sustaining image and fantasy.

Thus Tournier says that it is correct to imagine, as do the majority of heterosexuals, that homosexual relations are a "double and reciprocal masturbation." Again, there seems to be a vacillation, for saying that is to do injustice to the primacy of masturbation itself, its self-sufficiency, and its exclusion of the other. It is more likely, in this novel of reversals that are never complete, avowals that are never entire, and admissions that are never unfettered, that the terms here of "homosexual" and "masturbation" are "inverted." In a world that is the vision of an author who never allows all the variations on inversion to occur, there is still a wavering between the historical primacy and priority of heterosexuality and the ontological and epistemological primacy of homosexuality. Thus masturbation, which for Tournier would seem to be an activity on an equal footing with homosexuality, seems sometimes to have to pass through an imaginary realm of heterosexual definitions in order to arrive at its goal. So homosexual sex is not a double act of mutual masturbation, but rather masturbation in its purest form is the perfect homosexual relation. The penis is simultaneously that of the masturbator and that of the imagined other. The hand, simultaneously that of the self and the other, is alternately the other's mouth, anus, hand, his vagina, so to speak, as well as one's own. In this plethora of desiring machines with emitters and receivers constantly capable of transformation, like Barthes's erotics of the maculate and the mixed I discussed in *Alcibiades at the Door* (139–45), it is not necessarily the penis that is the sexual organ and the hand the adjuvant. Given the possibility of representing masturbation as the quintessential homosexual act, the male member, alternately imagined as one's own and as that of the other, acts as the receptacle for the fantasm. Willing participant in a game of changing identities, the erect penis can become the waiting male vagina for the imagined penis of the other. Moreover, as the point of contact between physical reality and ideated fantasm, it becomes the receptacle for the whole being of the other.

Constant through all this is the gift or dedication of the orgasm to a partner. It is a trait common to sexual intercourse and to masturbation when the other is at a distance: "Every sexual relation—homo- as well as hetero- —implies an offering to a certain person. It is true that this person can be far away, the dedication occurring at a distance, it is then that true masturbation comes anew to the fore." The distance of the other allows fantasy to reign uninhibited by any reality whatsoever except for the contact of two worlds, inner and outer, two sexual organs, hand and penis as parts of the same body. In a sexual coupling, the act itself serves as the act of communication with the other, an act within which other sex communications can take place: grunts, words, kisses, and so forth in a complex of kinetic, imagistic, and linguistic signs and sign systems. In masturbation, only one act of communication exists: the orgasm itself, dedicated and sent like a message in a bottle to one who will never receive it.

Sole communication and unique emission, the gift has the fact of *not* being received by the other as its defining quality. It is a gift of pure loss and a message of pure absence unhampered by any system of real exchange, unmediated by any transcendental sign, determinism, direction, meaning, or channels. Endlessly sought in various incarnations in his writing, all of which are avatars of this masturbation, this purity ironically defines this discourse. That irony punctuates the very page, for in the conclusion to his little disquisition on masturbation, Alexandre notes that he once received a postcard on which the following words were found: "Hi, friend! I have just emptied a stopcock [*burette*] to your health!" For masturbation to have a language and, *a fortiori*, a literature, it must be represented by language after the fact. Taken as the unmentionable transcendental signifier, masturbation can come to stand for any activity presented by a language that seeks to inscribe presence within its confines. In the final case, masturbation may be the taboo model for all or any literary activity that is not the act of writing itself.

If Tournier's novel at least partially celebrates the freeing of masturbation from the confining discourses of heterosexual drama, and in so doing, continues a longstanding tradition of associating masturbation with a kind of homoerotic activity, no such liberation occurs in *Portnoy's Complaint*, an amusing, yet resolutely steadfast paean to the neurosis commonly called heterosexuality, whose major symptom is an insistence on masturbation. Philip Roth's 1969 novel is framed as a life story told by a patient lying on his psychiatrist's couch. The psychiatrist is the ostensible implied reader of this complaint; in turn, he or she will go on and use the information of this case study to publish an article about a psychiatric disorder named "Portnoy's Complaint" in which "Acts of exhibitionism, voyeurism, fetishism, autoeroticism, and oral coitus are plentiful" (vii). Whether we accept psychoanalysis or reject it, whether the novel itself undercuts psychoanalysis even while touting it, through humor and outright laughter, every textual moment, every anecdote, and every confession of an act of masturbation is immediately seconded by a discourse of the most orthodox Freudian psychoanalysis. Roth leaves no stereotype unsullied; no figure remains exempt from what often amounts to a post–Borscht Belt translation of Oedipal drama into a series of one-liners. Every figure of the triangle is the best at his or her job of being part of the triangle. Thus Mrs. Portnoy is not only little Alex's archetypal Jewish mother, but also the most Freudian of

Jewish mothers, inquiring endlessly about her son's bowel movements, and acting as "the patron saint of self-sacrifice" (15). She is
moreover the castrating mother *par excellence*, armed with a knife
against her defenseless six- or seven-year-old son (16) and sure to
mention his "little thing" (54, 56).

Any recounting of masturbation is thus triply framed: by an Oedipal discourse, by the reader's recognition that poor little Alex failed
to overcome the Oedipal crisis, and by a humorous discourse that
endlessly replays the ambiguity of Oedipal trauma. Alex's body is
thus never his: it is the body of a subject battling to be a subject, the
body subject to the structures of Oedipal drama in a machine as
stringent as Poe's, a body subject to humor and to distortion through
that humor. Alex is endlessly castrated and recastrated; but it is the
repetition of that act that finally turns trauma into a situation com-
edy that one might entitle *Jocasta and Son*. Not simply the Oedipal
son, Alex is constantly overwhelmed by the absolute insistence of his
father as overwhelming father, even in his taciturnity; his father's obstinate maleness takes on a comic dimension, in his inability to diminish himself in any way: the father is constantly constipated. Not
only is there never any possibility of the reversal of the Oedipal blade
on the figure of the father, there is also a complete impossibility of
severing any part of the father's body, even his feces. Roth will not let
even a metaphor of castration enter the realm of the father.

Alex is repeatedly subject to a poking, prying mother and engulfed
in a sea of Freudian names for his failure. Alex is subject not to one,
but to two double discourses. One is the limited discourse of guilt,
shame, and double binds that is stereotypically that of the possessive
Jewish mother; the other is a theoretical discourse of Orthodox
Freudianism, which despite all its verbosity, can also be seen as being
limited to stories of "mommy-daddy-me" and "peepee-doodoo." In
the former case, the language of the other prevents that of the self
from occurring, existing, and assuming its rightful place. The famil-
ial language encodes the world into what is acceptable to the mother:
what is kosher, that is, clean. This realm conjures a mindboggling alterity that has no proper name, but only a series of improper descriptions that relate to taboos, uncleanliness, or the most heinous
category—"goyische," that is, non-Jewish.

In that world of Jew and other, the world of his parents, Portnoy's favorite activity of masturbation has no name. It passes furtively or is mistranslated into a language a mother can understand; he explains his constant trips to the bathroom: "Diarrhea! I cry. I have been stricken with diarrhea!" (20). Thus his metaphorized sexuality is the exact reversal of his father's naming of himself as the retentive, constipated uncastratable Other. Yet there is one point, one part, that despite Oedipus and naming, prying and misnaming, that remains his. Portnoy's digestive tract may be community property, but his penis is his, unnamed: "My wang was all I really had that I could call my own" (35). His hand, however, the other guilty partner in the bargain, is up for grabs: "My father plagued me throughout high school to enroll in the shorthand course. . . . Earlier it was the piano we battled over" (28). Again, implicitly, it is the father's longhand, the father's uncastratability in naming and in being that is contrasted with Alex's shorthand, a naming for a part of his body, for a homo-sexualizing of his body—one thinks of the army examination known as short arm—and with the sign of what is societally considered to be typically feminine: secretarial work, for which shorthand was considered a necessity. Alex refuses to take the course, resisting this insistence of an assessment of his own shortcomings by the radical act of continued masturbation.

Alex's penis may be his own, but he has not found a name for it outside his mother's belittling code. The Freudian discourse names every part of Alex's body and every one of his actions in a supposedly neutral and nonjudgmental discourse. But to translate is to decide and ultimately to judge, and the activity that Alex calls "whacking off" becomes necessarily, in the textual pattern of the implied auditor or implied reader, the name that the patient (protagonist, narrator) gives to autoeroticism. Yet it is a name that sits uncomfortably "on the edge": between the innocence of slang and the reference to castration that is the literal sense of the expression. Alex can name his complaint freely, uninterrupted by the discourse of another, but only on the condition that this naming be subject to an act of translation. The final imprimatur of Freudian discourse is never given because, aside from the humor that more than upsets the neat model of the family novel, Alex knows the language into which his plaintive song is being translated. Good little reader that he is, he can challenge an interpretation from within: "I have read Freud on Leonardo, Doctor, and pardon the hubris, but my fantasies exactly" (136). So for an instant, which I believe is the only such moment in the book, Dr. Spielvogel, perhaps named for Leonardo's fantasized bird, finds his narrative already translated. And it is no accident that the work is about playing with a bird: "this big smothering bird beating frantic wings about my face and mouth *so that I cannot even get my breath*! . . . Just leave us alone, God damn it, to pull our little dongs in peace" (136). Leonardo's fantasy of being smothered is reversed to shoo away the birds—the smothering mother and doctor. And interestingly enough, the homoerotic position eschewed for the psychiatrist/voyeur returns here as Portnoy makes Freud's image of a homoerotic da Vinci his own.[3]

The second reversal of Freud comes late in the book, where Freud is simultaneously the narrative of liberation and the double of the penis itself, image of a vying within Alex to find out whether his masturbatory activities are his death sentence or his prelude to an act of liberation:

> I have been putting myself to sleep each night in the solitary confinement of my womanless bed with a volume of Freud in my hand. Sometimes Freud in hand, sometimes Alex in hand, frequently both. Yes, there in my unbuttoned pyjamas, all alone I lie, fiddling with it like a little boy-child in a dopey reverie . . . even heedful of the sentence, the phrase, the *word* that will liberate me from what I understand are called my fantasies and fixations. (208–9)

Reducing Freud to an unwilling or at least an unusual partner in a game of one-handed reading, Roth rewrites Portnoy's complaint for him by providing an insoluble knot in translation: how do you say "Freud" in Freudian discourse? Though clearly Dr. Spielvogel can translate both these images of Freud into what Deleuze would call "mommy-daddy-me," it is an adequation at best and more likely than not a non-sense. There is no better image to upset the Freudian apple-cart than that of using Freud as a phantom penis, a turn-on narrative, as one-handed reading material.

In distinction to Tournier's solitude verging on a communicational system predicated on absence and silence, Roth's version is never silent. For him, the activity at hand is always part of a group, even as it escapes from the group. Masturbation is properly or improperly part of the socialization process—and thus safely heterosexual—even when the socius is a group of one. Not for him is the perversion of a circle-jerk, the recounting of which brings out in him the language of both his mother and his shrink. This time, though, they are not in a parodic form, but honestly and fully his, as if the desecration of his most sacred activity was so taboo in his own world that the only names for it were the proper ones of a Jewish mother ("pig") and the categories of sexual neuroses proffered by Freud and friends. Portnoy's acquaintance "is also a participant in the circle-jerks held with the shades pulled down . . . I have heard the stories, but still (despite my own onanism, exhibitionism, and voyeurism—not to mention fetishism) I can't and won't believe it. . . . What pigs" (194). And a circle-jerk includes the role of the masturbator intertwined with that of the homoerotic voyeur. For Portnoy, there is nothing more unkosher than being cast in either role: masturbator or voyeur, the participant in this kind of circle-jerk necessarily and unkosherly participates in a homoerotic game. And yet, contradictorily, he insists that we be there, women transfixed by a flasher and men exposed to their own homoerotic voyeurism.

Cradled and hampered by other voices in other rooms, the communicational system distinguishes sender and receiver. Roth's masturbator is performing as if he were talking to himself, but in a way that would be comprehensible were another to tune in. Whereas Tournier's version is imagistic and silent, Roth's is not predicated on the absence of the object of lust. At times he even flirts with what Dr. Spielvogel would call a tendency toward exhibitionism. At least the exhibitionist controls what is being seen, thereby negating the homoerotic voyeur. Hence there is one scene in which Alex masturbates on a bus and another in which, to reach orgasm while being given a hand job by a woman, "instead of making believe that I am getting laid, as I ordinarily do while jerking off, I make believe that I am jerking off" (202).

What remains to be seen is how Alex finds a language for his "whacking off." Whereas Tournier's theory of masturbation occupies a discrete part of his novel, an isolated section that takes its place alongside of other isolated discourses on sexuality, including one on a dry orgasm [coup sec], Roth's theory has its own spot, yet exceeds that locus to become a leitmotiv for the whole novel. Portnoy's problem is that very overflow. There is a continuous threat that masturbation will overflow form and contents, discourse and *récit*. For Portnoy's tale forms the basis for the discourse of another, be it his mother or his psychiatrist. Is this, we ask, siding momentarily with the Greek chorus of observers, the perpetual feel of adolescence: "half my waking life spent locked behind the bathroom door, firing my wad down the toilet bowl, or into the soiled clothes in the laundry hamper, or *splat* up against the medicine chest mirror" (18)? Or is it rather that the reader, too ready to agree with the chorus, though he or she is laughing and they are not, does not allow Alex to speak the pleasures of his whacking off without a translation waiting in the wings?

Separated from the discourses of Jewish motherhood and psychoanalysis, the reader does not know where to look and where to hide. Having refused the role of censor or therapist and having come upon Alex masturbating, the reader is in fact cum upon. We, he, or she, are the ones who receive Alex's jism. Having escaped from a proper socius of his friends or his family to be in his own socius of one, Alex allows the reader entry into this world, but at the price of being the *cloaca maxima* for Alex's cum: "Leaving my joint like a rocket it makes right for the light bulb overhead, where to my wonderment and horror, it hits and it hangs" (20). Occupying a middle ground in which he or she tries to see without being a voyeur, a reader is witness to the activity that even Alex is occasionally blind to: "eyes pressed closed but mouth wide open . . . not infrequently in my blindness and ecstasy, I got it all in the pompadour" (18). At least the reader will not go blind from Alex's jerking off, though the myth of going blind is present when Alex cums in his own eye—"I'm going blind" (203)—or worse yet, when this blindness means being unable to see women's genitals: "how I made it into the world of pussy at all, *that's* the mystery. I close my eyes, and it's not so awfully hard—I see myself sharing a house at Ocean Beach with someone in eye make-up named Sheldon" (140–41). Again, the eyes of the homoerotic lurk at the edge of the writing.

The reader, then, always with open eyes, sees even when Portnoy himself cannot. Even as yet unnamed, Portnoy's act of masturbation is one of proper vision and reflection. He does not see himself as performing some parodic version of *goyische tam*, non-Jewish taste (for example, pastrami on white with mayo), nor does he elevate his action into an act of "autoeroticism" coupled with "voyeurism" and "fetishism." Quite simply, he gets off seeing himself whacking off: "I stood in my dropped drawers so I could see how it looked coming out" (18). That complete self-absorption and self-reflection is the only perfect view. All other positions depend on a blindness of sorts, perhaps Oedipus' own blindness, a degree of dyslexia or a myopia that overreads or misreads a simple, innocent, though nameless act. For having accepted this role of focused observer, the reader, still distinct from the crowd, plays as Portnoy himself does: the reader is the recipient of the visual evidence. As in a porno film where the male actor withdraws before ejaculation so the viewer can see him shoot his load, the reader must see the cum as well as the violence of the orgasm. And in fulfilling such a role, the reader becomes expendable, like the water in a public urinal or the wrapper of a Mounds bar into which Alex's seed is spent (18), like a hollowed-out apple used as an adjunct for masturbation (19), like a leftover milk bottle (18), or even one of two pieces of liver, one presumably to be discarded (19) and the other to serve, two hours later, as dinner (150). Common to all these (and to the rhetorical reader as well) is that they are public property, taken in or thrown out, eaten or emitted. It takes, so it would seem, little talent to be a reader watching a character masturbate, even if he is "the Raskolnikov of jerking off" (21); it is a role that is self-consuming. As the rhetorical reader fulfills this obligation, he or she ceases to be of value until the next time. The reader mimes Alex himself, spent, no matter how briefly, after every session. And spent, the reader cannot channel his or her energy into the *continuity* of voyeurism. Finally, then, the inscription will have endured just as long and as episodically as the act.

Stripped of its translations into other discourses, masturbation becomes the event of the book and can serve as a general equivalent or a touchstone. Sex will be like masturbation, but working and living each day will also be like masturbation. Alex and the reader need to see a therapist, not because of some overnamed, overread neurosis, but because life itself and the reading of life itself are painfully close to the *acte gratuit* of masturbation which is an act of dispersal, dissemination, disappearance, and death.

Still we do not know what the proper name is for this activity, but it may only be necessary to listen. There is another voice in the writing, aligned neither with the discourse of guilt of the mother, the discourse of comprehension of Freud, nor even the silent, all-seeing assent of the reader, the light bulb of the writing. The voice is Alex's own, but one unsubjected to the discourse of domination. It is singlemindedly, "like some idiot microcephalic" (142), the pure desire of his libidinal excess, his penis itself: "'Jerk me off,' I am told by the silky monster" (143). But for all that, it is a singular libido at best, for though unsubjected to the constraints of an internalized voice of repression, a name/no of the father given status as a superego, it only wants what is not kosher: "'Just look at that nose.' 'What nose?' 'That's the point—it's hardly even there. Look at that hair, like off a spinning wheel. Remember "flax" that you studied in school? That's human flax! Schmuck, this is the real McCoy. A *shikse*!'" (143). The object of autoerotic longing, what the penis sees as a one-eyed jack spying on the world, has no reality as a subject. The object of this third eye is a collection of signs foisted upon the libido by some malefic anti-superego. So ultimately for Portnoy, there is always the hand of another moving his hand, always the voice of another in his ear or head, and always the space of another in which he improperly comes.

With no voice, there is no freedom. The book approaches its conclusion, which is the possibility of beginning psychoanalysis. But this beginning is nothing short of parodic, just as all of Alex's activities have, in the author's mind, in some way been parodies of healthy behavior. There are parodies of two cries for freedom: "Let my peter go!" and "Jerk-off artists of the world unite! You have nothing to lose but your brains!" (283–84). There is no voice other than one stolen; there is no language other than the borrowed tongues of repression. To them, we have just added the puritan consumer capitalism of WASP America. Alex is constantly in search of the proper name for his act; yet the more he looks, the more his action becomes that object for the others' discourses to include, explain, and spurn. After all is said and done, he would have done better to read Wittgenstein, and been silent about that which one cannot speak, only wordlessly continuing to play with himself.

It is only through a certain retrospective, tragic reading whose time is now that we see that these two novels were epiphenomenal. Now for us, masturbation has returned to the world of shared activity, as widely recommended now as it was denounced a hundred years ago. Who among us can read "masturbation" without immediately conjugating it with the practices and discourses of safe sex? Acceptable activity, outlet in the face of death, masturbation has taken on a virtue that it had never had through 2,500 years of recorded history. Though Tournier and Roth could not find the proper voice for masturbation, we can see that they came closer than anyone will now ever be able to. No longer innocent, masturbation has been endowed with a virtue that can never be shaken off. When all is said and done, it will have appeared on the horizon at one historic moment as a saving grace.

A final note on the subject of the representation of masturbation in literary discourse, and specifically on the representation of the male body caught in the act, comes from the quintessence of the postmodern, a short piece written in 1978 by the youthful Hervé Guibert, entitled "Le Journal de l'onaniste," included in *La Mort propagande*. This book is a collection of some of his early writings, a grouping he himself effected as he was dying of AIDS. But the work itself clearly predates the onset of the symptoms of Guibert's disease.

The word used by the postmodern Guibert for masturbation is onanism. In so doing, he recalls both the biblical concept of the spilled seed and the medical and scientific warnings against such self-abuse in the eighteenth century. Masturbation is part of an intensely ritualized recuperative activity that takes the self as the object of love, that finds a crystallization of that erotic attraction in the finest (and many would say most disgusting) aspects of recuperating the expense of the self: smelling his own body odors, be they from armpit or anus, by means of a well-placed finger, an inventory of snot, a weighing of shit, a gathering of sperm. And even if one part of the recuperation is rejected—the hairs cut from shaving—most of the activities relate to a making permanent of the outward flows at any given moment. So the onanist's activities are redoubled as displaced acts of masturbation as they themselves become figures of the masturbatory individual refusing to expire in an expense of spirit.

So too does masturbation itself take over as an activity better than sex with another individual. Even if the desire to French kiss or have oral sex remains (283), it is only at the level of the imagined other: "Only a dream satisfied me, by its brutality, but the possible severing of organs, by their only connection, separated from cruising, of a narration" (283). Narrating a story and retelling a dream are ultimately the same thing for Guibert. Here and well beyond the symbolic adequation, they become the equivalent of the masturbatory process: narrating oneself is a process of masturbation. And so finally, the recuperation of actions and effluvia, the telling of tales, and the act of masturbation become one and the same. For each flow that had simply been recalled two pages earlier, there is now a writing system recording and recuperating its contents, its essence. Toilet paper with souvenirs of bodily fluids are collated, notated, and inserted, not back into the self, though this is clearly the ideal, but into a book.

Writing long before he knew what was in store for him as a writer, the young Hervé Guibert ultimately hit the nail on the head: spilling his seed and recording the process, writing his body into a purely postmodern technological body of annotations, of parts, and of inscriptions, Guibert writes the last words on masturbation before it became the safest sex of all: "I began to collect my cum [crachats], to mark with a pen the stain they made on the paper, to give them titles, to sign them. I injected them with ink, strewed them with letters and hairs, arrows, as I noticed the progressive breakdown of matter" (283–84). Finally, then, to close, he wills his masturbation to the world and deeds his unique actions/stocks, the fruit of his masturbatory activity, to his inheritors, ostensibly those of us who read Guibert and realize the seed of his onanistic monologues will not have been wasted after all.

From Liberation to AIDS

In this chapter, I am interested in exploring the changing representation of the gay body as the object of discourse in French by starting with the rhetoric of gay liberation formulated by Guy Hocquenghem at the end of the sixties and the beginning of the seventies. After that, I shall focus briefly on a some work by Hervé Guibert that seems, along with Renaud Camus's *Tricks*, best to illustrate the liberation called for by Guy Hocquenghem. The latter parts of the chapter are devoted to Michel Foucault and to narratives about AIDS. Foucault provides a theoretical loop back to the writings of liberation by Hocquenghem, inspired as they were to a great extent by Foucault himself. For pragmatic reasons, I am limiting the investigation to French literature by reasonably well-known writers. This is not, I underline, a hegemonic move, given the nature of the discourse of gay writing. Certainly a Foucauldian reading of the subject would integrate famous and unknown alike, and my reading risks being considered exclusive, hegemonic, or unnecessarily discriminatory. But I would hypothesize that the very constitution of the object of the "gay body" is done through the rise and cohesion of discourses that dominate. The writers whose work I am looking at here, including Gilles Barbedette, Renaud Camus, Guy Hocquenghem, Dominique Fernandez, Yves Navarre, and Hervé Guibert, write the gay body publicly into existence. As I discussed in both *The Shock of Men* and *Alcibiades at the Door*, the gay body is constituted as an object out of a more general gay hermeneutic as the last object constituted by that hermeneutic developing over the course of a century. And for pragmatic reasons, rather than beg legitimate questions of national differences, I would prefer to stay within one national/linguistic tradition on this matter, because here especially, with the famous American closet having no real equivalent in French, the space can be more clearly circumscribed by a cultural, linguistic, and social context.

Consider the gay body for a moment. What could it be? What does it look like? What eyes see it? I do not mean the body of the male homosexual, defined biologically, genetically, sociologically, and behaviorally. I mean the body of a man, finding his gender as a man and attracted sexually to other men, and not measuring that attraction against some predefined normality or morality. Not the individual inhabiting that flesh, finding an identity within, but the phenomenology of that body, the person seen in the bar, the trick, the one-night stand, the body of the long-term lover still seen, now and again, as only a surface of pleasure. The gay body in other words. Object for eyes like its own, male eyes seeking the signs of assent in other male eyes, object for a similar subject, the gay body occupies a locus of its own definition, a locus where a phantom identity and an imagined reciprocity define the poles of the subject-object relation. The subject sees the object, who in his turn as the subject, sees the first subject as an object. And they see the same thing: not a man seeing the body of a woman, but a man seeing his own homologue, perhaps misrecognized, misrepresented, anamorphic, but a homologue just the same.

This is not to say that subjectivity ever fully disappears. In fact, the very possibility of seeing the other as homologue depends on the unvoiced belief that as a man, even as a gay man, this individual is a subject first. Western civilization tells every man that he can see, that he can seize an object with his eyes, and that he can possess. The gay man sees the other as object second, subsequent to his own constitution as a subject. In contrast, a gay woman, a lesbian, has endlessly been taught that as a woman, she is first an object for the structures of civilization, and thus, always already subjected to them. Thus she can assume her subjectivity only after having rejected the status imposed on her as an object.

Assured of his own subjectivity, no matter how alienated he might feel from the structures of the system, seeing his other as the same, the gay man seizes that other as a capturing of identity through the annihilation of alienation. Fragmentary, yes; repetitive, certainly; alienating at one remove, almost assuredly. The gay body is the representation of subject and object in a happy, timely mix, the "always already" existing hypostasis of subjectivity in search of the recognition of its own identity. The gay body is an object for the homologous other and for the self, both enunciated through a discourse of mirrored desires and a free play of seductions.

The gay body is a challenge, even a provocation to many. Set against the monolith of heterosexuality, the gay body is the incarnation of a refusal of the imposed weight of heterosexual discourse, its trappings, and its impolitic impoliteness or gestural liberalism: "*Heterosexual* is not a polite word. It is commonly used only in gay circles or in those liberal settings where there are a large number of professed *non*heterosexuals present" (Grover 23). The gay body refuses to be "the good homo," which Tony Duvert describes in *L'Enfant au masculin*: the one acceptable to heterosexual society, the one who doesn't act queer, the one who, as Duvert puts it, "keeps his anus closed [and] disdains penises" (67).

Consider the gay body for a moment longer. Made of the right stuff, well-packaged, well-assembled, it is an object for other objects, circulating in a system that tends to reproduce the concept of identity in its search for mirror images, even *en abime*, of itself. It is an object rejected by the world at large yet necessarily, if belatedly, accepted by a world that only recently has relearned to look at what it had forgotten: the male body in general as object. And yet, necessarily, the "heterosexual" structures of the system that organizes representation and signs—and by "heterosexual" here I mean, most impolitely, "*male heterosexual*"—find the object narcissistically and economically pleasing, part of the commodity exchange, yet erotically repugnant. If I look, worries the straight man, will it not make me queer as well?

Because the gay body is uniquely structured through homologous imagery, to consider the gay body then as an object, and not as a sign of an object that is safely packaged with the precautions of semiotics, the viewer must, if only momentarily, accept that his or her position of viewing is homologous to the position of another gay man. As a viewer, he/she must become a gay man looking at another gay man. For how else can the phenomenology of the subject-object relation be seen for what it is? That is to say, the very identity of the gay body is fundamentally dependent on the mirror image and the structures of narcissism, as are all structurings of identity, but it is also simultaneously dependent on the phenomenology of the other as perceived mirror image, the identity of the subject/object relation to its opposite. And even in cases where the sense of identity seems to come from complementarity (active/passive, s/m, fister/fistee), the complementarity is based on a sense of identity as well as on the structures in which one defines oneself in such a category and through which one implies a singular complement: in the world of the gay body, there is no sense to a fistee without a fister. But moreover, these attributes are preceded, I believe, by a general perception of the gay body, a perception in which the body of the other is "always already" defined in the definition of the body of the self and vice versa.

The gay body replaces the object of Gidean pederastic desire, the pure, adolescent ephebe who is neither woman nor man, more different from the lover than he is different from the female beloved. So too does the gay body replace the homosexual body, defined as the same as the heterosexual body, though merely with a different viewer. The homosexual is defined by the heterosexual community at large as that which is not in its realm. Defined as origin and center, that realm is the one in which the concept of identity seems to dwell. Homosexuality is difference from that realm, though the difference is based on the heterosexual concept of identity. According to that system, the homosexual body is the same as the heterosexual body, the only difference being in the desirer. It is no wonder then that the seeing the falseness of that image, as Dominique Fernandez notes, leads to a blaze of glory, of existential revolt. How could it not, when the "homosexual" is loathsomely defined relative to and secondary to a subject and domain that are not his own: "Genet is the last witness of an era in which the choice of a certain morality almost surely condemned you to revolt, delinquency, evil. His genius consists of making the magic associations of sex and blood, love and death, beauty and curse burn bright for one last time" (29).

The gay body, whose ramifications are described in George Bauer's article "Le Gai Savoir noir," replaces the homosexual body, as the definitions of the latter are finally seen to be derivative of a self-defined heterosexuality that determines its other. Of course, the two praxes overlap, and a gay sensibility, albeit in a form relative to the era, existed long before it is given a name. As I have tried to show in *The Shock of Men*, there are a number of writers, including Proust, Barthes, Tournier, and Renaud Camus, who do not accept the derivative nature of homosexuality and whose work is illuminated in a variety of ways by their refusal to accept secondary status. And indeed, it is not as if one praxis stops and another starts. Genet is certainly not the last example of the homosexual writer, for there is always Tony Duvert, who marries the image of the Gidean adolescent with that of the Genetian homosexual hero always in revolt. Among other remarks in his *Abécédaire malveillant*, note the following: "*He loves me* means plainly: he accepts that I capture him, tame him, rape him, kill him, and bury him" (11). By and large, though, at least in the public's perception of the situation, there was a sea-change in the sixties.

With the advent of gay liberation in the late sixties, the gay body replaces the homosexual body as the definitions of the latter are finally seen to be derivative of a self-defined heterosexuality that determines its other. Liberation tells us that the gay body must be equal, nonderivative, not accepted, but just there. As Dominique Fernandez pithily remarks, "Four million French people, who believed themselves to be homosexuals, woke up gay." It is no wonder that this new gay body, constituted by a discourse that has long struggled for the self-assertive validity of its subject, leaves many still in the dark.

The major architect in France of this liberation, and indeed its most visible and articulate spokesperson, was Guy Hocquenghem. Novelist, journalist, and militant, Guy Hocquenghem was born in 1946, a date confirmed by the author's close friend René Schérer in his afterward to Hocquenghem's posthumously published last writing, *L'Amphithéâtre des morts* (111), although *La Dérive homosexuelle* and the first translation of *Le Désir homosexuel* give 1944 as the date of birth. Among his novels are *L'Amour en relief*, dealing with blindness, and an AIDS novel, *Eve*. He is best known today for his writings on homosexuality, including *Le Désir homosexuel*, *La Dérive homosexuelle*, *Race d'Ep*, and *Le Gai Voyage*. A militant in May 1968, Hocquenghem was at the forefront of the French gay liberation movement, and in 1971 was one of the founders of the Front Homosexuel d'Action Révolutionnaire, the most visible and most militant of the French gay liberation groups, whose collected writings can be found in *Rapport contre la normalité*.

Fuck me in the ass, Guy Hocquenghem seems to be saying in his various writings on homosexuality, for it will be an act of liberation and liberation is what we need. Can liberation come at such an expense of spirit, such a simple expression of exulting, momentary freedom? For whom would this be an act of liberation, we ask, and for how long would it last? Who is liberated in this culturally coded, execrated, yet quite common, even banal action, perceived by much of the West as antisocial and still called sodomy, a name written with the wrath of God? Moreover, if we continue to divide the world, at least for now, into the subjects of Western metaphysics, ultimately the only subjects in question here—for we know that the culturally coded act is differently marked and differently remarked in other places and at other times—who exactly is liberated even by the call or invitation to such an event? In such an appeal, there are two figures, distinguishable for the moment until we contrast the stereotyped physical action with the voice of reason. Addressed and invited is the one interpellated by the wooing, commanding, yet ultimately passive militant; the individual who is told to perform an act of anal penetration is ironically the one who is first penetrated by the command of language itself. Calling the shots is the one anally penetrated; with perfect diction, he is still the one who is standing or lying there, his most private space open, available, penetrable, vulnerable.

For Guy Hocquenghem, writing what would turn out to be his best-known work, *Le Désir homosexuel*, the act of liberation of the homosexual begins with this gesture of vulnerability, this appeal to all that society tells us to shun. This invitation that is simultaneously a command is an affront to a capitalist system whose codes are those that name homosexuality, that frame desire within its borders, and subject homosexual desire to a controlling system that oedipalizes desire and in so doing controls it and deforms it at the same time. Whereas Hocquenghem is preaching a discourse of free desire as he invites the other to screw him, capitalist society endlessly remarks its own incapability for such freedom: "In the world of Oedipalized sexuality, there is no longer a free plugging in of organs or relations of direct *jouissance*" (*Désir* 59; 95).[1] We must start with that act of anal penetration, a "challenge to society," as Balzac writes in the last sentence of *Le Père Goriot* of the very straight Eugène de Rastignac's assault on Paris, because it is there that the act of suppression begins. Since the Oedipus complex is anal, as Deleuze and Guattari (168) succinctly remark, the best way to turn it on its ass is to make the most private of its components the public space of untamed desire. This, then, is Hocquenghem's avowed project.

For Hocquenghem, the act of liberation starts with the challenge to society as a whole, but the liberation is, perversely, always already detoured by a society—capitalist, modern, oedipal—that territorializes desire, that subverts desire through the creation of simulacra of desire, what Hocquenghem calls "the play of images" (*Désir* 59; 94). Just as they counterfeit desire, those simulacra are also figures of the speciously constructed independent subject of Western metaphysics and *his* (male, heterosexual) theories of desire. For this subject has erected himself as a cultural entity, and despite the fact that such a subject, necessarily, is historically produced, his greatest claim to fame is that he has universalized himself as transhistorical. As if his own phallus were the catapult moving him into some transcendental space, the white male heterosexual subject of capitalism declares himself the universal transhistorical subject of desire and its codes. For Hocquenghem, reading Deleuze, Lacan, and Foucault among others, the oedipal child of late capitalism has made himself the universal figure of the heterosexual male subject of desire, the figure from whose constructs all paradigms are produced. This subject, which is paradoxically the only subject Hocquenghem has to work with, precisely because it is a historical product, *his* historical product, constantly reappropriates the freedom of desire for its own purposes of perpetuating the oedipal mechanism that is one of the founding moments of the capitalist enterprise.

While Jonathan Dollimore (208–9) has summarized Hoc-

quenghem's indebtedness to Deleuze and Guattari's critique of oedipal psychoanalysis, one of my points in these pages is to show the
ambiguity of such a critique, because the critique of the oedipal subject depends on the oedipal structure. Moreover, I would like to
show Hocquenghem's program as not only being part of such a critique of psychoanalysis, but also as being part of the revolutionary
moment of May 1968 and part of a founding moment of discourses
of gay liberation. In other words, one of the important results of
Hocquenghem's writing is his participation in the founding of a new
discourse of gender studies. Flows of desire are called for by this system endlessly in the process of reproducing itself, but those flows are
detoured toward a series of guilt-provoking simulacra, an endless
stream of symptoms of the inadequacy of the ego to control the flows
of the individual's libidinal *jouissance*. The ego is always and already
subjected to the controls of an oedipal superego, the little tyrant that
is the metonymy of the family novel, the bourgeois family, the capitalist exchange system, the mommy-daddy-me mechanism under
which we all live, the tyrant that is discussed at length by Deleuze
and Guattari (60–162).

To overturn that mechanism, Hocquenghem starts with the same
historical subject, but literally turns him on his head, with his ass in
the air. Hocquenghem's gesture has a measure of the theatrical,
much like Jean-Jacques Rousseau's gesture of sweeping away all the
facts: "Commençons donc par écarter tous les faits [Let us thus begin by putting all the facts aside]," writes Rousseau in his *Discours sur
l'origine de l'inégalité* (132). But how else, in a world where images are
subjected to the laws of the phallus, can one overturn a system? To
found a new subject of desire—and ultimately a new set of discursive
possibilities—Hocquenghem begins with the last moment of the
subject. Since the past can never be fully swept away, the foundation
of a new subject, a new order, a figure and structure of deterritorialized desires, of nonheterocratic paradigms, of nonphallocentric *jouissances*, will depend on the abject body part of the capitalist variety of
homo erectus.

Following the arguments expounded at length by Gilles Deleuze
and Félix Guattari in *L'Anti-Oedipe*, Hocquenghem develops a critique of the channeling of desire into what society considers the appropriate territorial paths. These paths are the mechanisms neces-

sary for keeping the capitalist systems of production and exchange on the family plan. Desire is channeled into reproduction and reproductions to perpetuate the system; it neither reigns nor flows freely. In this system, desire cannot be fulfilled without the imposing influence of the oedipal structure being felt, without the phallocentric world of sublimated desire imposing itself on all desire (*Désir* 59; 95). Real desire is sublimated when it is bound by the phallocentric, capitalist, oedipal model; with such mediating structures in place, direct and immediate pleasure is safely kept at bay: "We are made ashamed of our bodies because they translate our desires" (*Après-mai* 144).

Following Deleuze and Guattari then means that Hocquenghem will accept the local validity of the oedipal model by saying yes, this phallic system does define our moment, or at least the institutions under which we live, the oedipal triangle of Freud, the Name of the Father of Lacan, the Ideological State Apparatus of Althusser, the realm of the practico-inert of Sartrean social history.[2] We are all subjected to that model and forced to sublimate our desire at the level of the production of desire as well as at the locus of sublimation, the anus subjected to the tyranny of the "despotic signifier" (*Désir* 60; 95) that is the phallus. The construction of a phallocentric model depends on the sublimation of that anus, the privatization of its functions, the sublimation of the zone of pleasure that it defines most intimately. Thus Hocquenghem and the authors of the *Anti-Oedipe* buy into the Freudian system as a schematic representation of the local— European and North American—system of ideology and exchange, though not of course as a general paradigm for all situations and all times. Indeed, the thrust of the argument is that the hegemony of the Freudian model needs to be challenged, the totalizing imposition of the phallic order needs to be subverted, outstripped, and overcome.

Le Désir homosexuel is a polemical book that seeks to overturn the "phallocratic" (60; 96) order of society as it now stands, the paradigms of a society that invests power and social value in the phallus, a society that lets the phallus rule over all others, women and homosexuals, alike. Society's problems are multiple and wide-ranging, yet they can be reduced to their metonymy in the reign of the phallus. Overturn that order and you will have overturned all the evils that are perpetrated in the name of maintaining the social structure, its ideologies, and exchange systems of postindustrial capitalism. And yet the polemic hides the real problem for Hocquenghem, the problem that goes beyond the focusing of this desire—whatever it may be—as a revolutionary activity. For homosexuality, or homosexual desire, is not merely the mark of a focused political action, it is also far more importantly the meaning of a drive or pulsion that he believes to be his. If Hocquenghem expresses his own homosexual desire, he is not only contributing toward a liberation of society as a whole, a liberation that is simultaneous with the political movement of May 1968, the women's liberation movement, and the recognition of the need for revising the freedoms of a postcolonial model that continues to maintain ex-colonials as second-class individuals at best. The author's homosexual desire is the impetus for his own act of self-liberation; the vehicle, a theatrical one to be sure, is his exhortation to buttfucking.

"Our assholes are revolutionary [*Notre trou-du-cul est révolutionnaire*]," writes Hocquenghem in *La Dérive homosexuelle* (42); we can use them to revolutionize the world. Fuck me in the ass, says Guy Hocquenghem, and in so doing we will liberate ourselves—or I will liberate myself as the possessor of a postcapitalist, post-oedipal, de-sublimated (or unsublimated) anus. Fuck me in the ass, exhorts Hocquenghem, and I will magically transform your catachretic phallus into a penis once more, a tool of free-flowing desire and not merely the simulacrum of power that that phallus is supposed to incarnate: by deprivatizing the anus, by refusing the social concealment, the *grand renfermement* will come to an end. The prison-house, the *stultifera navis* of which the anus was the last and most poignant prisoner, will finally have its doors opened wide. When libidinal energy is no longer shunted away from the anus, when it reaches its goal, then and only then will we all be liberated from the structures of capitalist thought and ideology, and more importantly from the hegemony of the heterocratic order that is the supremely reductive and reproductive sign of that ideological system (*Désir* 61; 97). In Hocquenghem's eyes, we are thus all—heterosexual and homosexual alike—the repressed products of that system, victims of an order that dominates, sublimates, and ultimately desecrates the individual's rights to his/her own body. Thus, we are all sublimated homosexuals to the extent that we are imprisoned in the order that forbids the pleasures of the anus. And it is up to true homosexuals, whoever and whatever they may be, to stand up for their liberation, to lie down for their rights, prone or supine figures of a desublimated zone of erotic bliss.

But what is homosexual desire? According to the Deleuzian model with which Hocquenghem starts in this book, there is no such thing as "homosexual desire." Just as Renaud Camus (138) writing a decade later in his *Notes achriennes* (1982), challenges the expression "homosexual writer," Hocquenghem finds the expression "homosexual desire" to be a meaningless one. If for Camus the expression is meaningless because the word "homosexual" is always defined secondarily to "heterosexual," for Hocquenghem the expression is meaningless because desire itself is not originally so labeled. Thus just as Hocquenghem needs the theatricality of building his model on the desublimated anus, he builds his argument for liberation on a title that *strictu sensu* has no meaning. Desire is not subdivided into homosexuality and heterosexuality:

Properly speaking, desire is no more homosexual than heterosexual. Desire emerges in a multiple form, whose components are only separable *a posteriori*, according to how we manipulate it. Just like heterosexual desire, homosexual desire is an arbitrary cut made in an uninterrupted, polyvocal flow. (*Désir* 12; 49–50)

Now it is clear that in such a model it is the institutions of society, including, most importantly, the bourgeois family of oedipal fame, that channel desire into the forms in which we recognize it. It also seems clear from Deleuze's work and from that of Foucault, whose concepts of categorization are akin to those expounded by the authors of the *Anti-Oedipe*, that, in the eyes of society and in the figures of its discourses, there are proper channels of desire—heterosexuality and its apotheosis in phallocratic, heterocratic order—and that improper channels are often a vague, confused, and unnamed mixture of leftovers. What is not white, male, heterosexual, and law-abiding—that is to say, phallocratic and phallocentric—is indistinctly other. As Hocquenghem notes in the article "Our Bodies Belong to Us": "fags, dykes, women, the imprisoned, the aborted, antisocials, the crazy" (*Après-Mai* 143). So that homosexuality, at least in the generative sense, is just one of many improper sexualities that are inappropriate vehicles for the reproduction of society, its ideologies, and its values. Insofar as homosexuality is concerned, thus always improperly named, its desires are manifestly channeled into two directions by the structures. Since desire is forced into an oedipal structure, homosexual desire becomes for Hocquenghem a bivalently framed drive. On the one hand, there is "an ascent towards sublimation, the superego and social anxiety." On the other hand, there is "a descent towards the abysses of non-personalized and uncodified desire" (*Désir* 59; 95).

It is no wonder then that Hocquenghem takes the position of revolutionary to overturn the hegemony with which heterosexuality girds itself; he is seeking the "proper" or the "genre" for homosexuality. Thus according to the model proffered by Deleuze and Guattari by which only unchanneled and undifferentiated flows of desire exist before a fictionalizing categorization, there is, nevertheless, for all intents and purposes, a proper and particular nature to homosexual desire. As Deleuze and Guattari write: "We are statistically or molarly heterosexual, but personally homosexual" (82). And why is that? Because instead of exclusions—the either/or of heterosexuality and binary logic—we are each playing with "differences that come back to the same without being differences" (82). Still, the divided desire framed within the structures of oedipal capitalist society hypocritically forces the homosexual individual into a situation of alienation. And yet that situation of alienation is not without interest; the best tools of the revolution are those that the dominant structure provides. Hence one of the sections of the book *L'Après-Mai des faunes* (144–77) will ironically and strategically be entitled "Fags" [*Pédés*]: strategically, because it uses the language of repression to underline the seriousness of the struggle; ironically, because the revolution failed.[3] After May fags are still fags.

If the revolution fails, does that mean that homosexuals are still condemned to live out their desire according to the heterocratic order impressed on them? By and large, Hocquenghem's essays and articles are a "defense and illustration of homosexuality" (*Dérive* 23), though, as he himself points out in the same location, they are not limited to that. And this defense and illustration—conveniently a phrase that comes from canonic literature—is no easy task. For there must be a defense of homosexuality as it is along with a defense against homosexuality as it is depicted. We will get to the illustration below as the proactive component in Hocquenghem's arguments, a forward-looking and even poetic guide for homosexual activity. But for the moment, it is the idea of a defense of homosexuality that is of concern here. A defense: a legal argument, a barrier, dam, or protection, a rationalization, a justification. The defense of homosexuality is all of these. Hocquenghem must not only take into account the practice of homosexuality, or what we would now, following Judith Butler, call the performativity of homosexuality (*Gender* 24–25). He must also take into account the categorization of homosexuality as a set of (antisocial) praxes, as a sexual drive split between sublimation and the impersonal, as a catch-all term wrongly yet insistently defined by heterocratic order:

> The "heteroclitic" nature of homosexual desire makes it dangerous to the dominant sexuality. Every day a thousand kinds of homosexual behavior challenge the classification one tries to impose on them. The unification of the practices of homosexual desire under the term "homosexuality" is as imaginary as the unification of the component drives in the ego. (*Désir* 119; 148)

It is thus that the defense of homosexuality takes place as a reactive remarking of perverse behavior, a provocation, an anathematic reading of heterosexuality itself. It is thus that Hocquenghem provocatively focuses on anal penetration, that most antisocial of acts, as the homosexual action *par excellence*, even though he knows that the act is not particularly limited to homosexuality nor is the performance of that act in and of itself a definition of homosexuality in any sense of the word.

So before focusing on the excess of homosexuality, its illustration and illumination, its poetics as expressed in many passages in Hocquenghem's work, we need to finish understanding the defense of homosexuality through the militant language and the focalization of the process on the asshole as a revolutionary organ. Because the anus is still, even in liberal bourgeois society, the unique remaining organ of shame of the body (*Dérive* 43), it is the focus of Hocquenghem's attention. Liberate it from the mechanisms of repression that make it both the "seat" of sublimation and the most private zone of the individual, that insist that it be both the metonymy of capitalist ideology and the shameful reminder of that system; in so doing, says Hocquenghem, you will be doing nothing less than liberating yourself or even society as a whole from the yoke of those structures. Be a homosexual, allow yourself to be the passive partner in an act of anal penetration. Do not think, however, that this is an act of feminization of the male individual. For Hocquenghem, even if anal intercourse seems to imitate the domination pattern of heterosexuality, the two actions are not the same because "it is still one man buttfucking another" [*c'est tout de même un homme qu'un autre homme encule*]" (*Dérive* 44). There is a difference: "shit will never be menstrual blood" (*Dérive* 44).

What makes shit better than menstrual blood? On the surface, the implications of such a remark should not and cannot be acceptable to the reader as a validating argument for what amounts to the difference and strength of homosexuality. For it seems, alas, still a story of phallic power, garnished with more than a slight tinge of misogyny. And that is odd in someone whose solidarity with the women's liberation movement was unfailing. Again, I would point to the theatrical nature of Hocquenghem's remarks: menstrual blood, one might surmise, is a visible reminder of the system of reproduction to which women are forcibly subjected and from and in which homosexuals, perverse beings that they are, find themselves both excluded and included. They are excluded because, as a rule, they do not reproduce; they are included, pathetic, limping oedipal failures, as the shit of a system that insists on its own production and perpetuation. There is nothing more theatrical than turning the tables on the system, by replacing the sign of the system's own apotheosis—menses—with its lowest and falsest equivalent.

It is this that Hocquenghem will raise up as a sign for all to see: it is clearly theory as performance art before the fact. The strength of the argument is rather in its bald statements: "our assholes are neither shameful nor personal; they are public and revolutionary" (*Dérive* 44). No, the value of the argument is certainly not to be found in the virtue of shit, though again, the reversal of the restraint or sublimation, that is, the anality, of capitalism as described by Max Weber in *The Protestant Ethic and the Spirit of Capitalism* provides more than a touch of irony to Hocquenghem's exuberant, desublimated prose. Rather, the value of the argument is to be found in the revolutionary action itself, in that Hocquenghem's concept of the asshole as public space and as a pleasure-zone becomes the paradigm for his concept of a revolutionary, homosexual body, which must now become public in its manifestations and pleasure-giving and -receiving in its behaviors. So it is our bodies that need to take their clue from Hocquenghem's extolling of one part of the homosexual body. This is not to say that we are free yet, even as this appeal to liberation occurs. Indeed, even as Hocquenghem makes this appeal, he is still caught in a capitalist paradigm when he is in this reactive mode: "Our Bodies Belong to Us" is a title of a 1971 article collected in *L'Après-Mai des faunes* (143–44). How does he get beyond belonging and possession to encompass the truly revolutionary act that homosexuality is for him? How can he escape the paradigms of capitalist, oedipal structures whose very vocabulary, catachretic though it be, infiltrates everywhere, even to our assholes?

Toward the end of *Le Désir homosexuel*, Hocquenghem writes of "sexual communism." The very choice of that word is far from coincidental, as he brings the whole enterprise under the aegis of a shared togetherness, a traditional revolutionary banner that builds on the idea that property is theft. Doing away with the personal, the proprietors, and the possessed is the best way of turning toward a joyous celebration of nonalienated behavior:

And perhaps some index of this state of primary sexual communism can be found in certain institutions of the homosexual ghetto, despite all the repressions and guilty reconstructions they undergo: I'm thinking, for example, of Turkish baths, where homosexual desires are plugged in anonymously, despite the fear that police presence is always possible. (*Désir* 76–77; 111)

Much earlier in the book, Hocquenghem has used the same situation as a contrasting example. In one case, we find the free-flowing sexual communism just mentioned. In the other case, we find the privatization of sexuality and the rape of the privatized individual by the mechanisms of the state:

One simply needs to stay too long in a street urinal to be convicted of indecent exposure; policemen may go as far as incitement (in Turkish baths, for instance) in order to provoke that crime. Repression does not merely take delight in poking into people's underpants, it seeks out the crime, provoking it in order to condemn it (such police behavior is frequent in the United States). (*Désir* 27–28; 65)

Homosexual desire is forced into its compartments of sublimation and shame, into its private spaces that are never fully private because what is private in this model effectively can be appropriated by the phallocratic order. Homosexual desire cannot be free unless public spaces are truly free, truly public, neither controlled nor patrolled by a mechanism that polices desire. Liberation then means freedom from oedipal morality, heterosexual repression, and capitalist shame. Let us celebrate, says Hocquenghem, and let us do so by shaking capitalism and the bourgeois family structure to its roots: "Cruising: let's steal its Oedipal moral coat" (*Dérive* 104). Hocquenghem redefines public space as a space for desire, pleasure, *volupté*, and the redefinition is based on a double outrage: his own outrage at the repression of the capitalist state and his outrageous position of making the anus the model for public space. For, in short, the model of deterritorialization he proposes is of one great pleasure zone, a universal asshole wherein all pleasures are henceforth possible.

Hocquenghem reorchestrates, or at least reorganizes his concept of space as a pleasure zone that is the generalized equivalent of the pleasure zone he has decreed the anus to be. Space is eroticized, homoeroticized in fact, though it was always gendered male by the powers that organized its private and public spheres: "Every social space is first a male space" (*Race* 158). One could say then that Hocquenghem is merely fulfilling the promise of the model he so despises by deeming space—and by this he generally means urban space—male, and uniquely male. But this eroticized model goes further, for the space he constructs is a utopia of sexual possibilities, of deterritorialized desires, of contacts, flows, couplings and uncouplings. Organs of pleasure meet other organs in an eroticized space where these organs, freed of any *phallic* order, are free to be organs of pleasure; not only is the asshole made a desublimated public space, but also the penis is freed of its onus of having to serve as the lightning rod for an entire civilization.

Now fully eroticized for each individual as well as for all individuals, space is remarked in a multiple reterritorialization in which each individual produces his own version of the territory, all of which coexist with one another. In that space, the very conception of an individual changes, as he—always "he"—reorders his very concepts of selfhood that came from the structures of the capitalist system.

Though *solidaire* with lesbian concerns and with the women's liberation movement, Hocquenghem tends to restrict his arguments to male homosexual desire without making an appeal to universalize his position. Rather, I think he attempts through his polemics to have "homosexual desire" stand on its own two feet, so to speak, neither subject to a dominant heterosexual other nor to a reproductive model in general. So that individual male subject no longer wants to be that individual, cut off from others, organizing his space territorially, phallically, and heterocratically, by definition. He wants to celebrate this erotic communism in the loudest possible way:

The annoying thing is that, for me "human being" and "respect for another's being," that's nothing to me; it's bull. I hardly want—OK, my situation is different—I hardly want to be a "human being"; I don't want to be respected, on the contrary. If someone puts his hand on my ass, I'm thrilled. If I'm whistled at in the street, I'm filled with joy. That's why I go to Morocco. Even the old, the unbeautiful offer pleasure. You can even get off with them. (*Dérive* 106)

Hocquenghem's map, which is his and uniquely his, is not a deed to possession and privacy, egotistical actions for which he continually reproaches the capitalist model, but is rather a map of his own version of a multiply-inhabited cyberspace *avant la lettre*, a happy hunting ground for the free flows of cruising: "A city map is a hunting ground. And cruising, a way of reading this map which soon covers it, crisscrosses it, makes it unreadable to everyone but me" (*Gai voyage* 9). What has changed is the perspective, the parameters, the orders of the space. In Hocquenghem's version of erotic space there is no definitive and permanent territorialization invested with power, inhibiting desire as it goes. Rather, the space becomes a space in which each player can determine a territory for a moment, can use it for his pleasure, for his desires, without that space ever having passed over into the realm of property. Space is for cruising, as the four incandescently lush pages of "Paris-Louxor" repeatedly show (*Gai voyage* 133–36). These are Hocquenghem's panegyric tribute to a movie theater on the Boulevard Barbès in whose balcony the various comings and goings of anonymous pleasure-driven men, both Maghrebin and French, make a permanent spectacle that one can watch or participate in. Space is where action happens. The space of a city, whose walls or institutions are easily recuperable markers for those who know how to read a generic gay map—"riverbanks, areas near railroad stations, public parks" and glory-holes whose "glorious nudity" Hocquenghem admires—is henceforth, at least for Hocquenghem, a space of and for homosexuality (*Gai voyage* 10; 181).

And that action, transforming space as it does, is itself revolutionary. Indeed, as much as he is driven by an Orientalism that is a means of liberating his desire within the model at hand, an Orientalism celebrated in *La Beauté du métis* and which, since Edward Saïd's work, has become a suspicious desire, Hocquenghem is also motivated by a sense of what the Sixties naively called "solidarity." Hocquenghem may be attracted to Maghrebin men because this marginalized form of desire is acceptable within the structures of heterocratic desire, as Foucault would read it, because the other is believed to be liberated, as Gide would have it, because of the stereotypes of that other as phallic machine, or at one remove and perhaps for the very same reasons, for the "beauty" of the individual. But he may also be attracted to the Maghrebin other, outcast of two societies, because of that sense of solidarity.

Projecting a revolution that goes far beyond the sexual liberation of the oedipally defined individual and buoyed by a sense of solidarity with the marginalized of society, Hocquenghem foresees a revolutionary new world. What could this world look like? Of course it is still a utopian concept: "The universe where the freedom of desire is realized is still to be built" (*Dérive* 57). And yet the very attempts at constructing the world, here and now, are not without their attendant successes, acts of liberation, acts of revolution for the militant who offers his most sublimated part, even as a sacrifice as well as an offering, to the world. It is a world where definitions are multiple, like the space they inhabit, a world in which, if something called "homosexuality" is still believed to exist, it is multiple in nature—as it always was, but it is now recognized as such (*Dérive* 19). It is, after all, a challenge: "name it, name it again, there will always be something left over" (*Comment* 210). To live as a homosexual in a homosexualized world, in a deheterosexualized world, will be the final challenge, the final success. But it will come with difficulty, for not only does Hocquenghem militate for the end of heterosexuality as an oppressive institution; he also wants the freedom to "remain homosexual."

And that is not the easiest task in the world. But how could someone who militates for "A Homosexual Conception of the World" settle for anything less (*Après-Mai* 158–66)? What shape this world would have taken for Hocquenghem we will never know, for his life, like so many others, was cut short by AIDS. But we should and must remember, and remember to celebrate the vision of a man who did so much to radically rethink the question of homosexuality during the sixties and seventies. Guy Hocquenghem ends his book *Le Gai voyage* with an image, mentioned by Robert Aldrich (191), no less striking than the oft-mentioned exhortation of *Le Désir homosexuel*. In Alexandria, a Greek is giving a blow job to an Egyptian slave. The latter grabs the Greek by the hair and makes him turn his head toward the city whose library is on fire: The Greek adolescent "wipes his mouth with the back of his hand, and answers thinking of the dead decomposing all around them: 'Yes, perhaps the night has just begun'" (*Gai voyage* 236).

This night, an American night as François Truffaut would have called it, is lit up with giant klieg lights. The gay body comes into existence as the object of discourse along with the desires expressed by, cathected onto that body. The body does not exist without the subject desiring and discoursing about the object: the body, a function of the man-as-object, and discourse, a function of the man-as-subject, meet, interweave, dance together in a field, not of Deleuzian desiring machines, but one of melded identities and unalienated subject-object relations. As Renaud Camus notes in one of the volumes of his diary, *Vigiles*, what he seeks is "the harmonious, muddled circulation of desire and gaiety in both senses of the word, happily confused" (13).

Consider the gay body again. The manifestations of its appearance were the events of 1968, the Stonewall riots, the Front Homosexuel d'Action Révolutionaire, the disco-fever of the 1970's. It is a body made of reflections of the self, a self that may be tautologically perceived as a reflection of that very same body image, image of self and other at once. The gay body is composed of its surfaces, projections and orifices, variously figured, neatly described, opened and closed, folded and unfolded in just the right way, *pli selon pli*. The gay body, object for the eye of the beholder who is himself ideally beheld in the same way, is always in the process of being undressed, if not already undressed when confronted. Skin is everything, substance, whatever that be, is there merely to fill out the skin in the right way. Muscle is the greatest misnomer in this world of surfaces. The body is its skin focused into zones of pleasure, of pain, of pain as pleasure. Discourse makes that body and frames those zones of pleasure; in this discourse of sexuality, the distance between the signifier and the signified is reduced to zero by the complete transparency of the discourse. While Camus's work offers a plethora of examples, including a whole book called *Tricks*, there is a poignant early one in Roland Barthes's *Incidents*, his 1969 jottings on some encounters in Morocco. Here Barthes quotes someone's come-on or pick-up line: "'I will do anything you want [*Je ferai tout ce que vous voudrez*],' he says, full of effusion, good will, and with complicity in his eyes. And that means: *I'll screw you* [*je vous niquerai*] and only that" (53–54). One always knows what the other wants—he wants to fuck—even in an approximate foreign language. The discourse is transparent, for the signified is the body, the body that desires, the body that has that desire "always already" inscribed for the self and the other to read, remark, reinvest with this reading.

Certainly the transparency of the sign system does not mean that the gay body is itself transparent. Far from it. Rather, the gay body, constituted as a reflection of the discourse of desire, is there in all its readability and all its flashy visibility as the demonstration of the locus of desire. Writing that body and rewriting the signs on that body, signs that circulate as simulacra of themselves—for the sign is always there, on the body—is the act of the gay writer remarking the gay body that is both not his and his. It is not his, as the body of the other, as yet untouched, but is his in its constant readability: "To write is to speak one's desire, and inscribing it is already to satisfy it halfway" (*Vigiles* 30).

Along with Renaud Camus's work *Tricks*, a series of short narratives about one-night stands, *aventures*, sexual encounters of all sorts, some of Guibert's early work best exemplifies the rhetoric of the gay body during the period of sexual communism called for by Hocquenghem. It is only in the sexual revolution of the last quarter-century, as I have shown in the previous pages devoted to Hocquenghem, that some sort of gay discourse can depart from the heterosexual norming from which it springs. Thanks to authors in the

French-speaking world like Renaud Camus, Yves Navarre, Guy Hocquenghem, Dominique Fernandez, and Tony Duvert, as well as critics like Roland Barthes and Michel Foucault, a modern gay discourse has developed. And only a few years later, it is because of AIDS, now part of daily life, that homosexuality becomes more and more normalized through the process of mourning that is ours. Homosexuality, of course, still remains distinct and different, but its marginalization both in Europe and in North America has diminished considerably.

For Hervé Guibert, who arrived at least a decade later on the literary scene than the other authors just mentioned, and thus, though coincidentally, at the same time that AIDS was making its first silent incursions, the chains binding a gay discourse to some dominant heterosexual model had already been broken. And although it is predominantly Guibert's autobiographical AIDS writings that have sustained the most interest among critics (including a chapter in my book *Alcibiades at the Door*), there were other works written before the recognition and representation of his seropositivity. In these pages I want to look at the register of the rhetoric of the body that Guibert puts into place in the works he writes before realizing his illness, and specifically in a synthesis of two short pieces: an early work entitled "La Mort Propagande," included in the collection of the same name, and the notorious "pornographic" piece entitled *Les Chiens*.

How can one write on homosexuality, for argument's sake, after Hocquenghem? For the stakes have become different. If the rhetoric before Hocquenghem was either one of idyllic liberation or one of internalized homophobia, the post-liberation but pre-AIDS rhetoric has become an opposition between that of Tony Duvert's "good homo" already mentioned and a recall of taboos, not so much of sodomy, fire, and brimstone, but of "pornography." Pornography in this case means a homosexuality that does not submit itself to the model of the closed asshole; it is a homosexuality where two or more guys fuck, where there are visible penises, where queer men just don't bother to keep their pants zipped.

The word "pornography" is insidious, and even Guibert himself (*Fou de Vincent* 85), perhaps unconsciously, uses the word to describe his short work *Les Chiens*. It is a word that can easily affect a critical discourse. Owen Heathcote, for example, seems to accept that *Les Chiens* is a pornographic work (61). And yet after an engaging reading in which he clearly shows how Guibert forces a deconstruction of all categories of psychological, narrative, and oedipal identity, Heathcote declares quite rightly that Guibert hardly does himself justice by describing the work as a "pornographic piece" (69). Heathcote is right, for in *Les Chiens*, all notions of the oedipal subject have been banished in favor of a rhizomatic system of desires. How can the self be distinguished from the other, the dominator from the dominated, in such a system? How can we qualify acts as sado-masochistic, voyeuristic, or indeed hetero- or homosexual if the lines between subjects are indistinct? I would suggest that the categorization of "pornography" in general depends on a primary distinction between heterosexuality and homosexuality, between self and other, that just does not operate in Guibert's work.

Murray Pratt aptly proposes the word "disidentification" to describe *Les Chiens*. As Pratt shows, Guibert's work is a refusal of categorization, for to be categorized is to be alienated (70).[4] Pratt is right when he affirms that it is possible in *Les Chiens* to "deconstruct the individual values of separation, of disjunction, and distinction and to imagine a writing of the self that goes beyond the limits of autonomy and which seeks to elaborate a plural 'I'" (74). As I suggest below in the pages on Foucault, there is a possibility of seeing the construction of a plurality of "sadian" subjects all acting in concert without having to fall back on outmoded, oedipal definitions of sadists and masochists.

Guibert is impassioned by writing the body, his or that of another, both remaining undefinable in their limits and borders, for the moment. As Derek Duncan writes, "Characterized by the writer's desire to inscribe his ego and through his intense identification with his means of expression, Hervé Guibert's work offers us the following challenge: the body, his body, is the locus in which identification points meet or fail to converge" (101). A body, his body, is thus constantly reborn and rewritten as the subject and object of bliss: "My body, whether because of *jouissance* or because of pain, is put in a theatrical state, a state of paroxysm, that I would love to reproduce, however possible: photo, film, sound-track" ("Mort" 183). A jouissance for himself, a reflection of himself, as if jouissance, which is itself unrepresentable, had become the single base of another representation, that of a sexuality that is no longer submitted to the law of tautological identity. Unrepresentable jouissance is still the transcendental signifier in a heterosexual semiotics, and becomes here the transcendental signifier, the post-logocentric guarantee of a discourse devoted to the representation of the self and the other in the state of jouissance, the state of loss and excess: "As soon as a deformation occurs, as soon as my body becomes hysterical, a mechanism of retranscription is turned on: burps, hurls, sperm from jerking off, diarrhea, spit, flows from my mouth and asshole" ("Mort" 183).

Jouissance and its path say what other discourses cannot: repetition becomes the representation of jouissance, a representation that is completely different at every moment, though without *différance*, aiming at the purity of the transcendental signifier until all is incorporated in the *jus*—juice and law, French and Latin—of Guibertian representation that is jouissance-producing, juicy, and jussive. For Guibert cum is the law: "Allow this convulsed, chopped, screaming body to speak. Put a microphone in my mouth, full as if with a cock, the juice deeply possible in my throat, in case of a crisis: seizures, ejaculations, or brutal expulsions of shit, groans" ("Mort" 183). Thus Guibert takes the usual formula for representation, that of identity and opposition, and deconstructs it to destroy this very idea of opposition.

It is in such a manner that Guibert fictionally categorizes *Les Chiens* under the sign of pornography or homosexuality, this story that starts with a description of heterosexuality, without one being tributary of the other: "He covers her and his sexual organ goes into hers, goes in and out, his/her buttocks [*ses fesses*] contract, my own sexual organ stands up uselessly at the thought of that butt, he withdraws from her and turns, he takes her from behind" (*Chiens* 9). Submitted to voyeurism by a man who is the narrator, this heterosexual couple becomes the variant of a homosexual couple in a universe where the only thing that counts is the relation of jouissance between subject and object. The fact that the man espied becomes the sadistic, dominating lover of the narrator/voyeur in the pages that follow changes nothing of the homosexual representation on which the scene is based. For Guibert, the heterosexual relation is always submitted to a structurally homosexual model as it becomes a juicy version of homosexuality:

> Later every thrust I give him pushes him ever more deeply in her, and it is at that very moment, through the flow of our sperm, passing from me to him, to his balls, and crossing the *corpus spongiosum*, from him to her, it is at that instant, through the flow of our sperm added to each other, that she becomes pregnant. (*Chiens* 36)

Submitted to the law of jouissance, the body speaks, representing itself through images and acts, indices of a range of activities that, on the one hand, challenge any classificatory system, and on the other, establish a fluid, undefinable movement of intensification or transformation that becomes the basis for Guibert's representation of sexuality. What heterosexual discourse would have classified under various sexual rubrics, especially one that would include "homosexual" and "bizarre," becomes for Guibert the most anodyne expression of the discourse of jouissance. Thus bondage for this narrator is merely a problem of arithmetic:

> I had calculated that I would need four strips [*bandes*], one for my feet, one for my hands, one for my sexual organ, a jugular, and a bit for my mouth. The scissors followed the dotted lines, as if they were a model or a pattern of my forthcoming pleasures. This job was enough to make my penis swell and to allow a thin brilliant stream to flow from it. (*Chiens* 10)

For Guibert, an object or the body itself does not exist except insofar as it is translated into being a sexual object, a sexual body capable of obeying the jussive command. Whether it be a dildo (*Chiens* 12–13), clothespins (13), a sheet (10) that will serve to make the strips for a game of bondage, or balls of yarn ("Mort" 194), anything can participate in the representation of the jussive law of orgasm. Taking everyday objects, including the dildo—for he does not distinguish—and transforming them produces, as Guibert himself writes, an "apotheosis" ("Mort" 203). Such is the name given to a varied, repeated pleasure that transforms the object each time, even the body itself, whose use value seems inextinguishable and whose worth seems ever increasing, as all these objects, and especially the body, metamorphose through their juicy representations into a flowing, spasmodically spewed liquid, into never-ending flows of cum:

Ramming my throat [*Me défoncer la gorge*] with their cocks, two by two in my mouth until they made a hole in it, nicking my neck with razors and coming in it, with their dirty, badly unsheathed cocks in the gash, buttfucking me in their reciprocal sperms, ramming me twenty times in a row, neglecting my jouissance, pissing their snot in my mouth, rubbing their filthy eyes on my face, farting in my mouth, assaulting me, stealing my clothes, selling me after having left their excremental odor of camel dung on my body. ("Mort" 203–4)

The intensification and the transformation occur on the body, on the body of the subject who is simultaneously the object of desire, the desired and desiring body at once. This intensification and transformation guarantee as much the movement of discourse as they do the possibility of reaching perfect jouissance. They are also the way of escaping from the heterosexual system that make bodies conform to a jussive command of clear subject/object relations. Heterosexual bonding, bodies, bondage means the law of the father that can only be dealt with through its perversion and upheaval: "A story told a hundred times already: the first sperm I had in my hands, my father's . . . a bizarre object, a little plastic package dripping with a sticky liquid, a transparent jelly, touching the rubber [*caoutchouc*] and letting it slip between my fingers" ("Mort" 215). Jouissance for jouissance, the act of fertilization that becomes the narrator is faced with pure jouissance, pure loss, spent sperm that will make no egg fertile. This pure jouissance that will not become another can only be thought pure because it is the law of the father. Elsewhere, with the narrator, the purity can come only with death, a death of drowning in one's own vital liquids: "During the night of 6–7 March 19 . . . , H. G. was found dead, bathing in his blood, in a room in disarray. Death silenced him" ("Mort" 210).

That this perfect jouissance of death is not tangible, that the transcendental can never become immanent—so be it. There is always the possibility of approximately reaching this moment of pure bliss through a sexuality that translates transcendence into new rules, a new code: "He told me: you must earn my penis, on all fours, you will try to release it from its wrapper [*gangue*], using only your teeth, trying never to touch it, never to get it dirty with your lips" (*Chiens* 16). On the next page, the narrator continues to receive such orders: "You will have to beg me, call me master, adore my penis, love it, stare at it, dream of taking it in your mouth, entreat me" (17). One's own body or that of another is the multiple, varied locus of thousands of micro-jouissances that can be infinitely varied, the locus of what René Crevel called "papillae of pleasure" (30, 145, 154, 155). The body is there where the transformations take place, on the skin itself, a locus of tactile erogenous pleasures: "My mouth is open to make your cocks cum, my cock is stiff to please your asses, I dilate mine for you to shake your dicks in. Come? Let's party! May each of our mouths devour two or three cocks at once! ("Mort" 202–3). Multiplied and intensified, sex organs and sex acts can be endlessly re-ordered through a *combinatoire*, one of whose most important rules is the endless specularity of representation: "I want you to watch yourself blow me, your mouth filled with my cock, I want you to see yourself swallow my cum [*jus*]" (*Chiens* 23).

This endless reflection of representation back onto itself, onto the body as its locus, medium, and fulfillment is a sign of the impossible conjunction of autofellation or autosodomization, seen and written about in the exact moment it would take place. Only then would the act of perfect jouissance and perfect representation be complete. But this is never to happen, and instead of that impossibility the body becomes a screen on which pleasure is registered. Screen and body are interchangeable loci for jouissance and for representation:

Being in a dissection room and taking apart an ass. Autopsying this spot of my body whose penetration by a cock, the nail of a calloused finger that writes and jerks off, scratches with delight my intestinal walls, or a raspy tongue that hardens, makes me get a hard on, cum, piss my sperm. ("Mort" 186)

The body become a screen unrolling endlessly, the locus is specular and spectacular, imaginary, a locus of jouissances past, present and future, all mixed into a whirl of an endless present:

I am going to spew my juice [*t'en juter*] in your mouth, and I'll save some to cauterize your ass, at the moment of orgasm, I pulled out of his mouth to spray his eyes that drowned in the milky white flows . . . I said to him: I am going to cover the surface of your skin that remains free with mustard plasters . . . so that every square centimeter of your body exults. (*Chiens* 29–30)

All of these positions, exchanges, changes, intensifications, and exaggerations are interchangeable. Every part of the body becomes a genital, a surface of pleasure that drinks it in or spews it out. And indeed, there is an interchangeabilty at the level of the body itself, that of the self exchanged with the other. The lines between them, the surfaces of intersection, intermingle: who cares who cums as long as someone does? Almost in passing, we see this through a grammatical ambiguity: "I follow/am [*je suis*] the guy who tried to buttfuck me" ("Mort" 204). We hesitate for a moment between the more sensible, but less common "je suis" of the verb "suivre," meaning "to follow" and the seeming nonsense of the more common "je suis" from the verb "être," meaning to be. But is it really nonsense? For one ambiguous moment, the perfection of self-sufficient sex and representation desired by Guibert seems to be there: "I am the guy who tried to buttfuck myself." Such is the bodily translation of the literary discourse in the process of being created: "I take a piece of paper to write something, I have gotten completely undressed, I write and it gives me a hard-on, I jerk off [*me branle*] with one hand, I have a loose tooth [*une dent qui branle*], there is blood on the paper" ("Mort" 205). Self-engendering and dissemination of that same sperm at the same time, a unique action accomplished in the representation of writing as interchangeable with jerking off, cumming, bleeding.

Guibert's *jus*, law and cum, is performative, a perlocutionary act that simultaneously brings about jouissance and its representation: "No, he has not yet pulled out of her, I see his cock free itself from her dripping labia, and I kneel to kiss their union, I lick his cock as he pulls it out, and it falls from her vagina into my mouth, I inhale their conjugated juices [*jus*]. My cock is erect" (*Chiens* 36). The action of Lafcadio in André Gide's *Les Caves du Vatican* is translated into a self-sufficiency in Guibert, a mixture of flows, some objective, some potential, some represented, some given in a name that spills and spells it out: "I tattoo cocks on my thighs with my Waterman" ("Mort" 207).

To annihilate the differences between the self and the other, between writing and violence, between writing and sex, between homosexuality and heterosexuality (as long as this last collapse starts from the primacy of the homosexual act, scene, and representation), is a radical way of changing a discourse and a representational system whose heterosexual markings are difficult to extirpate. Thus in a way, the erasure of the border between self and other is a way of dephallicizing the discourse, as any organ becomes a sexual organ and any act becomes a sexual act:

Henceforth, do you hear me, I forbid you to wash your penis. I will clean it, conscientiously, with my mouth, tongue, and lips; at your feet, I want to eat the gel of your sperm and your urine and all the musty odor [*remugle*] of the belly from which you pull out; I want her vaginal juice [*jus*] to flow in my throat through your cock. (*Chiens* 24)

Any discourse then is equivalent to a sexual act and vice versa; the body is body act and discourse. And the prediction of an act, in the form of an expressed desire, an obligation, a need, as well as the re-call of an act, are also legal and liquid *jus*, act, text, and body all to-gether. For Guibert the representation of the body in ecstasy would be a constant re-presentation of the body in a state of jouissance, where metaphor, metonymy, and even representability itself are all figured on the screen of the homosexual body.

And then: AIDS. Where does one start? How does one write (of) the gay body with AIDS or even of the gay body in the age of AIDS? To ask that question is to proceed too quickly. Indeed, there has al-ready been much writing on the subject, so it is not as if I were ap-proaching a completely untrammeled territory.[5] I would like to start, however, at a critical point, which is the death of Michel Foucault, the philosopher who theorized sexuality in so many different, indeed revolutionary ways, who influenced, as I have indicated, the sexual revolution of which gay liberation was such a salient part. Foucault's writing and his death are in a sense a fitting closure to the literature and theory of sexual liberation in the form of Hocquenghem's sexual communism. After that, after AIDS becomes a part of everyone's consciousness, there can be no return to that utopian space in which sovereign subjects desire and act.

Imagine a body, the body of the other lying in front of you. Through your perspective, by dint of your situation in the space you occupy, you have determined focus, gaze, vision. You have decided what is in your purview. Imagine that body neither alive nor dead, neither moving nor inert, defined neither as a *corps* nor as a corpse. Try to imagine it. It is someone, it belongs to someone, or perhaps it belonged to someone. To decide whose body it is, we must know if it is alive, if it is a subject, or the effect of a subject, or if it is purely and simply an object, just there, belonging to no one in particular. Belonging to someone else. Who does the body belong to when it is a corpse? It is an odd question, for in our time we think or believe that a human cannot belong to anyone else. We think or believe that the body is sovereign and specifically, that *my* body is *mine*. But when the *corps* becomes a corpse, we no longer know to whom it belongs. Is it, like some other inert chattel or object, the property of the inheritors, the legatees? Can one will one's body to be the property of another? Seemingly one can, and yet, no sooner does it belong to someone else than the body is more often than not cast off, buried, burnt, discarded.

The body of an other is an object that one wants only as long as that other, defined as some sensate being inhabiting or imprisoned within that body, is still resident. Once that soul, being, or heart is gone, once that body is only a body, no one wants it. The remains of the other cannot be his or her body, cannot be a body belonging to someone else. Necrophiliacs beware: you want what is willed to an other which that other does not want. Your desire is false, aberrant, unseemly, inhuman, because you do not desire according to the law of desire: you desire what no one desires.

To think of the body before it is categorized as living or dead means to rethink or to unthink a whole set of categories. Just for a moment, eliminate the thorny question of the subject, if only because the body has no necessarily resident subject. Perhaps the subject is only an effect of a subject, as fleeting in one way as it is evanescent in another: when the body is reduced to being the absolute object to be traversed, crisscrossed, barred, imprisoned by the discourses, powers, and grids that fix it, when that body has become an absolute prisoner of solitary confinement, the effect of subject is gone.

So think then of the body *neither* living *nor* dead or *both* living *and* dead. Imagine that body, think of it in your mind. See it then before you. To see that body, to gaze on that body is to make it yours, to appropriate that body for yourself. Living or dead, that body becomes the object of your gaze, the object of your coveting gaze, the appropriated thing that you now possess. You have watched the body of the other, you have made it yours, rightly or wrongly, you have gazed upon it. To conceive of it is to look at it, to possess it with your eyes. You have assumed the sadistic position. In your mind, you do with it what you will.

Consider the position in which you stand to look at the patient, the position you take to decide who is sane and who is crazy, the position you assume to look at a painting of some ladies in waiting. You dominate with your gaze: lying there lifeless or squirming from the torturous look by which you control her or him with your vision, the other becomes subject(ed) to your thought, politics, action, and discourse. The discourse of power translated into and translating your gaze confirms you as the master of what you survey. But wait—you too are in discourse, subject to the same language; you think you have the independence of a subject, the liberty or *disponibilité* of a free agent. Yet you are incapable of creating a position that is yours alone. Your mind and your body are subject to some other; you too are captive in a web or grid of discourse to which you are the tacitly assenting party. Wait again: what is at the center of what you see is not that subjected subject, captive of the grid. As you look into the center, you see yourself: you do not see the patient but the discourses you have proffered; you do not see the boy you love, subjected to your whims, but the logos describing what you can do, the same logos that you have appropriated for yourself (Foucault *Usage* 100–103). You do not see the redoubled reflection of something already there, but your own eyes, the eyes of the king that are now your eyes, the eyes of an absolute subject overcoming your own imprisonment by the returned reflection of your vision (Foucault *Mots* 24–25).

Look, then, as Michel Foucault looks. Share the scene of the body (of another, of himself as other) that he puts before you, as if it were his to give. And then and only then, look at his body to see if you too have appropriated a position, as I suggest. Foucault's study of the prison opens with what has become a famous description of the body of a condemned prisoner who in 1757 is put to death by being burned and then drawn and quartered (*Surveiller* 9). The public spectacle of torture, of *supplice*, the torture not to extract information, but the torture unto death, is a performance wherein the actor is always already the body that is neither living nor dead or both living and dead. Subject to the covetous view of the other, of all the others, the condemned prisoner is the figure of the common whore, belonging to all, subject to all possessive gazes, forced to go in every direction by the ones that have power over her or him. The body of the prisoner, usually male, is feminized by the power of the observer, sadistically and heterosexually male.

Not castration so much as the vision of a forced heterosexuality. To avoid the mimesis of the justly condemned homosexual position wherein the male looks at and possesses the *corps*, corpse of the male other, the prisoner becomes a woman, deprived of power, of phallic center, of an ability to move or to be. Sade—for his name has already appeared—is injudicious, obscene, improper in that he does not sublimate or disguise that homosexual position in a heterosexual mask. The eighteenth century that Foucault chooses as one of his privileged objects of study knows that order must be maintained. The male subject can look; the female subject must either be subjected, looked at, or, on occasion, may look away. But in no way can she look. Plate 29 of *Surveiller et punir* is an engraving from the end of the eighteenth century. It features a steam-run machine for the "correction" of little girls and boys. It seems to have a set of rods (*verges*) and whips (*fouets*) that are used to spank the children as M. Croquemitaine and Mme Briquabrac supervise. Interestingly enough, the adult male looks on, whereas the adult female is facing away from the machine and the supplicating child.

The nineteenth century universalizes that male position of vision and gaze while removing the direct use of power involved in the *supplice*. Am I wrong to suggest that this position is still a sadistic one, still a sexually sadistic one, and still a homosexual one? To look at the prisoner without killing him, to make your gaze the universal eye watching the other, is to desire according to the eyes of male vision, to make every position a homosexual sadistic one. René Girard, following Hegel, is right: if desire is effected according to the desire of another, that is, if I as a male desire a woman, it is because another male already desires her. Thus for Girard, desire is fundamentally homosexual: "Since the model rival, in the sexual realm, is normally an individual of the *same* sex . . . all sexual rivalry is thus structurally homosexual" (*Des choses cachées* 358). If, then, in the world of Foucauldian vision, I possess the other with my eyes, it is because I have imprisoned him in the structures of male dominance. The sodomy for which prisons are unjustly famous is a redundancy of the homosexual possession that the other makes of the body of the prisoner.

Foucault speaks of nothing else. Whether it is the creation of the medical gaze as the corpus of symptoms is created, or the invention of man, whether it is the effect of the subject imprisoned in discourses of general knowledge or the actual imprisonment of the body in a cell into which the eyes of the other can always penetrate, the discourse of Foucault repeats endlessly that the universal position, at least from the nineteenth century on, is one that is both homosexual and sadistic. The body of the other becomes the mutilated *corps* or corpse of Saint Sebastian, gay icon *par excellence*: "During the classical era, there was a whole discovery of the body as the object and target [*cible*] of power" (*Surveiller* 138).

Foucault relates the transformation of the body as an object for penology in which the "body itself is invested with the relations of power" (28) to the concept of the "king's two bodies" developed by Ernst Kantorowitz. Specifically, Kantorowitz considers that in the body of the king, there is both the transitory element of the individual who is born and dies and the transcendent element of the king that remains throughout time. Similarly, Foucault suggests that the "condemned prisoner is marked as the symmetrical and inverse figure of the king" (33). Thus, Foucault suggests, along with the body itself, there is a double, an incorporeal "soul" produced by punishment. This soul, unlike the Christian soul, is the locus where knowledge and power meet, "the effect and instrument of a political anatomy" and the "prison of the body" (34).

We might consider this soul, then, as the heterosexual construct, the "effect of the subject" within the structures of a homosexual and sadistic model. If the subject constructed by the discourses of society is presumed on the surface to be a heterosexual one, it is only after the internalization of the discourses of dominance. That is to say, one can become a fictionally free subject in this society of dominance and exchange by buying into the position of the discourses of power, by ingesting them, by internalizing them. One becomes a subject by eating the words of the father, by accepting that the consequences of the so-called oedipal model of capitalism are accession to a position of power by homosexually ingesting the Other of power and by passing oneself off thereafter as heterosexual.

Imagine a body, the body of an author. The body silenced in a way, a gag in his mouth, so that, puppet of the discourses of power, he silently repeats the discourses of the other as he stifles through the gag: "What matter who's speaking?" ("What Is an Author?" in *Language* 138). Bound and gagged, the author disappears behind the writing, behind the effects of a subject created, forced at that spot to perform as if it were a subject. What better retreat from being forced into a position where not only one's tongue is tied, but also one's body, than to pretend that the very body is not there. With no body there, there is neither *corps* nor corpse. With no body there, the space marked by no subject and no victim seems the uniform space of asceticism. In Foucault's writing, what could be loosely termed an ascetic approach to writing takes the form of the disappearance of the writer from the writing. This disappearance is double, not the single one that we would normally predict of the writer's consciousness. For it is also the author's body that disappears from the work. That body will come back with a bang toward the end of his life, as he realizes the fundamental importance of his body for his writing. As Miller notes, quoting Leo Bersani: "'There was something explosive about his fascination,' recalls Leo Bersani, 'I mean, the scene was fun—but it wasn't *that* much fun!'" (261). But before his body appears, can there be any doubt that he has to make it appear from within the walls of a Piranesian cell? "And while I was doing this project, I noticed that it was not working out. An important problem remained: why had we made sexuality into a moral experience? So I locked myself up, abandoned everything I had written on the seventeenth century, and started to work my way back . . . " ("The Return of Morality" in *Politics* 252).

It is thus understandable to find Foucault using a present tense that has a deictic component in the second volume of *Histoire de la sexualité*. Whereas the atemporal present, the habitual tense for scientific enquiry, is a commonplace, a temporal present is a rare occurrence in his writing. The present tense appears not only as the traces of an enunciative presence of mind, but also as that of the body of the author:

To say things quite schematically: we tend today to think that the practices of pleasure, when they occur between two partners of the same sex, relate to a desire whose structure is particular; but we admit—if we are "tolerant"— that this is not a reason to submit them to a morality [*morale*], even less to legislation, different from the one common to everyone. The point of our interrogation, we bring it to bear on the singularity of a desire that is not addressed to the other sex; and at the same time, we affirm that one must not accord to this type of relations the least value, nor reserve for it a particular status. (*Usage* 212–13).

No body, dead or alive, flayed or left whole, occupies the phantom locus. No subjection to the dualism of Christian and capitalist order need interfere with the production of writing or the realization of power grids. Dualism disappears, as does the division of soul and body, for without a body, the soul has no home. In *L'Usage des plaisirs*, Foucault contrasts Christian interiority with classical exteriority. Both imply a process of self-correction and self-work, but from vastly different perspectives. In Christian interiority, there is a "particular mode of relation to oneself that includes precise forms of attention, suspicion, *déchiffrement*, verbalization, admission [*aveu*], self-accusation, struggle against temptation, renunciation, spiritual combat, etc." (74). But the exteriority of classical morality relates to a set of external rules observed and followed, though without any interiorization of those rules.

And yet there is a body. At least a body is projected as a fantasy at the locus of the all-commanding, sadistic other: "I believe the great fantasy is the idea of a social body constituted by the universality of wills" ("Body/Power" in *Power* 55). There must be a body, but that universal body is a fantasy. It is the projection of some single position, some single sadistic other; it exists; Foucault knows it; is it any wonder then that the body of the subject returns? For the sadistic position to function, it requires fodder, meat, a body on which to operate.

No, perhaps the ascetic position is better, a position without a body: "Yet a fact is there: in a few dozen years what disappeared was the tortured, dismembered, amputated body, symbolically marked on the face or shoulder, exposed live or dead, given in spectacle" (*Surveiller* 14). No body is on stage on which to operate, no body need be present behind the words of the discourse that insists on the neutrality of its position—I would say, the singular neutrality of its position. Neither masculine nor feminine, neither heterosexual nor homosexual, the transmitter of discourse does not have to decide for himself or herself, can eclipse himself or herself from the stage, as observer and body alike disappear. If there is no body to punish, if there is no observer to categorize, the neutral disembodied observer can move from focusing on the repressive effects of discourse to seeing a series of positive effects (*Surveiller* 28). Neutrality means that one does not have to say, decide, or be; one can be moved off one's invisible mark, neither presence nor absence, neither alive nor dead. And that any movement, in any direction is a positive step.

Not saying one is gay, not having to say one is gay, pretending, not that one is not gay, but that that position can be a neutral one, this is the ascetic ideal in writing. Or at least in some texts, for in Foucault's writing there is both the espousal of a position of neutrality and, in select spots, a presentation of the position of a gay individual different from the scientific, neutral position often seen in the writing. There are two possibilities, then. The first is that the position of the individual caught in discourse and transmitting that discourse can be neutral, and that, specifically, the definition assigned by the general episteme to the genders of knowledge can be easily evacuated. In other words, there seems to be a belief in much of Foucault's writing that the marked position of transmitter of knowledge, which is white, male, heterosexual, can easily be neutralized.

But there is another position, a position that allows that the sexual position is an irreducible one, that despite all the sense of the social structuring of the sexual position, there is an irreducible mark or moment that cannot be voided or avoided. The gay position is always there, not as a variant of the heterosexual position, not as an opposition to it, but as a difference from it. And it follows then that the neutral position constructed at the point of discourse is necessarily different from the other neutral position, the evacuated heterosexual position. That neither then is truly neutral, and that both are always marked by the gendered, sexual signs of discourse and behavior, remains eminently clear as well. To be gay is to realize that there is another history, another discourse that is not so easily neutralized.

It also means that there are perhaps two versions of the same history, for example, the history of homosexuality, two versions of the same social construction, that do not necessarily correspond except in their surface phenomena. Take, for example, the tentative, neutral, dispassionate, scientific description of pederasty, the love of boys, that comes to the fore in the second and third volumes of *L'Histoire de la sexualité*. Now in part, Foucault needs to deal with what amounts to one of the great taboos of the contemporary Western world. And at least implicitly, the movement from exteriority to interiority brings about the complete repression of the possibility of the love for boys. Yet if Foucault's model and epistemological system are correct, the so-called repression of the love of boys, the construction of a taboo, is not part of a repression *per se* but is actually a means of channeling that same structure of desire. Hence Foucault's discussion of the love of boys must proceed delicately in order not to seem to be shaking the foundations of the taboo.

I would hypothesize that the fundamental ambiguity at the heart of Foucault's work relates to this sexual question. And we must ask ourselves how that ambiguity plays itself out. Does, for example, the fact that Foucault is gay have import for how we read his writing? Some would say that it has everything to do with it. On the other hand, some would say that while perhaps it is anecdotally interesting, Foucault's homosexuality in and of itself does not have much of an influence. Foucault's position could be described as being the absence of heterosexuality, it could be explained as being different from heterosexuality. But it could also be articulated as that from which a heterosexual position is different. A slight rhetorical move perhaps, but an important one. It matters what is defined first. The question is not "What matter who's talking?" but "What matter who talks first?" More precisely, if homosexuality is never defined as secondary to heterosexuality, then our perspective on the whole matter changes considerably.

In his biography of Foucault, Didier Eribon seems to consider implicitly or explicitly that the world of the reader is defined as being heterosexual, or at least that heterosexuality is the benchmark by which we read. As late as 1989, Eribon is hedging his bet by saying that he envisages a general public for whom there is a "scandal still constituted today by the evocation of homosexuality" (12). Eribon conceives of two possible sets of readers, those who might feel that he has said too much about the subject of homosexuality and those who regret "the absence of details or picturesque descriptions, on American life, for example" (12). He allows that he is more sympathetic to the latter, but that he does not want to shock the former. And it is this so-called American life, with its implicit freedom, abandon, and even danger, that Eribon evokes at the end of the book as well: "Foucault's American happiness: the reconciliation with himself finally realized. He is happy in his work. He is happy in the pleasures of the body. . . . But it is precisely there that the new plague was beginning to spread out its odious ravages" (338).

It is not at all "American life" on which the details are lacking, but rather "Foucault's gay life." Understandably so, from a legal point of view, for going much beyond the simple statement of fact could possibly have led to a libel suit against Eribon in France, since it would seem that it is in fact defamatory to go into detail about an individual's homosexuality. Though not subject to the same libel laws, Miller announces the same lack of information: "What exactly Foucault did in San Francisco in the fall of 1983—and why—may never be known" (29). We shall return to the dangerous implications of this black box of nonknowledge below.

Eribon's position is a safe one. He discusses Foucault's homosexuality from the point of view of the dispassionate, yet sympathetic reader who has adopted a view that sees the normative heterosexual position as the central one. Foucault's homosexuality must be understood as different from what is accepted by the dominant discourse, and when it is just one mode among others, it is not worth mentioning: "I decided to tell the facts, in their reality, when they had to be told to understand such and such an event, such and such an aspect of the career, work, thought, life—death—of Foucault. I passed over them silently when they concerned only the secret territory that each and every person arranges in his own existence" (12). So we could say that from the outset, Eribon's position seems unconsciously to mime the dualistic one that Foucault has set out for himself. On the one hand, there is a gay body, undeniably there, at the center of the crossroads. The effect of the subject produces the gay body because it is perceived as such, and swathes it in a set of discourses that define it as the gay body. On the other hand, there are times when, *from the point of view of the dominant discourse*, there is no need to mention the question of being gay, for it is restricted to a secret territory.

Where is this secret territory? Is it some recess of the mind safe from the dominant discourses that form the effect of the subject, that determine when and where something like a subject will come into place? One would think then that the secret territory is some area, some imprisoned area safe from and impervious to the discourses of dominance. Where does this territory speak? Does it have its own language? And yet, even that Foucauldian impossibility seems to pale in comparison to the more general question of universality: every one of us has such a territory. If this is a universal, not only is there a set of discrete idioms and praxes relating to that territory, but moreover that territory is part of a universal set. We are all sexual beings,

Eribon seems to be saying, regardless of the homo- or hetero- twist to the particular individual. Despite the secret yet universal nature of the territory, there is a name for it, and Eribon spells out the name of that territory in the very first pages: America. Yes, in fact, it is the description of the picturesque aspects of American life that is missing for Eribon, because America, for Foucault at least, is the fulfillment of the pleasure principle:

For Michel Foucault, the United States is the pleasure of work. But it is also just pleasure. He tastes the liberty that exists in New York or in San Francisco, with their homosexual neighborhoods, where there is a flowering of magazines and newspapers, bars, and nightclubs. . . . The gay community is uncountable, organized, and firmly decided to impose its rights. And also—this is not without importance—, the United States is a country where homosexuality is not marked by an age limit, by the severely defined criteria of youth. (336)

Thus one version of the story presents an idealized exteriorizing of an America where everything is possible, where there is a free play of sexual choices and sexual acts. It is an America that beckons, like a gay utopian paradise in which all acts somehow are possible, in which new games and new pleasures await. America is the pleasurable territory in which the body is not subjected to the arrest of discourse, where there is a flow of energies that is both a testament to an act of sexual liberation and a will to power. Certainly, as Lawrence Kritzman points out in the introduction to his collection *Politics, Philosophy, Culture*, commenting on Foucault's concept of homosexuality,

Gay sexuality is to be thought of as a dynamic mode in which the refusal of a more traditional lifestyle emanates from a sexual choice that transforms one's own mode of being; sexuality should be used to experiment, to invent new relations in which desire is problematized in a world of polymorphous perversions. For according to Foucault the ideology of sexual liberation is just another disciplinary technique for transforming sex into discourse and the homosexual into a species with a particular mode of life. (xxiii)

Homosexuality is and is not choice; is and is not a category into which one is thrust. The ideology of sexual liberation so necessary for the liberation to take place is just one more structure of discourses from which the individual never escapes, forced as he is then to be an "out" homosexual, constrained—Sartre would have said "condemned"—to his freedom. Just as there are two visions of the body in Foucault, an alternation between the subjected body and the absent body, there are two visions of homosexuality. One is the fruit of constraint, even if that constraint is named "liberation" and "understanding." The second vision is one of choice and option, freedom as opposed to liberation. The first vision depends on a heterocentric point of view, a sustained position that sees homosexual behavior as an acceptable (or not) variant of a dominant sexuality. Its main difference from heterosexuality—in fact, its unique difference from heterosexuality—is in the choice of the anatomy of the sexual partner. This is certainly the point of view that Eribon adopts for much of his book, because it is one that seems to reflect a certain strain in Foucault as an individual.

As a difference, as a variant, however, it is ultimately problematic, for the possibilities allowed it within the power grid of discourses limit it, constrain it far more than heterosexuality: there are far fewer acceptable modes of presentation, behavior, ostentation for the homosexual individual than for the heterosexual one. The homosexual individual has society against him or her: even if society allows him or her to practice his or her behavior, accepts it, the acceptance takes place from within the stronghold of heterosexism. It is an acceptance that the heterosexual never has to face for himself or herself, for he or she is that sexual object defined by society as identical to its dominant vision. When heterosexual discourse looks in, it sees a reflection of itself. For all others, at least for homosexuals, there is a crisis. The crisis has a name in current gender studies circles (in North America, that is): internalized homophobia. It used to be called "sensitivity." The gay individual internalizes the discourses of dominance and reacts to them, undergoing a crisis that the straight individual has no part of. So the gay adolescent or young adult, seeking his or her confirmation, is particularly susceptible to such a situation. Eribon mentions Foucault's homosexuality when he was at the Ecole Normale Supérieure: "And in fact, when he returns from his frequent nocturnal expeditions in cruising spots or homosexual bars, Foucault remains prostrate for hours, sick, annihilated by shame" (44). James Miller concurs. For him, the homosexual's life, often as not, is marked by a series of "self-destructive" behaviors that are symptoms of the internalized discourses of control that have entered the very being of the gay individual, who cannot see himself except as that figure constructed by straight discourse. Miller writes, for example, of Foucault and his lover that they "balanced their shared moments of Dionysian abandon through alcohol and sado-masochistic eroticism with their shared interest in unity and form" (90). Both Eribon's Foucault and Miller's Foucault are figures caught in a teleology of self-liberation. Miller's figure starts early: "Foucault as a young man made one small but telling gesture of revenge: in an act of self-assertion—and nominal self-mutilation—aimed directly at the bullying patriarch, Paul-Michel chopped off his *nom du père*, becoming simply 'Michel Foucault'" (63). As he goes through life, this Foucault, interested more and more in the discourses of power, seeks simultaneously to liberate himself from these constrictions and structures of power that imprison him behind a mask. For example, as Miller notes, in 1969, "He had changed his physical appearance as well: while living in Tunisia, he had Daniel Defert shave off all of his hair, which left him with a skull that gleamed like a spearhead. With his wire-rimmed glasses and smile of ivory and gold, he now looked faintly sadistic, like a bullying field marshal: for years, the *London Review of Books* would use his familiar image in advertisements ordering its readers to subscribe" (179).

So Miller's Foucault, involved in a process of self-liberation, exchanges one mask for another, seeks to find himself, to discover who he is through pushing the taboos and limits of the discourse that constrains him, by pushing back or crossing the barriers at the edge of experience. Miller remarks early on that he "was forced to ascribe to Foucault a persistent and purposeful self, inhabiting one and the same body throughout his mortal life, more or less consistently accounting for his actions and attitudes to others as well as to himself, and understanding his life as a teleologically structured quest (or, in French, *recherche*)" (7).

Eribon's second book about Foucault begins with a searing critique of Miller's approach, which is, after all is said and done, far more essentialist, far less sympathetic, and far more teleological than what Eribon himself proposes in the first biography. For Eribon, Miller takes the rumor of Foucault as the Typhoid Mary of AIDS and retrospectively builds a pathetic biography based on that fact.

Highly offended, Eribon pulls no punches: "As we have seen, James Miller's book is a novel, a disorderly [*échevelée*] fiction, a mythology of a negative hero, where one finds in spontaneous contact the American flavors for those great biographical frescoes founded on psychology, pathos, drama, sex, sound and fury" (69). David Macey has a well-researched, factual biography of Foucault that adds nothing to our understanding of the position of the sexual subject and sexual body in the latter's writings; it is like Miller without the more lurid aspects. Ultimately, as I discuss above, the positions of Miller and Eribon are not as far away from one another as they first appear, because of the complicated role of sexuality that neither seems willing to take at *Foucault's* word.

The second vision of homosexuality, one that involves choice, appears in the various interviews Foucault gave relating to homosexuality. In a sense, it also is the other face of Miller's view of Foucault: a Foucault who seeks to enact his own self, who wants *zu sich selbst kommen*, a Foucault who recognizes his difference and seeks to bring that difference to life and to light. It is that same Foucault with a purpose, but the focus is changed: it is not a movement of self-liberation, but one of self-actualization, what Ed Cohen, in his article "Foucauldian Necrologies," calls both a space of possibility and of creativity (91). As Kritzman states in his introduction to his volume of Foucault interviews, "Through his many articles and interviews Foucault supported, although never quite militantly, the imperatives of the gay movement which, like other experiences such as drugs and communes, situated the individual on the threshold of other forms of consciousness and inscribed him in the 'culture of the self'" (xxii). The key word is "other."

How so? The two visions of Foucault's concept of homosexuality seem to fall under the same general category of gay liberation. But there is a difference, I think, in emphasis, and in consequence. In the first, there is a process of liberation, of crossing of boundaries, and, ultimately, as we shall see below, the implicit idea of reaching limits and crossing them. In the second, the emphasis is elsewhere, on a distinct otherness, whose limits are not at all the same as the ones imposed on "sexuality" from the point of view or the position of dominant, normalized, vanilla sexuality. As we shall see, in the second view, sadomasochistic behavior is not at all a limit or an extreme.

In the interviews given to various journalists and other writers during the last decade of his life, Foucault provocatively formulates the concept of a distinct gay subject. In "Friendship as a Way of Life," Foucault discusses homosexuality with an interviewer for *Gai Pied*. Foucault says: "The problem is not to discover in oneself the truth of sex but rather to use sexuality henceforth to arrive at a multiplicity of relationships. And no doubt that's the real reason why homosexuality is not a form of desire but something desirable. Therefore we have to work at becoming homosexuals and not be obstinate in recognizing that we are. The development towards which the problem of homosexuality tends is the one of friendship" (*Live* 204).

So the two imperatives, the two views of homosexuality are simultaneously there. As something desirable, homosexuality is a goal, an object to be attained; as something that "we are," it is not homosexuality that is the goal as such, but the removal of obstinacy, the negation of all the impositions on the subject, all the constraints that are placed on him or her. It is understandable that the two views are linked, for there is no utopia, or seems to be no utopia, except the envisioned America as pleasure-palace, where the two worlds do not collide. Yet in order to understand homosexuality as such, Foucault insists that we think from within it, and not merely as we approach it. It is at that point that the separateness of homosexuality comes through, the multiplicity of difference and the multiplicity of different desires that are unmarked by the imposition of heterosexual models and values. As he notes in the same interview on friendship: "What we must work on, it seems to me, is not so much to liberate our desires but to make ourselves infinitely more susceptible to pleasure. We must escape and help others escape the two ready-made formulas of the pure sexual encounter and the lovers' fusion of identities" (*Live* 206).

For Foucault, the problem of homosexuality is not the sexual act itself, but the possibility that this sexual act is not a self-contained unit, but something with a consequence: the result being the formation of lines of order, power, and communication distinct from those of society at large:

One of the concessions one makes to others is not to present homosexuality as a kind of immediate pleasure, of two young men meeting in the street, seducing each other with a look, grabbing each other's asses and getting each other off in a quarter of an hour. There you have a kind of neat image of homosexuality without any possibility of generating unease, and for two reasons: it responds to the reassuring canon of beauty and it annuls everything that can be uncomfortable in affection, tenderness, friendship, fidelity, camaraderie and companionship, things which our rather sanitized society can't allow a place for without fearing the formation of new alliances and the tying together of unforeseen lines of force. I think that's what makes homosexuality "disturbing": the homosexual mode of life much more than the sexual act itself. (*Live* 205)

The consequences of this homosexual mode of life are clear: if the sexual act is not only an isolated, immediate act (though, of course, it can be), but some action with consequences for power, organization, and discourses, it stands to reason that even that sexual act, when found in a new set of contexts—that of the "homosexual mode of life"—means something else. In the vulgar sense, the sexual organs and orifices that heterosexual discourses define as those of homosexual intercourse are not the same as those defined by a homosexual power structure. From a Foucauldian point of view, contextual here as elsewhere, the penis and *a fortiori*, the anus, defined by homosexual discourse as the organs of its sexual acts, take on new values and new constraints. For Foucault, this difference already makes the penis and the anus "other." They are not the same sexual organs as they once were, just as, for example, the mad are not the same as they once were, or the sick, or the condemned, and so forth.

It is clear that it is a short step from this position of homosexual sex to Foucault's concept of sadomasochism. Obviously, Foucault's idea of s/m is wholly distinct from some pathology of sexuality. If there is an inspiration it is perhaps literary, but in the most banal sense: the idea of s/m is its multiplicity and the control of that multiplicity by the sadistic self. Asked about his interest in Sade in an interview conducted in 1973 entitled "An Historian of Culture," Foucault says, "It is evident that if I want to make love (or rather, when I want to make love) I do not resort to Sade's prescribed methods, to his combinations; not so much because I wouldn't like to try, but because I've never had the opportunity" (*Live* 82).

The sadistic self meeting the sense of homosexuality that Foucault sees in the freedom, as opposed once again to the act of liberation, of some imaginary, finds the extension of gay sexuality to some multiplicity the most natural consequence:

> S & M is not a relationship between the one who suffers and the one who inflicts suffering, but between the master and the one on whom he exercises his mastery. What interests the practitioners of S & M is that the relationship is at the same time regulated and open. . . . This mixture of rules and openness has the effect of intensifying sexual relations by introducing a perpetual novelty, a perpetual tension and a perpetual uncertainty which the simple consummation of the act lacks. The idea is also to make use of every part of the body as a sexual instrument. ("Sexual Choice" 20)

For Foucault then, s/m, sadomasochism, is misnamed. It is a question of two or more sadistic subjects, two individuals who both control a sexual situation. It is as far as possible from the game of dominance and submission traditionally associated with heterosexual intercourse. For Foucault, again in the vulgar sense, to take it up the ass is as sadistic a sexual action as any other. Perhaps it is the most sadistic, for symbolically it is the enclosure of the organ of power, the capturing of the phallic penis, the imprisonment of the violent within a larger, controlled violence, yet with no will to reproduce the self in the realm of the imaginary, as in heterosexual coitus.

If we turn then to Miller's vision of Foucault's s/m sexuality, and his patient explanation of that behavior, we wonder at the limited vision that this explanation implies. It is perhaps the best illustration of what David Halperin calls "this instance of heterosexual pathology, The Passion of James Miller" (178).[6] Miller explains in great detail, for example, the details of s/m behavior. Miller gives the list of s/m techniques, as he finds the catch-all "etc." of Larry Townshend's book The Leatherman's Handbook, "the most widely read gay s/m manual," woefully inadequate: "gagging, piercing, cutting, hanging, electric-shocking, stretching on racks, imprisoning, branding, blindfolding, mummifying, pissing on, shitting on, shaving, burning, crucifying, suspending, clamping, suffocating, fist-fucking" (264–65). Following Geoff Mains in Urban Aboriginals, Miller explains each activity in detail and adds that s/m is not necessarily a sexual activity whose ultimate goal is orgasm (265–67).

But is this Foucault's s/m sexuality? Is it Foucault's sadism? I think not. To detail these activities is to give in too easily to a nomothetically defined sexuality that accepts the definitions of sexual behavior offered by dominant heterosexual discourse, to see homosexuality perhaps as an acceptable variant, but to see s/m as an extreme. No, I think for Foucault, s/m, at least as it appears to function for him as an eroticizing of the entire body, is the most normal sexuality imaginable. For it is only in a world that puts logical and discursive chains on a discourse that sex becomes focused on a discrete set of genitalia, some of which are acceptable for use when coupled with others, some of which are not. But why do I say discourse? Because, in the world wherein we all live, in which murder is ostensibly still prohibited, s/m has to be discourse: it cannot go to the logical conclusion that Sade implies in his writing of sacrificing a person for *jouissance*, of making a corpse from a *corps*.

Sade makes (it with) a dead body. Could Foucault, the voices ask, have gone as far? It is tempting to fall into an easily laid trap and think that the extreme sexuality that s/m represents to the "normal" lay reader means a complete violation of ethical norms, of the human condition, of the social contract. Violation of one set of norms means perhaps that others were violated. Listen to Miller's repetition of the innuendoes. Miller's postscript deals with the rumor that Foucault, in full knowledge of his being sick with AIDS "had gone to gay bathhouses in America, and deliberately tried to infect other people with the disease" (375). He continues, for the explanation seems to make some sense to him: "I was immediately struck by the fact that the stories were leading me to pay attention to aspects of Foucault's style and historical argument that I had previously ignored" (376). And then a final hint, rhetorically put: "I now had to wonder whether the rumor that had gotten me started was closer to the truth than I had come to think possible" (381). Yet it concludes that this was not humanly possible. Foucault could not have knowingly done this, not because of some philosophical truth about Foucault, but because Foucault just was not sure if he had AIDS: "Everything that I had learned, from Defert and others, persuaded me that it was highly unlikely that Foucault would (as the rumor depicted him) go around deliberately trying to infect—and hence, in effect, murder—innocent people. Evidently he had been uncertain, perhaps to the day he died, whether or not he actually had AIDS" (381).

Such a comment, such an exculpation, begs the question. Before

Miller, Eribon also put Foucault's knowledge of his own illness into question, only to come down on the side of knowledge: "Foucault knew. And did not want to know: in his diary, in November, 1983, he noted, according to Paul Veyne, who was able to read it after Foucault's death: 'I know I have AIDS, but my hysteria permits me to forget it'" (348). For Eribon, then, going on secondhand evidence, Foucault knew he had AIDS; writing later, Miller is not so sure. So Miller ultimately clears Foucault because the latter may not have known if he had AIDS. Thus, Foucault could have continued to have the same sexual encounters as he had previously had, and though sick, he was ignorant of that fact: he thus could not have knowingly infected someone else.

All that is well and good. But what if Eribon is right? What if Foucault knew he had AIDS? Did he then go around and "murder innocent people"? Inconceivable, hard to envisage even for a moment, unless of course we fall into the same old trap of thinking his sexuality as an extreme. Yes, he discovered this s/m sexuality over a period of time when he was a mature adult. But no, this s/m sexuality does not imply a breaking of all the rules. In fact, as I have said, for Foucault, this s/m sexuality ultimately occurs in discourses and etiquette (rules of behavior). It is not translated into a simplistic game of power whereby the sadist has life-or-death control over the imprisoned masochistic other. No, for Foucault it is a game for two sadists to play; to cheapen it by turning it into a game wherein one controls the true destiny of the other would be to repeat the unfortunate structures of power that Foucault had long sought to combat. To think that Foucault, like some child lashing out, willingly brought others down with him, is to forget Foucault's lessons, Foucault's thought, Foucault's beliefs from one end of his writing to another. Foucault may very well have been the "postmodernist sphinx" that Miller (320) believes him to be, but he was a sphinx always already faced with Oedipus, two sadists caught in a dance and game played among friends: "Homosexuality is an historic occasion to re-open affective and relational virtualities, not so much through the intrinsic qualities of the homosexual, but due to the biases against the position he occupies; in a certain sense diagonal lines that he can trace in the social fabric permit him to make these virtualities visible" (*Live* 207).

Of course, as Miller says, one can never say for sure. But I would add: "of the man Foucault." Of the philosopher, I think that we can be certain that he did not willingly kill the object he loved.

The great touchstone in writing about AIDS is a set of narratives by the late French author Hervé Guibert, whose renown in this matter came with the book *A l'ami qui ne m'a pas sauvé la vie*, and was followed, most notably, by *Le Protocole compassionnel*, and the poignant short narrative *Cytomégalovirus*. As I have dealt with these extensively in *Alcibiades at the Door*, I shall not spend much time here with Guibert's AIDS-related works. His work seems to resume some of the themes that are found elsewhere, and the decrepitude and physical impotence, the psychological scarring and changing interpersonal relations he describes, are often echoed elsewhere. But other writers have other things to say and we need to read the rewriting of bodies in their work as well. Indeed someone like Cyril Collard, the other media darling, though this time the bad boy *par excellence* of the world of French literary AIDS, seems slightly hurt to be put in the same category as Guibert. Comparing himself to Guibert after having read an article that links the two of them, Collard says: "Our paths and our actions are completely opposed: Guibert is on the side of death and I am on the side of life, without that being a value judgement on my part. He tells of a forced march toward death, and me, the difficult life of someone who changes nothing when he learns he is HIV+" (*Ange* 192).

Both in the world at large, and in literature, the person with AIDS or the protagonist in the universal story and individual stories of the disease, more often than not, is gay, a protagonist given various roles of subject, that is, victim; agent, that is, Typhoid Mary; and object, that is, medical patient. Yet it is not true that he has become the disease and that the disease has become him. It is not my concern *here* to dissociate the gay man from the disease or the disease from him: AIDS affects everyone, period. No, I am trying to describe what may now or still be the gay body despite AIDS and/or faced with AIDS. Indeed, one might convincingly state that AIDS is the war of the individual to remain himself in spite of the disease. In his narrative about his own struggle with AIDS, Alain Dreuilhe makes such a point. Dreuilhe's essay on his AIDS develops a poetics based on an extended metaphor between war and the battle of his body: his writing is filled with military metaphors, with analogies to great battles and strategies, and this starts from the very first, his title, *Corps à corps*, which recalls "body to body [or hand-to-hand] combat." And caught in a Hobbesian vision of the world, Gilles Barbedette sees the war as generalized and goes so far as to call himself and Daniel Defert "war widows" (110).[7]

Here I am trying to see what gay writing of that body might be under these wartime conditions. Where desire and discourse once enjoyed free play in which they unmistakably, clearsightedly, and penetratingly aimed at and reached their targets, there are now barriers, blindnesses, precautions, aversions, and diversions. The adjectives and adverbs modifying the transparent fulfillment of desire have given way to nouns, impediments, and solidities; in any case, the transparent has disappeared. One cannot look, and if one looks, one does not see through to the target that is already known, conquered, and internalized. For Yves Navarre, a Frenchman writing in Canada, AIDS has rewritten the body and its representation in writing:

If I then shave myself, with the privilege of standing in front of the sink, I cut myself because I no longer dare to look at myself. I am covered with shaving cuts [*Je suis tailladé*]. I tremble even while writing. These lines are like my cheeks, my chin, my neck, the blood pearling here and there. The press clippings [*coupures*] that Rachel gathered as so many signs as well. (99–100)

When one looks, one sees someone else, one sees the signs of illness and death. As the Belgian Pascal de Duve writes in *L'Orage de vivre*, "Have the Promethean ambition to be an example. You will see that the mirror will become more beautiful each day even if it is spotted with purplish stigmata or the black patches of Kaposi's sarcoma" (163).[8]

AIDS has figured a martyrdom, the death of a thousand cuts, a slow death of a Saint Sebastian for a new age. AIDS rewrites the literary work, rewrites desire, or sends it packing. In place of the flows of desire and the *loquèle* of textuality, a veritable litany of conquests, is the body, slowly ebbing away, as its reintroduced solidity fades. The body reappears where there was the skin, the surface of desire. Now the body is undeniably there, sick and visible; the body is reintroduced only to fade away in a gradual unreading, a slow or rapid

flow toward death: "AIDS equals death. In three months or in two
years, by rotting, smothering, asphyxiation, melting away, any way
possible, but always without a hope, without a reprieve" (Fernandez
175).

It is perhaps only a coincidence that two of the writers here, Guy
Hocquenghem and Hervé Guibert, both now dead of AIDS, wrote
books on blindness. But with the appearance of the gay body in all its
solidity, tenuously constituted now between the transparent skin of
yesterday and the dissolution of tomorrow, blindness is no longer a
free choice. And still, as Duvert points out, blindness can mean invisibility (26). One can be willfully blind and not see the gay body.
One can look away, pretend that the disease and the body are not
there. Motivated by a detour in vision, the body as object undergoes
a transformation. First of all, it is no longer the transparent skin, the
continuity of flow and pleasure. The knowledge necessarily knows
and/or shows the detour from a body and not from a flow. Now
more than ever, the body is the fragmentary series of palpable body
parts dissociated from a whole that one pretends does not exist. Camus writes of an American, whose look "did not come from an exaggerated uneasiness about the scourge, in any case, for if he didn't
mind me fucking him, on the contrary, he didn't want me to put on
a rubber" (*Vigiles* 262).

Willful blindness also means the destruction of reciprocity in the
subject-object relation. The other is different from me; yet I deny his
difference in turning away from it. There is no direct flow of vision
and desire to the accomplishment of desire through the repetition of
a discourse defined *grosso modo* as the language of the clone zone. No,
the body in front of me cannot be seen as a body. I must retain my
will to the other's invisibility at all costs. One knows, though, that after the mid-eighties this turning away, this refusal to see the body, itself changes into something belated. For the turn comes after having
seen the body. So it is equally clear that in turning away or *in not
turning away*, the subject recognizes that the other is potentially different and that the body of the other is not undeniably there.

And certainly once there is the sign of disease, there is often the
will not to see in order to pretend that AIDS does not exist. Notable,
of course, are the various reactions of the press, that now seem
shameful and have entered the literature in that way. Fernandez

notes, with irony, that *"Libération,* the champion of virtue, raised its voice against the rumor that Michel Foucault died of AIDS" (144–45); he goes on to lambast the now defunct gay weekly *Gai Pied,* which also started out denying "the seriousness of AIDS" (145). Of course, in retrospect, it can be said that at the time of Foucault's death, little was really known about AIDS, and it is perhaps somewhat unfair to criticize *Libération,* even despite its strange coverage of the death of Michel Foucault. At the edge of the discursive praxis I am examining, Michel Tremblay's *Le Coeur découvert* is the story of two men, the older Jean-Marc and the younger Mathieu. Early on, Jean-Marc peremptorily speaks of his will to blindness: "I'm also deathly afraid of AIDS, but I've decided to think about it as little as possible" (24).

One can avert one's eyes, a turn that Hervé Guibert, in one of his last works, seems to make into an allegory. In a series of AIDS narratives that I have discussed at length in *Alcibiades at the Door,* Guibert faced, as squarely as possible, the problem of an AIDS-ravaged body, his own in this case, or at least that of his rhetorical narrator, virtually indistinguishable from the author. Yet one late work, *Mon valet et moi,* is not the story of a young man dying of AIDS, but of an old, feeble man merely fading away. And whereas one could not talk of Freudian denial where Guibert is concerned, one could certainly see this work as the narrative about denial. The character is not gay: "They say that homosexuals are attracted by uniforms, those of sailors, firemen, legionnaires. I'm not homosexual [*qui n'en suis pas*], I have always been fascinated, almost erotically, by the outfits of flunkies of all sorts [*larbins de tout poil*]" (21–22). He has never dressed in drag: "The only thing that has value nowadays is compromising photos, taken in one's youth, hidden away in strong-boxes. Photos where one is dressed as a woman, if you see what I mean. Now, not at all, I answered, such photos don't exist in my past" (32). He participates in the narcissism of subject-object identification and even sees himself as a woman: "I can no longer figure out if he is on the left or me on the right, as if we were only one person duplicated. Sometimes I discover us in the mirror transformed into women. Quite a comical [*cocasse*] picture" (59–60). He wants to have his temperature taken rectally, which is obviously neither here nor there but seems of a piece with the rest of the remarks: "My valet always wants to stick the thermometer under my arm, though I want it in the hole like in the good old days" (50). He refers to the dimensions of his valet's genitals, a taboo in straight fiction, except, I believe, in self-referential first-person and often erotic or pornographic narrative: "I discovered he had a big penis, much bigger than mine was when I was young" (85). And he even accepts water sports: "He pissed on me to teach me to shut up, he said" (84). The symptoms are the same in this narrative that is "not about AIDS": "He never looks at my emaciated body, it is as if I didn't have one" (48). For now, I would just say that this is, in many ways, a metanarrative about the turning away from the reality of AIDS, an allegory about denial. I shall return later to this figure of nonhomosexuality.

If we look directly at the gay body now in the age of AIDS, what we see first, in this skin made flesh, is the decomposition of the body. Inside and outside are laid bare, but it is always the signs of decomposition that we see rather than a silent dilapidation of the body: "faces half blue with Kaposi, skeleton-like thinness, endless herpes, swollen lymph nodes" (Hocquenghem, *Eve* 232). The scene is the same in almost every narrative, with the obligatory description of the visible sign of the disease: "He had slipped off the sleeve of his pajamas and showed a purple flow that started at the top of his shoulder and ran down to his elbow, as if a monstrous eggplant had flowered on his flesh" (Fernandez 189). On the other hand, when the signs are not visible, even if the person is known to have AIDS, it is again as if AIDS itself were not there:

I was glad to see and say hello to Jean-Paul Aron who was having lunch yesterday at La Coupole. He seemed to look the same as usual and had none of the cadaver-like appearance given him by the photographs and even the comments of the *Nouvel Observateur* last month, when he made his famous public declaration of having AIDS. (Camus *Aguets* 38)

One could hardly accuse Renaud Camus of willful blindness or self-delusion, though one could say that the wishful thinking is what Camus himself calls a hope: "He had been infected for several years. But he represented a sort of medical miracle, and, of course, a hope: he had no symptoms of the illness, and up until a few months ago felt completely chipper" (*Vigiles* 233). Nor could one level such an accusation at Hervé Guibert. Camus and Guibert, each in his own way, have been at the forefront of the "normalization" or dedramatization of being gay. And whereas Camus has not published much on AIDS, Guibert faced the problem squarely in *A l'ami qui ne m'a pas sauvé la vie, Le Protocole compassionnel,* and *Cytomégalovirus.* So it becomes necessary to look further: I would hypothesize that the construction of the gay body is such that it is perceived necessarily with its signs affixed. Before and during the age of AIDS, the gay body is a hybrid of body and sign, the homographesis discussed by Lee Edelman (5–10), who considers the homosexual body the site of writing and the same body as the object of desire I have discussed in reference to Barthes in Morocco (*Alcibiades* 139ff). Before AIDS, if there is no perceptible sign one cannot see that it is a gay body: it is only a homosexual body, indistinguishable from a heterosexual one. With AIDS, if there is no perceptible sign, one cannot see the disease. If one cannot see it, read it, and thereby seize it, its invisibility remains its most constant and insidious feature. Unreadable and unsigned, AIDS is the phantom object that seems a product of rightist xenophobia, incipient paranoia, or both: "Besides, given such promiscuity with faceless, anonymous, unknown people, you could get any illness, in particular the one whose importance was exaggerated by the rightist press, but which appeared even more dangerous because the way in which it was transmitted was still unknown" (Fernandez 64).

Thus the gay body, no sooner constituted as such, as an object for the gay observer (subject, reader of signs) soon metamorphoses into something unimagined for it as it came into being. Whereas one might have thought that the gay body would eventually become an object among other objects, especially in a postmodern consumer society, chosen or unchosen by the masses, but certainly not invisible to them, it has become equated with its incipient disappearance. In the general imagination, the gay body equals the AIDS-infected body. For the gay subject, this means the realization of the dissipation of the flesh; for the nongay reader, the fearful heterosexual, this means the specter of the pariah himself, Typhoid Mary for a new generation: "in the butcher's mind, homosexual has become the synonym of infected by AIDS" (Fernandez 142).

Given the readability of the sign, the full-fledged presence of visible AIDS, the danger for most, save the most paranoid, seems to have passed. If one has tested positive, and—must one say it?—one continues to participate in the social contract, one takes precautions to prevent another from getting AIDS. If one is visibly sick, say with Kaposi's sarcoma, the sign is there for all to read. Sick, the gay body fully signed anew, though with a series of signs of death, has once again become its surface. Two series of signs are generated at this point to fill out the various works: one series relates to the gradual dissipation of the body, as the gay body shrinks like some latter-day *peau de chagrin*. This series is itself actually double, consisting on the one hand of a series of symptoms, most often visible or readable signs of the disease, and on the other of a gradual perceptible decline of the body, a recognition of decrepitude. The second series consists of the various medical attachments and procedures appended to the body. If the first consists of two sets of signs that signify subtraction, the second consists of augmentations. The body is transformed.

When underlining the general dissipation of the sick body, classical narratives of illness tended to use the symptom as a sign of an order of discourse other than medical (Sontag, *Illness*). To wit: a narrative of tuberculosis in the nineteenth century or even cancer in the twentieth underlined symptoms to talk about morals, ethics, repressed passions, or existential isolation. In works like Mann's *The Magic Mountain* and Dumas's *The Lady of the Camellias*, the afflicted character undergoes moral change, ethical reflection, or participates in a system that relates the dissipation of an individual to his or her social/societal function. Contemporary fiction about cancer changes the scenario somewhat in its description of the sick body by augmenting the figures of illness with an overlay of medical science. The radical otherness of cancer discussed by Sontag is figured in the list of symptoms, which may serve to show the distance of the individual from the cold, alienating establishment of knowledge and/or be a metonymy for the inexpressible ravaging of the subject.[9]

Certainly AIDS literature shares with cancer literature the attempt to express the pain of the subject through a list of symptoms and signs concerning the body-as-object. Yet in the literature of AIDS the litany of symptoms serves in a different capacity as well. Symptoms are listed to test the reader's mettle, to force the reader to view what he or she would not willingly see. And the litany of symptoms, in its evident mastery of the language of medicine, pushes the limits of the literary. Specifically, the very idea of a list of symptoms and signs or interventions, such as in Hocquenghem, who in *Eve* provides both a list of daily medical interventions (269–70) and a list of occasional procedures (274), seems to test the limits, not of the representable, but of the interesting; along the same line, Christophe Bourdin devotes well over a page to discussing how the AIDS-infected character studies his shit (48–49). If we continue to read, we must look and we see the gay body anew. Under these conditions, we are being asked to suspend our aesthetic interest in favor of another pleasure of the text. Who, one would ask quite crudely, wants to read a litany about intubation and resuscitation, about biopsies and excisions, about pharmacopoeias and etiologies, about spinal taps and EEG's, about intravenous drips and endless needles? In his first AIDS narrative, Guibert provides a mix of drugs and symptoms, as if the very integrity of the body were now always threatened by a double discourse:

I had various secondary diseases that Dr. Chandi had treated, often over the phone, one after another: patches of eczema on my shoulders, treated with a 0.1% Locoïd cortisone cream, diarrhea treated with Ercéfuryl 200, one pill every four hours for three days, a doubtful stye treated with Dacrin eye-wash and an Aureomycin cream. (*Ami* 167)

The very idea of such a list being a literary object or even an element of an ongoing narrative seems to reach right into our received ideas of normative textuality. It is not every subject that is able, or willing, to cooperate in being re-viewed. In such cases, the author paints an abject individual whose gesture is a hollow effort at rebellion: "A young man who could be Marc's age, his neck and arms stuck with tubes and needles, had the strength to turn his eyes toward them and glared at them" (Fernandez 182). But in general, if we are viewing the body once more, it seems that the gay body cannot resist the final dissolution of its subjective component into its objectivity. It has become its own corpse, offered up to the reader who witnesses that death. If only it were possible, the last act of this tattooed individual in the throes of death would be a final defiance of this all-penetrating, but hardly pleasing, gaze. Raphaël de Valentin's remark in Balzac's *La Peau de chagrin* about "delivering an undecipherable body to society" becomes Hocquenghem's speculative musing: "Perhaps I shall die of an unknown illness, scientifically intestate" (276). But as Lévy and Nouss (108) point out, that corpse is worthless: "The sacred nature of the body, moreover often lauded in homoeroticism, having been affected by the illness, the dead body no longer bears any value."

Pierced, repierced, and remarked, the gay body is given as the object that no one would willingly look at, but which is, endlessly, tragically fascinating in its dissipation. Less a body than a collection of signs that cohere through the discourse of the individual narrative and through the mutations of the protean disease itself, the body with AIDS itself takes the form of a narrative: so many signs, so many ways of reading the checkerboard pattern of the flesh. And to be sure, the AIDS narrative turns the body into the limit of the representable, in a turn in Western narrative that no one would have predicted. Still at the center of the narrative, the individual object, living and simultaneously dying, becomes almost a black hole defying representation as a whole, defying description. No moral system links the individual signs, no substance links what was once just the surface object of the narcissistic gaze.

Each individual symptom, too, even in its benign form, seems to test the possibility of a continuously linked textuality. So in Guibert's AIDS allegory, *Mon valet et moi*, it is a question of dissipation with each individual symptom that tends, on the one hand to insist on the corporeal, and on the other, to diminish that corporeality in its very announcement. Thus the protagonist says that "I've rediscovered the pleasure of incontinence" (70) and is expecting that soon "it will be my diarrhea, even warmer than urine" (71). He notes, almost with pleasure, that "I farted more and more at parties" (10) and that, in short, he has become so emaciated, there is "nothing left" (16). The body appears, where once there had been nothing more than the folds of skin forming the illusion of the law of the phallus, or its various invaginations of buttocks, anus, pectorals, and so on. But once there, that body immediately begins to melt. Fernandez notes: "His cheeks, which must once have been full, had fallen, and hung in flabby wrinkles beneath his eyes ringed in gray pouches" (188). And Hocquenghem shows the very image of a confused subject and object melting in the mirror:

One day I saw myself, naked from the waist up in the mirror as I got up. You'd think it was a concentration camp photo. My ribs stick out under the skin as if they were going to puncture it. My arms are matchsticks, my legs have melted away. I have no buttocks left. And I'm covered with bed sores from living lying down. And, especially, I have the fearful look of a hunted animal on its last legs. (*Eve* 266)

Compare Guibert's description in *Le Protocole compassionnel*:

This confrontation every morning with my nudity in the mirror was a fundamental experience, renewed each day, I cannot say that the perspective it offered helped me get out of bed. Nor can I say that I had pity for this guy, it depended on the day; sometimes I have the impression that he'll make it out alive since people returned from Auschwitz; other times, it is clear that he is condemned, ineluctably heading toward his grave. (15)

The mirror as the locus of alienation is a frequent motif in these narratives, almost a shorthand way of describing the differences between a struggling internal subjectivity and the abject body in view. See Hocquenghem (43–45) or Navarre, where the narrator serves as a mirror into which one cannot look: "The most difficult thing is to shave David in the morning without cutting him" (99).

In the age of AIDS, the gay body cannot maintain the liberty of its subjectivity. And as such, the very objectivity of the body examined changes: the specific nature of the gay body as object was predicated on the reciprocity of the subject-object relation. Now, though, the object is forced three times to be a nonreciprocal object: forced to be a collection of symptoms, treatments, and tubes for the reader; forced to be the object of a nonreciprocal other within a literary narrative; and forced finally to be the object of the vision of the medical profession. Once under control, the medical gaze is as multiple as the procedures, as diverse as the symptoms. For each, there is a fractional glance, the attempt to codify a profusion of signs that can be looked at but never fully seen. Of an EEG, Hocquenghem writes that it was a "spider-like network of sine-waves, the map of my mind is for specialists only" (280). Guibert's version of the map in *A l'ami* is quite comparable: "I have never suffered as little as when I learned that I had AIDS; I am very attentive to the manifestations of the virus's progress; I seem to know the cartography of its colonizations, its assaults, and its retreats, I think I know where it waits and where it attacks, I feel the zones as yet untouched, but this struggle within me, quite real organically, as the scientific analyses show, is for now nothing, wait a while good fellow, given the certainly fictive ailments that assail me" (45). The medical glance, ironically enough, comes to stand in the locus of the original observer, the one involved in a reciprocal relationship with the object. The medical gaze is not the negation of the homoerotic glance. It is as if in reverse, through a mirror, through the wrong end of the telescope, the photographic negative of a former objectivity. Once the gay body was all skin formed into illusions of the ideal phallus and its incarnations. Now, subject to the medical gaze, the gay body is all symptoms and insides: "It's a scopic madness: endoscopy, sigmoidoscopy, rectoscopy, I'll skip the details. You think you've become a thing, a model [*mannequin*], a toy that is opened up and whose insides spring out at the investigator from such explorations" (Hocquenghem, *Eve* 275). The flesh that once was invisible, if not to say phenomenologically nonexistent, has now been brought to the surface, new sex organs for the scopophilic glance that fulfills the most abject of relations for the body. And finally, the scopophilia is a necrophilia of sorts, as the doctor, or the medical gaze, sees the person who used to be gay, the person who used to have a gay body. Or as Hocquenghem dramatically puts it in the same novel, "one to whom love is no longer made [*celui à qui on ne fait plus l'amour*]" (139).

What of sex, what of the sex organs, what of the mythical partial object: the condom? Again, if we consider the gay body as the generalized object of investigation, broader than any division into passive and active, any *a priori* separation of bodies into seronegative and seropositive individuals, we can logically imagine three kinds of sex with another individual: unsafe sex, safe sex, and no sex. The first two terms are obviously open to interpretations outside the scope of this book: on the one hand, the term "unsafe sex," or a somewhat nicer if equally inaccurate version, "unprotected sex," is just old-fashioned sex. It is sex before AIDS, sex that does not take AIDS into account as a watershed; it is therefore, at least in the minds of many, the cause as well as the mode of transmission of the disease. It is the version of sex found to be "morally repugnant" to some, as Leo Bersani notes in his article "Is the Rectum a Grave?" (214–25).[10] On the other hand, there is safe sex, protected sex, safer sex, *sexe sans risques*. And there is, of course, the only *truly* safe sex: chastity, abstinence, no sex at all. Thus, through an introduction of the concept of chastity in the gay world, sex becomes one possible behavior among others. Where sex was heretofore an activity in a set with no other members, it now becomes part of a generalized pattern of behavior. Is this a renormalization of sex or a simultaneous removal of its specificity and its purported dangers? As Fernandez remarks:

Among those directly threatened by the epidemic, in the "at risk" categories of the population, I foresee an infinite variety of reactions. Some will give up all sexual activity, some will become maniacal about precautions, some will change nothing of their habits, out of fatalistic resignation or selfish threat, some will light a candle in church, some will send their checks to the Institut Pasteur to hasten the discovery of the vaccine, some will think that the danger is only for others, some will seek it out willfully, some will play Russian roulette and others will act like mystics running toward immolation. (160)

The generalized body of the gay individual of indeterminate retrovirus status is visualized as composed of potentially dangerous parts mixed with innocuous parts. If we return to the model of the gay body as a surface phenomenon versus the body itself as a permeable solid, we see that in some parts of the physique the skin remains skin, in others it seems to have a "secret architecture." Take, as a case in point, Tremblay's novel, in which AIDS barely makes an appearance. In fact, the only sustained discussion occurs in conjunction with the mention of the male body as such. Jean-Marc is speaking about his ex-boyfriend Luc, who turns heads: "when he leaves a subway car . . . erections are rather badly hidden" (245). Compare Guibert's remark in *A l'ami*: "I attacked his nipples anew, and rapidly, mechanically, he kneeled before me, his hands imaginarily tied behind his back, to rub his lips against my fly, begging me in his tremblings and groans, to give him my body again, to free him from the pain I was imposing on him. To write that today, so far from him, gives me an erection in an organ that has been inactive and inert for weeks" (156). Erections now occur only in the safe absence of the other. The presence of the male body, its undeniability, is really the only occasion for an integration of AIDS into the work. The subjectivity of the anonymous passengers is somehow challenged, for if they let their bodies appear, they may in fact become prey to this mysterious illness that will make them abject cases as well.

The penis, votive lingam of gay liberation, becomes the tool, organ, weapon of potential death. Bersani asks, "Is the rectum a grave?"; we must ask as well, "Is the penis a weapon?" Certainly this is the case for the radical feminism on which Bersani focuses, but what of the gay body? I do not think the reorganization of material in the new semiotics of gay sex return the penis to its traditional, heterosexist role of penis-as-sword. But quite frankly, it is difficult to tell. Always a phantom member of the language of the body, the penis well-nigh disappears in post-AIDS gay writing. In attesting this disappearance one notes that the penis, deprived of its sexual function, can simply become one organ among others, one bodily part among others, all of which are undergoing the same gradual decrepitude (*Valet* 48; 85). And at the very least, the penis loses its phallic power and thus its potential to kill another: as Michel Manière bluntly writes: "I no longer get hard-ons" (23).

Renaud Camus offers, I think, the clearest overview of this phenomenon. Now, obviously, his writing is not focused on AIDS, whereas the novels in question, with the exception of Tremblay's, all take AIDS as their subject or as part of their subject. For that reason, Camus is especially helpful here: though Camus certainly writes less about sex in the later diaries than in the former ones, he still views the gay body as sexual object, whereas most of the others have taken their narratives to a locus "beyond" sexuality. Rare, then, are the remarks in any work that engage the question of the penis. Aside from the decrepitude mentioned above, the penis appears in two guises. In one incarnation it remains vaguely visible, a taboo zone between the safety of the surface and the danger of the body: "He didn't give a fig about 'precautions.' And besides, later, he started to come in my mouth, without warning, and I had barely the time to pull back my head and, as well as I could, to spit out his first cum, whose passage over my tongue still bothers me a bit now. Later with the light back on in the sauna, I observed many completely imprudent scenes, which seems unimaginable to me" (*Vigiles* 415–16).

If oral sex is not dangerous then it can be part of the now nostalgic view of sex as the possible complete reciprocity of subject and object. It is in a vague no-man's land (or every man's land) between the absolutely forbidden action of anal intercourse without a condom and safe sex, like mutual masturbation: "I wasn't going to take precautions for him; but if he never took any more, was he putting me at risk? Is it dangerous to have one's cock sucked?" (*Vigiles* 274). In Camus's case, his sexual preferences have always tended toward what we now call safe sex (mutual *frottage*) and away from anal penetration: "Decidedly, I have no anal eroticism. This zone of my own body, rather unsensitive, except to pain, offers me only reduced pleasures" (*Vigiles* 90). In *Fendre l'air*, Camus calls *frottage* the act that is closest to "pure homosexuality, the least stained with resemblance to the other love" (224). Thus, Camus's work is the least likely to be affected by the changes in sexual practices. Still, his notes are the only ones we have to go on.

The other appearance of the penis, be it one's own or that of one's partner, is in its immediate disappearance into a condom: "I fuck him with two rubbers obligingly offered by him and which he put on me himself" (*Vigiles* 365–66). A condom returns the body to where it was, for it makes the penis a skin once again: only surface, no substance, and no danger. The sheath, a word used both for condoms and for the protective envelope for swords, makes sex medically safe. It also gives life to the illusion that gay sex is still the same thing, a play of surfaces, of endless foldings and unfoldings: "He spread out a rug, and on that rug, aside from his own spread-out body (moreover, pleasing to the eye) a bottle of poppers, rubbers, a tube of lubricant; all quite meticulously aligned, very visible, like in a store window. A good-looking boy, *safe sex*, amyl nitrate, up-to-date technology, all that suits me just fine" (*Vigiles* 321).

The condom is a *paroi* of complete division, radical deconstructive other for the membrane such as the tympanum or the hymen that join and separate, as Jacques Derrida has shown in "Tympan" and "La Double Séance." The condom joins two skins, separates, denies, closes off what they might contain. If it is penetrable or permeable, the condom is not a condom. And finally, the condom almost miraculously makes the rectum an impermeable surface once more, now nothing more than the sheathing invagination of the surface skin. For if a seropositive individual is responsible enough not to have sex, it is nonetheless logical to assume that the penis of the other may potentially be dangerous. So the condom makes his penis a skin once more, through which nothing can be transmitted, and the subject's anus, cast as the object of the gaze/penetration of the other, an equally impermeable locus.

One category of sexual activity remains: sex between two seropositive individuals. Not surprisingly, the body as object seems entirely to disappear in the two references to the situation. In one, in Guibert's writing, AIDS itself looms up as the object, against which two helpless, lost subjects seem destined to lose: "It had become difficult for Jules and me to screw again, of course there was no longer any risk except for a reciprocal recontamination, but the virus stood there between our bodies like a ghost pushing them off/away" (*Ami* 155). In another, the body itself dissolves into its own disintegrations, the empty spaces between the loci where the folds used to be: "We made love, with devotion, almost like before, almost. We like each other's wounds, faults, beauty marks, scars, lacks, rushes, excesses, humors, dizzinesses, wanderings" (Navarre 109). In both cases, the gay body disappears, not simply as it does when only one body is at stake, but in an act of transsubstantiation, metamorphosis, transhumance, metempsychosis. The body falls into its scars, its absences, its own subjectivity. Grounded in that act of sex, in a first-person plural that is itself disappearing, heading toward oblivion, the act of sex completes the recognition that the self, constituted as other, is fading away.

One final point, odd to realize, necessary to announce. The change in the gay body through the eighties brings a return of non-homosexuality within gayness. In Tremblay's novel, Mathieu is married and has a four-year-old son. As I have noted, *Mon valet et moi* is, at least superficially, about a heterosexual old man; the lover in *A l'ami* and *Protocole compassionnel* is bisexual. Though *Le Gloire du paria* remains steadfastly gay, the AIDS infection comes from tainted blood, not from gay sex (241). *Eve*, too, turns to heterosexuality (and incest, to boot) and away from gay sex. And in Navarre's novel, David, the character dying of AIDS, has fathered a son with a Japanese woman. Of the authors I am examining in this short study, only Camus seems to have no nostalgia for some heterosexual utopia, a world, one presumes, uninfected with AIDS. Yet even he makes a remark that moves him from the mark of free, unbridled gay sexuality that he always seemed to cherish unconditionally: "*Tricks*, tricks: it's a practice that is interesting only if one's heart is anchored elsewhere. They can't be the totality of a sex life, and even less of an emotional life" (*Aguets* 216).

Some would undoubtedly say that this seemingly obligatory turn away from the gay body in its sexual identity and availability for free play is part of the internalized homophobia of all gay men, though I would find it difficult to speak of homophobia in the case of Camus and Guibert, among others. Some would see it as the necessary corrective to the rampant sexual freedom of the seventies, a textual eschatology and morality play, a punishment for promiscuity. And still, it seems that a third solution, the one limned above, is perhaps more appropriate. If I am correct in these hypotheses, the gay body defined by its free play no longer exists. Its objective correlative is now split between the partial object that is the condom, an object impossible—yet necessary—to fetishize, and a transcendental signifier still attached to the object: the imaginary, pure, heterosexual body, the myth of virginal love we were all once taught as children. We are thus in the process of witnessing some of the symptomology of the formation of the dialectical antithesis of the gay body.

Will there be another gay body? A synthesis? Assuredly. What form will it take? It is too soon to tell. Will the gay body once more be a sign of *la gaya scienza*, of life and of love? One can only hope.

Reference Matter

Notes

INTRODUCTION: ON PLEMYSTOGRAPHY

1. Peter Schwenger (107–8) discusses *Io e lui* briefly in his article entitled "The Masculine Mode," but as Earl Jackson, Jr. (9) quite rightly notes, Schwenger conflates penis and phallus, and sees Moravia's novel as a reinforcement of the myths of heterosexual dominance.

2. As will be seen in the last chapter, in his radical call for gay liberation Guy Hocquenghem posits the anus as the locus of liberation. It is another call for the overthrow of the phallic order in favor of a system of pleasure.

3. See also Naomi Schor's article, already mentioned, "The Portrait of a Gentleman: Representing Men in (French) Women's Writing," included in *Bad Objects*.

π

1. Many of the works involved in the French Poe debate, including those of Lacan, Derrida, and Johnson, can be found in Muller and Richardson. The anti-Lacanian French psychoanalyst, François Roustang, refers to the chain with a book title, *Un Destin si funeste*, in which he quotes Lacan quoting Poe.

2. Again, I would wonder what Lacan might make of a detective story like "The Murders in the Rue Morgue," where the doubling insists in all its forms. Still, one might find a suitable moment of language or writing, some

of which I have mentioned above, to form the basis for such a hypothetical reading.

3. Mentioning the Lacan-Derrida debate, Mark Seltzer notes "Laplace's announcement . . . that the number of dead letters in the Paris postal system remained constant from year to year. The discovery of such regularities irreducible to individual intentions, and the generalization of the statistical method, are closely bound up with the emergence of a biopolitics of populations, with the possibility of a social science" (105).

4. In German, an *Ohrwurm* is both literally an "earwig" and an "insistent melody." In a completely different context, Jeffrey Mehlman has discussed an image of the literal earwig in the work of Michel Leiris: "The passage from the *perce-oreille* fantasy to that of the phonograph might best be viewed in terms of the relationship between the phonic and the graphic" (115).

DESIGNING MEN

1. As for Flaubert, we should consider that the description of Frédéric in *L'Education sentimentale* indicates merely that he has long hair (2:33) and that the character that comes closest to being the male without a penis and the opposition to the narratorial phallus is Emma Bovary.

2. Hence the justification for my somewhat unusual choice of calling the protagonist "Georges" throughout this chapter, for it is the only name that is always his.

3. The reader should recall the scene in *Faust II* (ll. 6161–72) in which Mephistopheles introduces the Fool to paper money, yet another version of the phallus, and decides that the Fool is not that much of a fool at all.

THE WRITER'S HAND

1. As I have pointed out in *Flaubert and Sons* (203–23), the model of literature as an activity like masturbation, and simultaneously of masturbation as an activity like literature, is what propels a good part of *Du côté de chez Swann.* Several readings of Proust link these activities: Paul de Man's *Allegories of Reading,* Jeffrey Mehlman's *A Structural Study of Autobiography,* and Serge Doubrovsky's *La Place de la madeleine.* Additionally, the pages on Rousseau in Jacques Derrida's *De la grammatologie,* as well as the commentary on them in de Man's *Blindness and Insight,* might prove useful.

2. The excellent edition done by Slatkine in 1979 of this now forgotten work, which is the edition I am using, is a reprint of the 1888 edition, which has a singular advantage over the first edition: all the passages cited at the obscenity trial in which Bonnetain was acquitted are printed in italics.

3. Significantly, the other bird in the story involves a recitation of Yeats's

poem about Leda and the swan, after which the auditor, Portnoy's erstwhile girlfriend, is so turned on that she insists he perform an act of cunnilingus (216–19).

FROM LIBERATION TO AIDS

1. In references to *Le Désir homosexuel*, the second set of numbers refers to the recently reissued English translation, *Homosexual Desire*, published by Duke University Press in 1993.

2. These complicated concepts are by no means the same. Suffice it to say that Hocquenghem for one would view all of them as manifestations of the same "phallocratic" power structure against which he is proposing his revolution (*Désir* 60; 96).

3. As Peter Starr shows, the very figure of the revolution that failed, what he calls the figures and logics of "failed revolt" itself, becomes part of the metaphoric field for the post-1968 theorists of liberation, literature, and philosophy.

4. I do not wholeheartedly agree with some of Pratt's conclusions, for three reasons. He seems tacitly to accept as given the automatic internalized homophobia of any homosexual. Secondly, some of his comments could only charitably be accepted under the sign of what would seem to be a misplaced irony. He writes of someone "whose writing is criss-crossed with a catalogue of homosexual representations along with other unspeakable practices" (70) and of the "dastardly character of the homosexual" (72). And finally, having insisted correctly on the idea of disidentification, Pratt simply makes the other character in the story out to be a "heterosexual," whatever that is, this despite the fact that the narrator inserts a dildo into the anus of the so-called heterosexual.

5. Two works of criticism stand out in my mind relative to the French situation. For an excellent study of the discourses of AIDS in contemporary France, see Robert Harvey's article "Sidéens/Sidaïques." Harvey looks at the multiple discourses of AIDS, of which the literary is only one set. Elsewhere, Joseph Lévy and Alexis Nouss have written a comprehensive overview of what they call a novelistic anthropology of AIDS, which involves an examination of a variety of French and American novels. They look at the thematics of the depiction of the illness, the descriptions of the various stages of the disease, the relations between the illness and death, the depictions of death and its social constructions, and the relation between AIDS and sexuality—specifically, homosexuality. As anthropologists they take the novels as so many artifacts, signs of a social structure. If I have a quarrel with this book it is that what we might consider a more literary side is eschewed in favor of literature as testimony.

6. Halperin's critique of Miller and Eribon in his excellent book (which appeared after this study was complete) is highly recommended. If Halperin is excessive, it is for polemical reasons, as a corrective against a normalizing vision of Foucault. To wit: "So let me make it official. I may not have worshiped Foucault at the time I wrote *One Hundred Years of Homosexuality*, but I do worship him now. As far as I'm concerned, the guy was a fucking saint" (6).

7. Joan DeJean's book, *Literary Fortifications*, is a study of the function of military strategy in eighteenth-century French literature. David Bell's work on tactics and strategy in nineteenth-century narratives, *Circumstances*, also relates literature to the structures of the battlefield.

8. I point out Navarre's and de Duve's nationalities because the responses of the newly negotiated figure of the gay body and AIDS do vary from country to country. While including a Francophone Belgian writer and a French expatriate writer does not seem egregious, I shall draw the line, somewhat arbitrarily in a no man's land, between them and the Québecois writer Michel Tremblay. Still, as we shall see below, Tremblay has a similar reaction, at least on one count, to the phenomenon in question.

9. Susan Sontag's two works on illness are formidable studies of the relation of the language of illness to the subject. As she says in the book on AIDS, "As tuberculosis had always been regarded sentimentally, as an enhancement of identity, cancer was regarded with irrational revulsion, as a diminution of the self" (12). In distinction to Sontag, I would remind the reader that I am attempting to focus on the structuring of the body. Obviously the two fields are not completely distinct.

10. In his construction of a gay-focused argument, Bersani is speaking specifically of Andrea Dworkin's and Catherine MacKinnon's views about heterosexual intercourse. I think his point is valid (as does he) for the rhetoric around homosexual anal intercourse. Both this article and Jan Zita Grover's come from a special issue of *October*: "AIDS: Cultural Analysis / Cultural Activism," edited by Douglas Crimp. In a world where the information about AIDS changes almost daily at the scientific level, and where, even as I wrote the first version of this material, the very definition of the disease had just changed in the United States, this collection remains absolutely compelling for the acute perceptions of its various cultural analyses.

Bibliography

Adams, J. N. *The Latin Sexual Vocabulary*. Baltimore: Johns Hopkins University Press, 1982.

Aldrich, Robert. *The Seduction of the Mediterranean: Writing, Art, and Homosexual Fantasy*. New York: Routledge, 1993.

Althusser, Louis. *L'Avenir dure longtemps. Suivi de Les faits. Autobiographies.* Paris: Stock/IMEC, 1992.

Anderson, Sherwood. *Winesburg, Ohio: A Group of Tales of Ohio Small Town Life*. New York: The Modern Library, 1919.

Anzieu, Didier. *Le Moi-peau*. Paris: Dunod, 1985.

Aron, Jean-Paul, and Roger Kempf. *Le Pénis et la démoralisation de l'occident*. Paris: Bernard Grasset, 1978.

Balzac, Honoré de. *La Comédie humaine*. Ed. Pierre-Georges Castex. Paris: Gallimard [Pléiade], 1976–80. 11 volumes.

Barbedette, Gilles. *Mémoires d'un jeune homme devenu vieux*. Paris: Gallimard, 1993.

Barthes, Roland. *Incidents*. Paris: Seuil, 1987.

———. *S/Z*. Paris: Seuil, 1970.

Baudelaire, Charles. *Le Peintre de la vie moderne*. In *Oeuvres complètes*. Ed. Claude Pichois. Paris: Gallimard [Pléiade], 1975–76. 2: 683–724.

Bauer, George. "Le Gai Savoir noir." *Contemporary French Civilization* 16.2 (1992): 194–213.

Bell, David F. *Circumstances: Chance in the Literary Text*. Lincoln: University of Nebraska Press, 1993.

———. "The Random Walk in Poe's 'The Mystery of Mary Rogêt': Probability and the Nineteenth-Century Detective Story." *Oxymoron* (forthcoming).

Benjamin, Walter. "Der Flaneur." In *Gesammelte Schriften*. Vol. 1, part 2. Frankfurt: Suhrkamp Verlag, 1974. 537–69.

Bersani, Leo. *Homos*. Cambridge: Harvard University Press, 1995.

———. "Is the Rectum a Grave?" *October* 43 (1987): 197–222.

Benveniste, Emile. *Problèmes de linguistique générale*. Vol. 1. Paris: Gallimard [TEL], 1966.

Bloom, Harold. *A Map of Misreading*. New York: Oxford University Press, 1975.

Bonnetain, Paul. *Charlot s'amuse*. Geneva: Slatkine Reprints, 1979.

Bory, Jean-Louis, and Guy Hocquenghem. *Comment nous appelez-vous déjà? Ces hommes que l'on dit homosexuels*. Paris: Calmann-Lévy, 1977.

Bourdin, Christophe. *Le Fil*. Paris: Editions de la Différence, 1994.

Brittan, Arthur. *Masculinity and Power*. London: Basil Blackwell, 1989.

Brubach, Holly. "Medium Rare." *The New York Times Magazine*, May 8, 1994, p. 49.

Butler, Judith. *Gender Trouble: Feminism and the Subversion of Identity*. New York: Routledge, 1990.

———. *Bodies That Matter: On the Discursive Limits of "Sex."* New York: Routledge, 1993.

Camus, Renaud. *Aguets. Journal 1988*. Paris: P. O. L., 1990.

———. *Fendre l'air. Journal 1989*. Paris: P. O. L., 1991.

———. *Notes achriennes*. Paris: Hachette P. O. L., 1982.

———. *Vigiles. Journal 1987*. Paris: P. O. L., 1989.

Carrouges, Michel. *Les Machines célibataires*. Paris: Arcanes, 1954.

Chion, Michel. *La Voix au cinéma*. Paris: Editions de l'Etoile, 1982.

Cohen, Ed. "Foucauldian necrologies: 'gay' 'politics'? politically gay?" *Textual Practice* 2.1 (1988): 87–101.

———. *Talk on the Wilde Side: Toward a Genealogy of a Discourse on Male Sexualities*. New York: Routledge, 1993.

Cohen, William A. "Manual Conduct in *Great Expectations*." *ELH* 60.1 (1993): 217–59.

Collard, Cyril. *Les Nuits fauves*. Paris: Flammarion, 1989.

———. *L'Ange sauvage. Carnets*. Paris: Flammarion, 1993.

Connell, R. W. *Gender and Power: Society, the Person and Sexual Politics*. Cambridge, England: Polity Press, 1987.

Crevel, René. *Mon corps et moi*. Paris: Pauvert, 1979.

DeJean, Joan. *Literary Fortifications: Rousseau, Laclos, Sade*. Princeton: Princeton University Press, 1984.

Deleuze, Gilles. *Proust et les signes*. 4th edition. Paris: Presses Universitaires de France, 1964.

——, and Félix Guattari. *L'Anti-Oedipe. Capitalisme et schizophrénie*. Paris: Minuit, 1972.

——. *Mille plateaux. Capitalisme et schizophrénie*. Paris: Minuit, 1980.

De Man, Paul. *Allegories of Reading: Figural Language in Rousseau, Nietzsche, Rilke, and Proust*. New Haven: Yale University Press, 1979.

——. *Blindness and Insight: Essays in the Rhetoric of Contemporary Criticism*. 2nd edition. Minneapolis: University of Minnesota Press, 1983.

Deneys-Tunney, Anne. *Ecritures du corps. De Descartes à Laclos*. Paris: P. U. F., 1992.

Derrida, Jacques. *De la grammatologie*. Paris: Minuit, 1967.

——. "Devant la loi." In *La Faculté de juger*. Paris: Minuit, 1985. 87–139.

——. "La Double Séance." In *La Dissémination*. Paris: Seuil, 1972. 199–318.

——. "Tympan." In *Marges*. Paris: Minuit, 1972. i–xxv.

Dickens, Charles. *David Copperfield*. Ed. Trevor Blount. Harmondsworth, Mx.: Penguin Books, 1966 [rpt. 1979].

Dollimore, Jonathan. *Sexual Dissidence: Augustine to Wilde, Freud to Foucault*. Oxford: Clarendon Press, 1991.

Donaldson-Evans, Mary. *A Woman's Revenge: The Chronology of Dispossession in Maupassant's Fiction*. Lexington: French Forum, 1986.

——. "The Harlot's Apprentice: Maupassant's *Bel-Ami*." *French Review* 60.5 (1987): 616–25.

Doubrovsky, Serge. *La Place de la madeleine. Ecriture et fantasme chez Proust*. Paris: Mercure de France, 1974.

Dreuilhe, Alain Emmanuel. *Corps à corps*. Paris: Gallimard, 1987.

Duncan, Derek. "Gestes autobiographiques: le sida et les formes d'expressions artistiques du moi." *Nottingham French Studies* 34.1 (1995): 100–111.

Duve, Pascal de. *L'Orage de vivre*. Paris: J. C. Lattès, 1994.

Duvert, Tony. *Abécédaire malveillant*. Paris: Minuit, 1989.

——. *L'Enfant au masculin. Essais, livre premier*. Paris: Editions de Minuit, 1980.

Eagleton, Terry. *The Rape of Clarissa*. Minneapolis: University of Minneapolis Press, 1982.

Edelman, Lee. *Homographesis: Essays in Gay Literary and Cultural Theory*. New York: Routledge, 1994.

Eribon, Didier. *Michel Foucault*. Paris: Flammarion, 1989.

——. *Michel Foucault et ses contemporains*. Paris: Fayard, 1994.

Fernandez, Dominique. *La Gloire du paria*. Paris: Grasset, 1987.

220   Bibliography

Flaubert, Gustave. *Oeuvres*. Paris: Gallimard [Pléiade], 1951–52. 2 vols.

Foucault, Michel. "Des caresses d'homme considérées comme un art." *Libération*, June 1, 1982, p. 27.

———. *Foucault Live*. Ed. Sylvère Lotringer. New York: Semiotext(e), 1989.

———. *Histoire de la sexualité*. Paris: Gallimard, 1976–84. 3 vols.

———. "L'homosexualité dans l'antiquité." Interview with J. P. Joecker, A. Sanzio, and M. Ouerd. *Masques* 13 (1982): 15–24.

———. *Language, Counter-Memory, Practice: Selected Essays and Interviews*. Ed. Donald F. Bouchard. Ithaca: Cornell University Press, 1977.

———. *Les Mots et les choses. Une Archéologie des sciences humaines*. Paris: Gallimard, 1966.

———. "Non aux compromis." Interview with R. Surzur. *Gai Pied* 43 (1982): 9.

———. "Un plaisir si simple." *Gai Pied* 1 (1979): 1.

———. *Power/Knowledge: Selected Interviews and Other Writings 1972–1977*. Ed. Colin Gordon. New York: Pantheon, 1980.

———. *Politics, Philosophy, Culture: Interviews and Other Writings 1977–1984*. Ed. Lawrence D. Kritzman. New York: Routledge, 1988.

———. "Sexual Choice, Sexual Act: An Interview with Michel Foucault." Interviewer James O'Higgins. *Salmagundi* 58–59 (1982–83): 10–24.

———. "Sexuality and Solitude: An Interview with Richard Sennett." *London Review of Books*, May 21–June 3, 1981, pp. 3–7.

———. *Surveiller et punir. Naissance de la prison*. Paris: Gallimard, 1975.

Gilbert, Sandra M., and Susan Gubar. *The Madwoman in the Attic*. New Haven: Yale University Press, 1979.

Girard, René. *Mensonge romantique et vérité romanesque*. Paris: Grasset, 1961.

———. *Des choses cachées depuis la fondation du monde. Recherches avec J. M. Oughourlian et Guy Lefort*. Paris: Grasset, 1978.

———. *La Violence et le sacré*. Paris: Grasset, 1972.

Glucksman, André. *La Fêlure du monde. Ethique et sida*. Paris: Flammarion, 1994.

Goddard, Jean-Christophe, and Monique Labrune, eds. *Le Corps*. Paris: Vrin, 1992.

Goethe, Johann Wolfgang. *Faust*. Ed. R.-M. S. Heffner et al. Madison: University of Wisconsin Press, 1975.

Goldstein, Laurence, ed. *The Male Body: Features, Destinies, Exposures*. Ann Arbor: University of Michigan Press, 1994.

Gooder, R. D. "Edgar Allan Poe: The Meaning of Style." *The Cambridge Quarterly* 16.2 (1987): 110–23.

Goulemot, Jean Marie. *Ces livres qu'on ne lit que d'une main*. Aix-en-Provence: Alinéa, 1991.

Goux, Jean-Joseph. *Les Iconoclastes*. Paris: Seuil, 1978.
———. *Marx, Freud. Economie et symbolique*. Paris: Seuil, 1973.
Green, Martin. *The Adventurous Male: Chapters in the History of the White Male Mind*. University Park: The Pennsylvania State University Press, 1993.
Grover, Jan Zita. "AIDS: Keywords." *October* 43 (1987): 17–30.
Guibert, Hervé. *A l'ami qui ne m'a pas sauvé la vie*. Paris: Gallimard, 1990.
———. *Les Chiens*. Paris: Gallimard, 1982.
———. *Cytomégalovirus*. Paris: Seuil, 1992.
———. *Fou de Vincent*. Paris: Minuit, 1989.
———. *La Mort propagande et autres textes de jeunesse*. Paris: Ed. Deforges, 1991.
———. *Le Protocole compassionnel*. Paris: Gallimard, 1991.
———. *Mon valet et moi. Roman cocasse*. Paris: Seuil, 1991.
Halperin, David M. *Saint=Foucault: Towards a Gay Hagiography*. New York: Oxford University Press, 1995.
Handy, Bruce. "What's It Worth to You?" *The New York Times Magazine*, February 13, 1994, p. 82.
Haraway, Donna J. *Simians, Cyborgs, and Women: The Reinvention of Nature*. New York: Routledge, 1991.
Harrowitz, Nancy. "The Body of the Detective Model: Charles S. Peirce and Edgar Allan Poe." In *The Sign of Three: Dupin, Homes, Peirce*. Ed. Umberto Eco and Thomas A. Sebeok. Bloomington: Indiana University Press, 1983. 179-97.
Harvey, Robert. "Sidéens / Sidaïques: French Discourses on AIDS." *Contemporary French Civilization* 16:2 (1992): 308-35.
Heathcote, Owen. "*Les Chiens* d'Hervé Guibert: analyse d'une "plaquette pornographique.'" *Nottingham French Studies* 34: 1 (1995): 61-9.
Hocquenghem, Guy. *L'Après-mai des faunes*. Préface de Gilles Deleuze. Paris: Grasset, 1974.
———. *La Beauté du métis. Réflexions d'un francophobe*. Paris: Editions Ramsay, 1979.
———. *Le Désir homosexuel*. Paris: Editions Universitaires, 1972.
———. *Eve*. Paris: Albin Michel, 1987.
———. *Homosexual Desire*. With a New Introduction by Michael Moon. Preface by Jeffrey Weeks. Translated by Daniella Dangoor. Durham: Duke University Press, 1993.
———. *La Dérive homosexuelle*. Paris: Jean-Pierre Delarge, 1977.
———. *Le Gai voyage. Guide et regard homosexuels sur les grandes métropoles*. Paris: Albin Michel, 1980.
———. *Race d'Ep. Un siècle d'images de l'homosexualité*. Avec la collaboration iconographique de Lionel Soukaz. Paris: Editions Libres / Hallier, 1979.

Hofstadter, Douglas R. *Metamagical Themas: Questing for the Essence of Mind and Pattern*. New York: Basic Books, 1985.

Huisman, Bruno, and François Ribes, eds. *Les Philosophes et le corps*. Paris: Dunod, 1992.

Irwin, John T. *American Hieroglyphics: The Symbol of the Egyptian Hieroglyphics in the American Renaissance*. New Haven: Yale University Press, 1980.

———. "Mysteries We Reread, Mysteries of Rereading: Poe, Borges, and the Analytic Detective Story; Also Lacan, Derrida, and Johnson" *MLN* 101.5 (1986): 1168–1216.

———. *The Mystery to a Solution: Poe, Borges, and the Analytic Detective Story*. Baltimore: Johns Hopkins University Press, 1994.

Jackson, Earl Jr. *Strategies of Deviance: Studies in Gay Male Representation*. Bloomington: Indiana University Press, 1995.

Jardine, Alice. "Men in Feminism: Odor di Uomo or Compagnons de Route?" In *Men in Feminism*. Ed. Alice Jardine and Paul Smith. New York: Methuen, 1987. 54–61.

Jarry, Alfred. *Le Surmâle*. Paris: Editions Le Terrain Vague, 1977.

Kelly, Veronica, and Dorothea E. von Mücke, eds. *Body & Text in the Eighteenth Century*. Stanford: Stanford University Press, 1994.

Kofman, Sarah. *Lectures de Derrida*. Paris: Galilée, 1984.

Kosinski, Jerzy. *Cockpit*. New York: Arcade Publishing, 1975.

Kronick, Joseph G. "Edgar Allan Poe: The Error of Reading and the Reading of Error." *Literature and Psychology* 35.3 (1989): 22–42.

Lacan, Jacques. *Ecrits*. Paris: Seuil, 1966.

Lacqueur, Thomas W. "The Social Evil, the Solitary Vice and Pouring Tea." In *Fragments for a History of the Human Body*. Part 3. Ed. Michel Feher et al. New York: Zone, 1989. 334–42.

Le Diraison, Serge, and Eric Zernik. *Le Corps des philosophes*. Paris: Presses Universitaires de France, 1993.

Lehman, Peter. *Running Scared: Masculinity and the Representation of the Male Body*. Philadelphia: Temple University Press, 1993.

Lévy, Joseph, and Alexis Nouss. *SIDA-Fiction. Essai d'anthropologie romanesque*. Lyon: Presses Universitaires de Lyon, 1994.

Lingis, Alphonso. *Foreign Bodies*. New York: Routledge, 1994.

Lyotard, Jean-François. "Discussion, ou: phraser 'après Auschwitz.'" In *Les Fins de l'homme*. Ed. Philippe Lacoue-Labarthe and Jean-Luc Nancy. Paris: Galilée, 1981.

MacCannell, Juliet Flower, and Laura Zakarin, eds. *Thinking Bodies*. Stanford: Stanford University Press, 1994.

Macey, David. *The Lives of Michel Foucault*. New York: Pantheon, 1993.

Mallarmé, Stéphane. *Oeuvres complètes*. Paris: Gallimard [Pléiade], 1945.

Manière, Michel. *A ceux qui l'ont aimé.* Paris: P. O. L., 1992.

Martin, Robert K. *Hero, Captain, and Stranger: Male Friendship, Social Critique, and Literary Form in the Sea Novels of Herman Melville.* Chapel Hill: University of North Carolina Press, 1986.

Marx, Leo. *The Machine in the Garden: Technology and the Pastoral Ideal in America.* New York: Oxford University Press, 1964 [1pt. 1981]

Mathews, Harry. *Singular Pleasures.* Normal, Ill.: Dalkey Archive Press, 1993.

Maupassant, Guy de. *Romans.* Ed. Louis Forestier. Paris: Gallimard [Pléiade], 1987.

Mehlman, Jeffrey. *A Structural Study of Autobiography: Proust, Leiris, Sartre, Lévi-Strauss.* Ithaca: Cornell University Press, 1974.

Melville, Herman. *Redburn, White-Jacket, Moby-Dick.* New York: The Library of America, 1983.

Meyer, Richard. "Robert Mapplethorpe and the Discipline of Photography." In *The Lesbian and Gay Studies Reader.* Ed. Henry Abelove, Michèle Aina Barale, and David M. Halperin. New York: Routledge, 1993. 360–80.

Middleton, Peter. *The Inward Gaze: Masculinity and Subjectivity in Modern Culture.* London: Routledge, 1992.

Miller, James. *The Passion of Michel Foucault.* New York: Simon and Schuster, 1993.

Mirbeau, Octave. *Le Jardin des supplices.* Paris: Gallimard [Folio], 1988.

Mishima, Yukio. *Confessions of a Mask.* Trans. Meredith Weatherby. New York: New Directions, 1958.

Moravia, Alberto. *Io e lui.* Milan: Bompiani, 1971 [rpt. 1991].

Muller, John P., and William J. Richardson, eds. *The Purloined Poe: Lacan, Derrida, and Psychoanalytic Reading.* Baltimore: Johns Hopkins University Press, 1988.

Murphy, Peter F. *Fictions of Masculinity: Crossing Cultures, Crossing Sexualities.* New York: New York University Press, 1994.

Navarre, Yves. *Ce sont amis que vent emporte.* Paris: Flammarion, 1991.

Nye, Robert A. *Crime, Madness, and Politics in Modern France.* Princeton: Princeton University Press, 1984.

Osborne, John. *The Entertainer.* In *Three Plays by John Osborne.* New York: Bantam, 1977. 99–203.

Paglia, Camille. *Sexual Personae.* New York: Vintage Books, 1991.

———. *Vamps and Tramps.* New York: Vintage Books, 1994.

Poe, Edgar Allan. *Poetry and Tales.* New York: The Library of America, 1984.

Pratt, Murray. "De la désidentification à l'incognito: à la recherche d'une autobiographie homosexuelle." *Nottingham French Studies* 34.1 (1995): 70–81.

Prince, Gerald. "*Bel-Ami* and Narrative as Antagonist." *French Forum* 11.2 (1986): 217–26.

Quéran, Odile, and Denis Trarieux, eds. *Les Discours du corps. Une anthologie.* Paris: Presses Pocket, 1993.

Remy, Jacqueline. "L'institut qui soigne les criminels sexuels." *L'Express International* 2229 (March 31, 1994), 28–31.

Ringe, Donald. "Poe's Debt to Scott." *English Language Notes* 18.4 (1981): 281–83.

Robinson, Doug. "Trapped in the Text: "The Pit and the Pendulum.'" *Les Cahiers de la nouvelle* 7 (1986): 63–75

Roth, Philip. *Portnoy's Complaint.* New York: Fawcett Crest, 1967 [rpt. 1990].

Rotundo, E. Anthony. *American Manhood: Transformations in Masculinity from the Revolution to the Modern Era.* New York: Basic Books, 1993.

Rousseau, Jean-Jacques. *Les Confessions.* In *Oeuvres complètes.* Paris: Gallimard [Pléiade], 1959. 1: 2–656.

Roustang, François. *Un destin si funeste.* Paris: Minuit, 1976.

Safire, William. "The Horny Dilemma." *The New York Times Magazine*, February 6, 1994, p. 10.

Scarry, Elaine. *The Body in Pain: The Making and Unmaking of the World.* New York: Oxford University Press, 1985.

Schaal, Jean-François. *Le Corps. Cours préparation HEC.* Paris: Ellipses, 1993.

Schehr, Lawrence R. *Alcibiades at the Door: Gay Discourses in French Literature.* Stanford: Stanford University Press, 1995.

———. *Flaubert and Sons: Readings of Flaubert, Zola, and Proust.* New York: Peter Lang, 1976.

———. "The Homotext of Tournier's *Les Météores.*" *SubStance* 58 (1989): 35–50.

———. *Rendering French Realism.* Stanford: Stanford University Press, 1997.

———. *The Shock of Men: Homosexual Hermeneutics and French Writing.* Stanford: Stanford University Press, 1995.

Schor, Naomi. *Bad Objects: Essays Popular and Unpopular.* Durham, N.C.: Duke University Press, 1995.

———. *Breaking the Chain: Women, Theory, and French Realist Fiction.* New York: Columbia University Press, 1985.

Scott, Sir Walter. *Anne of Geierstein.* In *The Waverley Novels*, vol. 21. New York: Peter Fenelon Collier & Son, 1900.

Schwenger, Peter. "The Masculine Mode." In *Speaking of Gender.* Ed. Elaine Showalter. New York: Routledge, 1989. 101–12.

Seidler, Victor J. *Rediscovering Masculinity: Reason, Language and Sexuality.* London: Routledge, 1989.

Seltzer, Mark. *Bodies and Machines.* New York: Routledge, 1992.

Serres, Michel. *Feux et signaux de brume. Zola.* Paris: Grasset, 1975.
———. *Le Parasite.* Paris: Grasset, 1980.
Sibony, Daniel. *L'Autre incastrable. Psychanalyse–écritures.* Paris: Seuil, 1978.
Siebers, Tobin. *The Romantic Fantastic.* Ithaca: Cornell University Press, 1984.
Silverman, Kaja. *Male Subjectivity at the Margins.* New York: Routledge, 1992.
Simpson, Mark. *Male Impersonators: Men Performing Masculinity.* New York: Routledge, 1994.
Sontag, Susan. *AIDS and Its Metaphors.* New York: Farrar, Straus and Giroux, 1988.
———. *Illness as Metaphor.* New York: Farrar, Straus and Giroux, 1978.
Starr, Peter. *Logics of Failed Revolt: French Theory After May '68.* Stanford: Stanford University Press, 1995.
Steinberg, Leo. *The Sexuality of Christ in Renaissance Art and in Modern Oblivion.* New York: Pantheon Books, 1983.
Stendhal. *Romans et nouvelles.* Ed. H. Martineau. Paris: Gallimard [Pléiade], 1952. 2 vols.
Tournier, Michel. *La Goutte d'or.* Paris, 1985.
———. *Les Météores.* Paris: Gallimard [Folio], 1975.
———. *Vendredi ou les limbes du Pacifique.* Paris: Gallimard [Folio], 1972.
Tremblay, Michel. *Le Coeur découvert. Roman d'amours.* Montréal: Leméac [Bibliothèque québécoise], 1992.
Villiers de l'Isle Adam. *L'Eve future.* Paris: José Corti, 1987.
Žižek, Slavoj. *Looking Awry: An Introduction to Jacques Lacan through Popular Culture.* Cambridge, Mass.: MIT Press, 1991 [rpt. 1993].

Index

In this index, an "f" after a number indicates a separate reference on the next page, and an "ff" indicates separate references on the next two pages. A continuous discussion over two or more pages is indicated by a span of page numbers, e.g., "57–59." *Passim* is used for a cluster of references in close but not consecutive sequence.

Library of Congress Cataloging-in-Publication Data

Schehr, Lawrence R.
  Parts of an andrology : on representations of men's bodies /
Lawrence R. Schehr.
      p.   cm.
  Includes bibliographical references and index.
  ISBN 0-8047-2919-0 (cloth : alk. paper). —ISBN 0-8047-2920-4
(paper : alk. paper)
    1. Body, Human, in literature. 2. Men in literature.
3. Andrology in literature. 4. Generative organs, Male, in
literature.   I. Title.
PN56.B62S34   1997
809'.9336—dc21   96-49744
                                                            CIP

  ⊚   This book is printed on acid-free, recycled paper.